The Cadet Experience

MIKE JUDD

First published 1999

Published by Fisher Miller Publishing
17 The Drive
Oakley
Basingstoke
Hampshire RG23 7BA
United Kingdom

Printed by Redwood Books, Trowbridge

Perfect bound

Text and photographs © Michael R Judd 1998

ISBN 1–899077–07–3

A catalogue record for this book is available from the British Library.

Contents

List of plates

Acknowledgements

Photographs 1 and 6 are the copyright of Mike Judd. The author and publishers are grateful to Andrew Bathie and David Brown BA(Hons) ABIPP for permission to use other photographs of which they hold the copyright. The author acknowledges the assistance provided by the following individuals and organisations who have contributed information or assisted in the publication of this book:

The Commanding Officer, RAF Manston
The Commanding Officer, RAF Oakington
Harrow Public Library
Margate Public Library
Imperial War Museum
National Army Museum
Public Record Office, Kew
British Museum Newspaper Library
Royal Air Force Museum, Hendon
Spitfire Memorial Museum, Manston
Hall of Aviation, Southampton
78 (Wembley) Squadron Air Training Corps
94 (Feltham) Squadron Air Training Corps
444 (Shoreditch) Squadron Air Training Corps
2366 (Bletchley) Squadron Air Training Corps
217 (Hornsey) Detachment Army Cadet Force
Mr Andrew Bathie
Mr Barry Brooks BSc
Mr John Brooks
Mr David Brown BA(Hons) ABIPP
Mr Paul Creese
Mr Saqub Inam
Mr Richard G King
Mr Donald Matheson
Mr and Mrs Andrew Miller
Mr and Mrs Stephen Rees
Mr John E Spinks MITD
Mr Graham Vincent
Mr Darren Whitfield

Preface

Much has been written about World War II with its funny moments as well as its human horror. At the time, I was trying hard to become educated, in the hope that the war would soon end and I could go out to earn a living. I was dragged into being a cadet in my spare time, which also had its funny moments and not quite so serious horrors. I am writing about my own memories, which I now relate to you with a degree of nostalgia. They are all true, though I have had many problems in getting the details exactly right, because of the great difficulties with the unrecorded incidents that rely solely on human memory. I made many friends – both as a cadet and when I rose to become an officer in later years – but to preserve any possible embarrassment to those whom I hope are still alive and well, I have changed most of the names and some of the locations.

You may well be shocked when you read about what happened in those days. I can only assure my young readers that there have been great changes since I was a cadet, and it is now one of the best youth organisations in the world. It is commanded by a professional team of men and women who do their best, in their own – mainly unpaid – time, for the younger generation despite the actions by successive governments. Whether you intend to join the uniformed services as a career or to take up employment in private industry, being a cadet is one of the experiences that are recognised by prospective employers, and one that you ought not to miss. It can offer you a wealth of experience which, although you may not recognise it at the time, turns out to be extremely valuable in years to come.

1

It Was Wartime

Ilived with my parents and younger sister in one of those semi-detached houses, built in the early 1930s, which made up the outer suburbs of London. My father had worked hard to get the deposit for the house and would now be struggling for many years with the mortgage repayments. Our house was in the middle of a terrace of four situated in a quiet road with grass verges, a few small trees and lamp posts for street lighting that had been converted from gas to electricity just before the outbreak of war in 1939. When the war started, some brick air-raid shelters were built which started on the grass verges and extended over the kerb to make the road slightly narrower. It spoilt the charm of the area, but a few strokes of white paint on the end walls marked out a goal for our occasional games of football.

From my parents' and sister's bedrooms we could see part of the golf course rising above the tops of the houses on the other side of the road. We had a small front garden with a patch of grass that frequently suffered severe cutting by the lawn mower, a border of not too expensive small flowers that my father had grown from seed, and a concrete path along one side leading to the front door. The back garden, which could be seen from my bedroom, was much larger. It stretched for a good distance towards the gardens of the houses in the next road, with access at the rear just large enough for a small car. However, a car was quite beyond the reach of my father's pocket, even if wartime conditions would have allowed sufficient supplies of petrol for it. The garden at the back was divided in two. The part nearer the house was dominated by a lawn with a wide border of flowers at one side of it. Further away from the house, the rest of the garden took on a more commercial atmosphere with its fruit trees, vast crop of vegetables and one massive blackberry bush which hung on our boundary fence, making it lean at an angle. My father had built a shed to house his gardening tools and other household items that were considered too undignified to be in the house. The remains of my rabbit hutch were next to the shed. Its occupants had been slaughtered for food in the early months of the war, providing some delicious meals at a time of severe shortage of meat supplies. The rabbits had made several attempts to escape by gnawing away at the hutch but the more substantial remains of timber were earmarked for the dining room fire when the need arose.

My mother was fully occupied, attending to domestic household duties, with the principal tasks of shopping for what little food was available and trying to make the best of cooking it, and of keeping the house warm and tidy. She also maintained the garden, looking after the flowers and pulling up the weeds for disposal, often taking part in a neighbourly chat to exchange items of local news.

My father was a clerk employed by the London, Midland and Scottish Railway Company. He travelled daily to his office which was set in the heart of a London goods depot. His times of leaving in the morning and getting back home from the office were totally predictable. The bus service did not venture within half a mile of our house, so my father had a 20-minute walk to the station. There were a few occasions when my mother wanted him to get me out of the house for a day, so as my father regularly went to work on a Saturday morning, it was a convenient arrangement for me to accompany him to his office. I was kept out of the worst mischief by being allowed to compose something intelligent on the railway company's ancient typewriter, and before being carted back home I was taken out for a meal. It was all a rather pleasant interlude in the routine of a normal weekend.

World War II was still in progress in 1943. The constant reminder was a substantial Morrison shelter in the lounge, rather like a metal cage the size of a big office desk, that did not fit in with the décor of the room. The Morrison was designed so that we would be safe if the house collapsed on to it, and it served as our sleeping area. It had to be approached very carefully in the dark, everyone crawling on all fours in the direction of their allocated space and trying to avoid a collision with the upright corner posts. I had several such collisions which resulted in many cuts and bruises. Once all four of us were inside my father secured the remaining side with a heavy mesh panel. The process was reversed in the mornings. It was also necessary to black out the windows using heavy curtains, so that light did not escape and it would be difficult for enemy aircraft to locate areas to shed their bombs. The only news from the outside world came via an antiquated wireless set that my father had bought on our arrival in 1933, and the newspapers that were sold at the station bookstall. Once, while in one of my inquisitive moods, I tried to find out how this wireless worked, but having removed the back panel from its varnished plywood case I was baffled by the collection of glowing valves and the mass of wiring inside. I never plucked up enough courage to investigate further in case I created a permanent electrical disaster. When I asked my father how it worked, his knowledge seemed to extend no further than the trial and error method of fiddling with the knobs.

Food was in extremely short supply and many items were only available on a ration basis, upon presentation of coupons supplied by local government offices. Many items of food that up until 1939 had been imported from overseas, were missing from the food shops, as shipping was being used for essential supplies for the war effort. My mother spent a good part of her time in devising meals from what little there was available, and our hunger was satisfied mainly as a result of her splendid efforts. There was a problem with clothing. Because of a temporary government order recognising the shortage of cloth, I was required to wear short trousers until my twelfth birthday, then this was extended by my parents for a few years, until I passed my exams at school. I never found out what penalty they were likely to inflict upon me if I failed these exams. I was also promised a watch and a bicycle, thus guaranteeing that my homework was regularly finished.

Inspired by the thrill of watching steam trains going through our local station at breakneck speed, with the steam hugging the tops of the following carriages as it met the opposing flow of air, I wanted to be an engineer of some sort when I left school. My father had told me about the disadvantages of being a train driver and he had often lectured me on the horrors of having to be a fireman first. During my junior school days I was given a model train set as a Christmas present, and although I had acquired a few accessories by dropping hints just before a birthday was due, toys were not often available so I frequently modified it using scrap odds and ends. This, plus a basic knowledge of electricity, although I was still confused about the wireless set, added to my great interest in engineering.

The day came for me to take the entrance examination to the technical college. I did not do at all well, nowhere near achieving the success that my father and I had hoped for. Although I had not gained sufficient marks for a place in the engineering department, there were places left in the building department of the college. No further options were open to me. I was sent to the technical college, kitted out with the approved clothing including, to my delight, my first pair of long trousers, briefcase, fares and dinner money.

One of the many friends I had made at school was Donald, who lived next door, and we always met at a fixed time before setting off in the mornings. Coming home was different as our times of departure from school depended upon whether we had earned a period of detention or had to wait for the cane to be laid across our backsides first. Donald's father was in the Army and had not been in the country for several years. The family always became very concerned every time the postman called, hoping that it was further confirmation that he was still alive. Donald often brought his sister into our house for company when his mother was out at work. He had been in the Cubs and had later graduated to the Scouts. He made many attempts at getting me to join, but natural physical fitness and a love for the fresh air were not important parts of what I considered to be normal activities. I always rejected his offers in favour of the dreaded homework, and in the safe knowledge that it was insurance against wearing short trousers again. He liked camping and fishing at weekends, which fitted in quite well with his scouting activities, and, of greater importance, it gave him a ready-made reason for avoiding Sunday school.

My other close friend and great mad-brain was Tony, who lived on the other side of the road at number 19. He had a much older brother and sister, with parents who were always pre-occupied with the maintenance of their property. As a result, Tony was often left to his own devices for much of his spare time, and if there was ever any opportunity to embark on mischief, Tony was usually involved. He was a considerable duffer at school and he often came to see me, in the hope that I could get him out of a scrape with his homework. He spent quite a lot of time thinking up a variety of impossible ideas, then trying to persuade me to go into partnership with him. He had a wandering mind and could not concentrate on anything for very long. The discussion of any plan within the hearing of my parents was usually sufficient to prevent it from proceeding any further before the anticipated disastrous results set in. I think that Tony's influence over me owed a lot to his lovely smile and feverish activity. We became good friends, mainly because he was so dominant and I could not successfully avoid him when I wanted to. There was no doubt that he had very firm ideas on where he was going when he left school. I remember his fervent desire to join the Navy so that he could see the world, with the alternative of becoming a lion-tamer in a circus. He was fascinated by anything of a military nature and he often used to drag me along to see a local camp where the German prisoners of war were accommodated. He wanted to leave home eventually, having realised that his parents did not really accept him as part of the family. His only moments of relative sanity occurred in the periods following the good hidings he earned for doing something quite outrageous.

As the area where we lived was of some interest to the German airforce, the wailing noise of the air-raid sirens frequently warned us of the approach of German aircraft. Consequently, the college authorities had sensibly decided to hold lessons in the air-raid shelters. As well as providing a degree of safety, this certainly saved us from possible injury by flying glass, in the event of windows being blown in. Lessons were being interrupted much too often for comfort and one of these raids was particularly violent. Fear grew with every shriek of another descending bomb, and I clearly remember a morning when one of them was meant for us. Nearly deafened by the explosion on the other side of the wall of the shelter, I found myself within a mass of loose bricks, unable to move and with my class mates close at hand in a similar predicament. I tried to wriggle free but with every movement I became more firmly wedged. I thought about shouting for someone to dig me out, not that it would have helped because the rest of the class was already doing that, but as the air was laden with brick dust I decided to keep my mouth shut, if only to keep that out. I really wanted to know how badly I had been injured. My toes and fingers seemed to operate normally, but my head was sore and painful and I could not get my arms free to carry out any investigation. I wondered what other damage there might be and how soon it would be before someone arrived who could release us.

I was beginning to feel cold. Nearby, someone was panting amid the debris, probably trying to free himself. One young voice began reciting an anti-German poem, which made us a good deal more cheerful, then this was followed by some revoltingly artistic adaptations of some current songs. It all came to a halt when a teacher told us to be quiet, then from some distance away we heard the sounds of bricks being moved. By now I was really shivering and my head was hurting a lot more. My next recollection was a sensation of floating in fresh air and looking upwards at the sky, which was soon exchanged for the view of a classroom ceiling. I was covered with a woollen blanket and starting to feel pleasantly warmer. I guessed that I had been unconscious for a short while, but apart from a few small cuts and bruises, I seemed to have avoided any other damage and was now beginning to understand what was happening. Eventually some refreshments were available from the canteen, although the cheer of the free-of-charge tea was much greater than its quality. Soon I was declared fit enough to go home. I waited a while to see if any of my friends had been seriously injured, and discovered that four students and a teacher had been taken to hospital. When I went to see the remains of the shelter I saw a lot of minor damage to the adjacent buildings. The caretaker's precious garden was a mess, with a rather large hole in it. I went home that day with a story to tell. My father wrote it off as one of the real hazards of living near London and pointed out just how necessary his effort in the Home Guard was.

During the summer of 1944 the Germans changed their method of attack on south-east England and began using their unmanned aircraft, commonly known as the V1 or 'doodle bug'. After that they developed the V2 rocket. Although it was extremely nerve-wracking, at least you could hear the doodle-bug coming. The silence when its engine failed gave warning to take cover and wait for the explosion. By contrast, the rocket arrived silently and delivered a hefty explosion. My first experience of a rocket was one morning, on the first stage of my journey to college. Passengers were persuading the conductor of the bus that there was room for a few more to stand in the gangway, despite the legal limits, when from somewhere very close by there was an almighty bang and a rush of air that rocked the bus. This was immediately followed by the splitting of timber and the tumbling of brickwork. As is the case with such catastrophes, there were a few seconds of tense silence before full appreciation of the circumstances dawned. The road ahead was clear for about 200 yards but, not far beyond that, a cloud of dust was slowly settling to reveal a heap of debris that had, only a few minutes earlier, been a line of modern semi-detached houses. Within moments, people were seen running to help and a policeman arrived. The bus driver was advised to find another route to continue his journey, helped by the locals who knew their way around the obstruction.

I still had plenty of time to get to college so, instead of my usual determined walk, I took a leisurely stroll from the station. Before I reached the college gates, there was another fearful bang but with no immediate sign of any damage. Residents opened their front doors and looked for signs of disaster, but none was to be seen, so they chatted for a moment before they went back to their morning routine. I was puzzled. There must have been an explosion and some damage close by. The college caretaker was walking round the front of the building, looking just as puzzled as I had been. I went round to the back of the row of college workshops where I discovered the battered remains of a rocket, some ten feet high and still very warm from its journey through the atmosphere. It had missed the workshops by only a few inches and was now firmly embedded in the tarmac. My first reaction was to run like hell but on second thoughts I decided that this was not very sensible. My nervous system had to settle down first, and I had to try to recall what I really should do. At school we had been taught what to do if we discovered a German soldier or a live bomb, and how to take cover during an air attack. I did not remember being taught what to do about a rocket that had fallen and obviously parted with its other half before reaching the ground. I knew nothing about the characteristics of these things, so panic took over for a moment while I wondered if this lump of rocket would explode again. Then I remembered the notices that were posted up at college, advising people to tell a policeman or other official. That was not a very practical idea either, but perhaps the college caretaker would know what to do.

I found one of the masters first, and I blurted out the story. His face went a few shades paler than its usual colour and then he broke the college rules by running at breakneck speed down the corridor to the school office. Then the fire alarm rang and those few who had arrived went to the place appointed for just such a situation as this. There was another administrative crisis when it was discovered that the roll could not be called to check whether everyone had been accounted for. The college rules did not seem to have been written to cater for events that took place at this hour of the morning. When the caretaker and yet another master arrived, we were left to our own devices while they went off to investigate my report. After a quick review of the situation, they told us to go home. Some of us stood outside the station waiting for more students to arrive, and then passed on the news that college had been closed for the day. Knowing the practical jokes that were often played at college, most of them ignored us.

On the way home, I could not resist getting off the bus where it had been diverted earlier, to have a look at the devastation caused to the houses. When I saw the remains of the houses, with their contents spilled out on to the road, I asked if I could help with the clearing of debris and my offer was gratefully accepted by a policeman who seemed to be in charge. It was the first time that I had ever seen such a collection of mutilated bodies. I was offered many cups of tea during the day, and eventually walked home, satisfied that at least I had done a worthwhile task. I arrived a little earlier than I normally did and my mother commented on the filthy state of my college uniform and the dirt and grime on my face and hands. She cried a little while the first aid kit came out and my hands were bandaged. My mother must have guessed what had happened but did not ask. She offered me food but after the day's experiences I could not face it. I drew my legal limit of five inches of water from the hot tap into the bath, washed myself clean and went to my bedroom. I spent most of the evening thinking over the horror that was associated with this wretched war. I should have liked to get hold of Adolf Hitler and make a mess of him, but my military knowledge was very limited and I had to accept that my chance might come when I was older. When my father arrived home, he came up to my bedroom to see if I wanted anything, and then left me alone while my brain was pondering the events of the day and what tomorrow was likely to bring.

2

The stamp of approval

One very particular warm evening the French windows were open and the soft spring breeze was keeping the temperature in the house within comfortable limits. The evening meal was over and the washing up had been done. Our suburban family's settled evening routine was well under way, with my mother, having put my younger sister to bed, concentrating on her knitting. My father was deeply engrossed in a good book. Over many years he had acquired a good library of leather-bound literary works that occupied most of a polished hardwood bookcase situated conveniently close to his favourite chair. I had made many serious attempts to match his love for reading these books, but I found them far too heavy-going to give me any pleasure. At least his reading enabled him to ignore the occasional minor household troubles when they arose. The radio was tuned in to some very pleasant background classical music, the cold winter weather had been almost forgotten and Germany had not sent us a V2 for several weeks. I had a good pile of homework that evening and my reference books were scattered on the floor, with the rest of the work distributed over the dining table.

After a while, this relaxed and pleasant atmosphere was disturbed by the loud crashing of the knocker on the front door, which was Tony's trademark demanding entry. My mother, having accepted that my homework was far more important than her knitting, got up and went to let him in. As he came into the room I recognised on his face the expression which usually indicated that yet another of his madcap ideas was about to be launched. He sat down, facing me across my homework, obviously trying tactfully to choose a suitable moment to interrupt proceedings. Eventually his excitement overcame him and he boldly announced that he was hoping to go flying in a few months' time, and wanted me to join him. My mother dropped the knitting into her lap and my father looked up from his book, peering over the top of his spectacles. Flying was considered to be a fairly hazardous activity, and my instant reaction was that it was another one of Tony's mad passing ideas.

Tony's face was glowing with delight. He announced that he had joined the cadets during the previous week. Now it was most unusual for Tony to keep such a proposal secret from me, and even more startling that he had actually joined and was still enthusiastic after one whole week. His flow of conversation was quite unstoppable for nearly a quarter of an hour, and I did not know what to make of it all. I was picking up the message that, for the first time in his life, Tony had actually landed on a practical idea and my father was paying a lot of attention to what he was saying. It was possible that this particular plan might have some merit and could even have longlasting results. My father had joined the Home Guard only because the railway company or the government demanded that he should and I had quickly learned to keep my distance when he was putting the final touches to his uniform, ready for an evening duty. Perhaps the chance of getting someone else in the family into a military uniform was an opportunity that my father would not miss. It would certainly relieve the embarrassment that he seemed to suffer before he went on duty. Meanwhile, it was gradually becoming very clear to me that I was in danger of being cajoled into joining the Air Training Corps, with both Tony and my father becoming more and more determined that they were not going to let me escape. At that moment I did not really have much of a clue what it was all about, except perhaps that it might somehow contribute to the war effort, and I might eventually have to do that in any case. The hazards of warfare went flashing through my mind and I had an awful recollection of the destruction of houses and the death of innocent human beings that I had seen while on my way home from college. Then I thought about my own experience at college when I had been temporarily buried in the air raid shelter, quite apart from all the other various threats to my normal lifestyle.

When Tony's flow of words was finally exhausted, my father was silent for a while. He looked at my mother, perhaps hoping for at least a little inspiration from that direction, but my mother seemed to be determined to avoid the issue and continued with her knitting. Tony had delivered his planned attack on us, and nothing was going to happen now until my father pronounced judgement on the matter. Tony knew this from previous experience and he now sat on the edge of the chair in uncanny silence, watching for my father to say or do something. For him, the torment of waiting must have been similar to being caught misbehaving at school and wondering if his backside was in for another caning. After a few grunts and the leisurely lighting up of his favourite pipe, my father indicated that he thought it was a jolly good idea, despite the fact that it might interrupt my studies, but I should have to deal with that problem as best I could. Tony's face brightened immensely as my father turned to me and told me to join as soon as I could. There was no way of contesting what he had decided and by the end of the evening it had been collectively decided that my father would allow me just a few days to discover what the cadets were like, and to report back to him with my comments. Firm arrangements were then made for Tony to call for me on the following evening. Tony was now well on the way towards a successful outcome for one of his ideas.

I went to bed that evening thinking about all that Tony had said. I knew that if I gave it a try, I might be able to find a suitable reason for opting out, assuming that I could persuade my father that my reason was valid. The obstacle that I might not overcome quite so easily was my father's enthusiasm to get me involved. I had noted that my mother said very little in the matter, but it was likely that my parents would discuss the plan further before they went to bed and while I was out of the way.

At college the next day, during the boring parts of formal instruction, I thought more seriously about the matter. I even asked some of my fellow students if they knew anything about the cadets. The majority belonged to the Army Cadets, with a major interest in anything of an explosive nature, but they all seemed rather short of any details. On my way home from college that afternoon, I decided that I would have a go at this cadet organisation and see if I could make a success of it. I had worked out that I could just about rearrange my plans so that college homework would not interrupt my attendance at cadets. My mother, having properly anticipated a revised evening routine, had organised my meal much earlier than usual. After that I was resigned to being tarted up for the occasion. My mother's only concern was that her little son should be outstandingly presentable. My only suit was surveyed and approved before she issued the very positive command that I should go and polish my shoes to an even higher standard than I normally did. Then there was a thorough search for tell-tale signs of my not having washed myself properly. Only when I was up to 'family wedding' standards of presentation and cleanliness was I released to meet Tony, who by that time had arrived and was annoying my sister. There were the usual last minute warnings for us to keep to the footpath and not to walk on the grass, and to be sure to come straight home afterwards. My sister waved from the window as if I were departing for good. Tony was quite confused by all the fuss. He always did look rather scruffy and my mother's efforts with me had quite nicely accentuated the point.

Thankfully, it was a reasonably pleasant,warm evening. I hate to think what precautions my mother would have taken if it had been raining. Tony wanted to get me there as fast as possible while the enthusiasm lasted, so I was forced to proceed in moderate haste. Although I was quite familiar with the geography of the local area, I had not known of the existence of some buildings that were tucked away behind the houses and flats fronting one particular road. Tony led me up a driveway to a collection of timber huts surrounded by a tarmac area and a patch of good quality grassland. He explained that the whole complex had previously been a tennis club and had been requisitioned some years earlier for 'military purposes'. It looked as if this quite tatty old tennis club had been heading towards financial disaster when the war took away its premises and its members. The six courts, now without any protective fencing, provided the tarmac area that was now designated as the parade ground. It was not very military in its style but, with lots of cadets milling around, it certainly gave the impression that intense activity could happen at any moment.

Tony ushered me past the several groups of cadets, all very smartly dressed in their uniforms, and into an area within the building which seemed to be the foyer. From here I could see many poorly-painted office doors. I understood the significance of the one boldly labelled 'Commanding Officer', but the word 'Adjutant' made me wonder. While I was silently racking my brain for a possible explanation, two more boys appeared who both seemed to be in a similar position to mine. Tony had since disappeared somewhere, but that was quite usual for him. I exchanged 'hellos' with the two new arrivals then, in the true style of English gentlemen who have not been formally introduced, the conversation ended abruptly at that point.

A variety of posters had been stuck rather carelessly to the wall. These may have strategically covered the worst of the patches of grubby paint. One particular poster that caught my eye was advertising the Air Training Corps to young men over fifteen and a half years of age. Tony was certainly nowhere near that age, and I was just over fourteen. A mild crisis was developing in my mind. One half was telling me that I should not be here at all, in which case there would be long and complicated explanations when I got home, with the near certainty that the full force of any disapproval would fall upon Tony, assuming that his parents were sufficiently concerned about it. I was not at all happy with the idea that I might let Tony down. The other part of my mind suggested making an 'accidental' adjustment to my date of birth. At least, it would let Tony off the hook, and I could explain it either by saying that I had not been aware of the age limit or that I had made a genuine error. I decided on the latter plan, assuming that there were no other complications to consider once I was inside the office.

We all stood there, wanting to have a good look at each other but not quite managing to pluck up enough courage to do so. Perhaps someone had forgotten that we were waiting, or perhaps there were bets being taken on how long we would last before one of us did something positive about it. I looked around for the unlikely signs of a spy hole in the woodwork in case our movements were being observed, but there was none. As I turned round I caught sight of the smaller of the other two potential recruits. His nose was showing signs of serious impact damage, and he had unsightly thick ears that stood out almost at right angles to his head. His fists looked as if they were used to coming into contact with other people. I made a mental note to keep well clear if ever he got upset.

I was wondering about all this when Tony appeared again. He walked boldly up to that door labelled 'Adjutant', gave it a good, hard knock with his knuckles, opened the door, roughly signalled us to go in and quite firmly shut it behind us. This was the officer whose title had so puzzled me. He was wearing a uniform made of superior quality cloth, spoilt by a rather distorted hat that had been consigned to the 'in' tray on his desk. There was a matching wooden 'out' tray on the other corner of the desk in which there was a ragged pile of loose paper.

We were asked to sit down. It was funny to see how his bushy moustache twitched as he spoke. I started to watch it with fascination, but quickly realised that this was not quite the thing to do. His face wobbled around, too. He was plump, and he panted away quite seriously as he gathered up his thoughts. He introduced himself and then very effectively welcomed us to the squadron. He told us a little about the progress of the war and how the Air Training Corps fitted in with the general plan to provide training for the armed forces. The proceedings were punctuated by a few hefty blasts of smoker's cough, with further facial instability, as he went on to explain about the cadet service, training, sports, music and flying. During his ritual of lighting up a cigarette, I had the chance to cast my eye over some very nice drawings of aircraft adorning the walls. There were explanations of discipline and foot drill, and details of subscriptions that had to be paid in order to belong to this organisation. Suddenly it all came to a stop as he started to rummage through his desk to find forms for us to fill in. I wondered if one of us would dare to ask how long we were supposed to sign on for but, after writing down my name, address and date of birth, I was relieved to see that there was no space for a signature on the bottom of the form, neither was there any clue about my commitment with the cadets. I heaved a sigh of relief when the details of my age were not pursued. There was a weekly contribution of a few pence to be paid into the squadron funds, and we were warned that we might have to pay some extra money to take part in camps and other outside events.

It all seemed to be very interesting and pleasant. Even in my earlier years, I had been trained to look out for a catch somewhere in any offer that seemed too good to be true. I was not really sure how I was going to cope with this major rearrangement to my social life, but to reject the ATC at this stage might cause problems at home between my parents and myself. Somehow, the signal that one of the more senior cadets was required was transmitted to the outside of the office. There was a positive knock on the door of the office and a very smart cadet appeared. I was impressed as he came to attention, saluted, and just stood there as smart and as stiff as the guardsmen I had seen outside Buckingham Palace. He was commanded to conduct the three of us round the premises, after a free cup of tea.

We got our awful cup of tea. It came in a metal cup that had almost certainly seen some wartime service, judging by the damage around the rim. The canteen lady had not been very generous with the milk and sugar, but these commodities were scarce. The cadet who had been appointed to look after us had two stripes on his arm. I knew it meant that he had some authority, but I was not sure how much. He gave us a very good talk on the history of the squadron which, luckily for me, was brief. History was my worst subject at school, but I found that this little bit of additional knowledge was worth listening to. We were invited to peer into one room after another where we found cadets being taught a variety of subjects. Some were trying to make musical sounds on band instruments, others were attempting to identify aircraft types from pictures and, for the rest, it looked more like an extension of lessons at school.

In one room, a small group of cadets had found a set of tools and they were trying to work on a piece of metal. Tony was among them, intent on larking about with a box of matches. I then had my first thrill of the evening when the cadet who was showing us round shouted at Tony to behave: I instantly learnt that cadets with two stripes had to be addressed as corporal. Tony was not very pleased about being caught out and his usual mischievous smile rapidly changed to a look of horror. The time seemed to pass very quickly until, during a period right at the end of the evening, we were taken to see the clothing store where some very essential measurements were taken and recorded on the forms that we had completed earlier. Before I was released to go home, I was taken aside to watch the parade, during which the formalities of notices and dismissal of the cadets took place.

After the parade when the cadets were leaving for home, Tony found me again. He was bubbling over with his usual excitement, trying to find out what my reaction was to the evening's events. I was genuinely impressed with it all, but I was not going to tell him very much until I had given the matter some more serious thought. Rather like my father, I was never one to pass instant judgement. On the way home, Tony tried to press the point, but I was determined to delay my answer until later.

I had not long qualified to have my own key to the front door, and how useful it was to my plans that night. I did not want to be cross-examined by my parents just yet, so I decided to creep upstairs to bed without being detected, but then I realised that I might be missed, my parents might even go in search of me – and there could be some supper on the table. The lounge light was on, so I went in. My father was in his usual chair, reading a book. He glanced up, but did not say a word. My mother had already gone to bed but had left the usual tit-bits of food that I so dearly liked to eat at the end of the day. I polished off the food, said a polite 'good-night' to my father and went to my room without any undue delay. I liked my bed and, having had many disturbed nights during the war as the result of enemy activities, and some very unpleasant bouts of earache, I welcomed the chance to lie amongst the bedclothes, hoping to sleep continuously until breakfast. But tonight was different. Before morning, I had to collect my thoughts about this cadet venture. Even if my parents tactfully decided to say nothing until I mentioned it, there was a good chance that my sister would start up the conversation out of sheer curiosity. The first point was whether I was going to like it. Perhaps I could put up with sitting down in a classroom and learning about engineering and aeroplanes, but could I put up with wearing a uniform, with all my friends looking on, and would Tony still be there to support me if my confidence failed? The thought of being in the squadron band was rather attractive to me, as I had liked music at school despite the fact that I detested the teacher. Was I going to cope with foot drill and being shouted at if I got it wrong more than once? Doing drill with a heavy rifle on my shoulder, and with that sharp bayonet near my ears, looked rather dangerous. On the other hand, I had not seen any cadets with damaged ears or bloodstains on their tunics, so I guessed that it was safe enough. Then there was a threat of an annual camp that I was supposed to attend. I was very unsure about that. It might be quite hazardous too.

By now I was getting really tired. I had been awake far too long already that day. Further thoughts about all these matters would have to wait until tomorrow.

3

Blue for Sunday

One Friday evening my father told me he wanted to speak to me in my bedroom. That usually meant that the rest of the family were not allowed to interfere or join in the discussion. On these occasions I was often in trouble for something or other. My father did not show any signs of being annoyed by anything in particular, and this meeting began to develop into a questionnaire about my future. My father spoke of his concern that Tony was beginning to dominate my actions in many ways. He pointed out that I had got myself well established in a college of building, and he understood that, although I was nowhere near the top of class in my studies, I was taking those studies seriously. At the same time, though, he noticed that, mainly under Tony's influence, I was taking an increasing interest in military matters. He was looking for some assurance that the money that he might need to spend on my building studies was not going to be wasted by my joining the Army. I made it clear that joining the cadets seemed to be a worthwhile alternative to sitting at home, kicking my heels. There was also the very real possibility that I might be conscripted to the armed forces at some time and I wanted to be ready for that eventuality if it came. The conversation then changed direction as I found myself being pressed to become a perfect little cadet. I was seriously persuaded to follow his strict code of practice, from maximum attendance to perfect politeness at all times. My first task was to acquire a uniform. This was quite clearly under the control of the squadron warrant officer, but my father wanted to ensure that all the accessories I needed were going to be funded by a slight increase in my pocket money, and to this end I was given temporary possession of a book of clothing coupons.

On the following morning I was commanded to go on a solo expedition to the shops to try to find some socks of the right colour, and a pair of army boots to the same specification as the pair of Home Guard boots that my father had to wear. I had already worked out that I needed boots, firstly by looking at what the other cadets were wearing, and secondly through several pointed remarks by the warrant officer. I never felt totally confident about going shopping for clothes without some general guidance from my parents, but I knew my father would be at work, and my mother would be clueless on military matters. I had been given an address where I could get the boots and socks, so I decided to catch the bus to the station and then complete my journey by tube to investigate what was available. As I left the tube station in a busy market area, I noticed a lot of young people forming a queue outside a newsagent's shop. I watched for a while until some of them came out, each complete with a satisfied smile and a large ice cream. I had seen few ice creams about, so after joining the queue and handing over a portion of my pocket money, I tasted my first ice cream for several years. The address I had been given was somewhat elusive at first, but I eventually found a small plate fixed high up on a corner of a building, pointing the way down a narrow alley between two other old buildings.

A board suspended over the alley was gently swinging in the light breeze and making occasional screeching noises. The name was not easy to read as the weather had attacked the original signwriting quite seriously, but I was certainly in the right place. I pushed the door open to hear the jingling of a bell somewhere in the rear of the premises. The very high counter in front of me that suggested that some of the customers were guardsmen. It was so high that I could just about rest my arms on it. When the cobbler emerged from the room at the rear I carefully explained what I wanted. He looked as if he had been in the Army and readily understood my needs. There was very little space in front of the counter, so I was invited round the back. Amongst the debris of leather cuttings was just one chair. He offered me several varieties of long black socks, then some boots to wear over them. On the third attempt, I had a pair of solid leather size sevens, each complete with thirteen metal studs and leather laces in accordance with the regulations. Once the cobbler had confirmed that both socks and boots fitted properly, I parted with my money and the deal was done. No clothing coupons were surrendered for the boots, so I bought another two pairs of socks. I later discovered that this cobbler still had some army contacts and their cast-off boots had been cannibalised and rebuilt, so coupons were not necessary. On the way back home, on the tube, I could not resist admiring their sheer solid construction and weight. As I placed them back in the paper bag and peered through the gap in the canvas stuck on the carriage windows, I was aware of several passengers in adjoining seats being very interested in what I had bought.

When my father got home from work at lunch-time and inspected my purchases, he seemed satisfied. My mother was even more pleased to discover that during my shopping the only coupons surrendered were for the socks. In the afternoon, having been given precise instructions on the use of a hot spoon, water and polish, I raided my mother's supply of cotton wool and got busy. Soon the evidence shown by my fingers of the effort of smoothing off the leather and polishing it was well compensated by the most beautiful shine. I took the boots upstairs to my bedroom, mainly to ensure that my sister would be at a safe distance, but also with the intention of trying them on in front of the mirror. First

I compared them with my shoes. The boots looked miles better. I tried them on. My feet were now very comfortably encased, and I was a little further off the ground than before.

Little sister had gone out to play. My father had taken his gardening fork and spade to attend to his allotment and to ensure a supply of vegetables. My mother had been attending to the flowers in the garden, but was now in the lounge working away at her knitting again. I went downstairs and made several return journeys to the bottom of the garden. Marching was going to be my next new experience. I needed to become accustomed to the metal studs — negotiating the right angle turns in the garden path made me feel very unstable. After only half an hour of marching around my leg muscles were beginning to complain, and they certainly did not like stout leather boots. I went back to my bedroom and considered the situation. My father had already subsidised my boots, through a temporary increase in my pocket money, although this did not quite cover the cost. The warrant officer had demanded boots, so there was absolutely no chance of wearing shoes with my uniform. I was in a no win situation again. Those leg muscles, already with fourteen years of valuable service, just had to be conditioned to stand the strain.

A knock at the front door was followed by the sound of a wad of newspapers landing on the doormat. Only fifteen minutes earlier I had heard the sneeze of the horse and the rattle of milk bottles. There was a delivery of milk and newspapers every morning of the week, but on Sundays these noises dominated the background of relative silence. I turned over between the sheets and stayed where I was until I heard my mother working away in the kitchen, and the lovely smell of cooking breakfast wafted up the stairs. It had the same effect on me as rattling a tin plate when you wanted the cat to come in. I had managed to time my washing and dressing so finely that my breakfast was ready to be eaten as I landed on the ground floor.

Today's plan was that Tony would call for me and we would go to the squadron together. However, Tony had not appeared by the appointed time and I was becoming concerned. A quick look out of the bedroom window in the direction of where he lived failed to reveal any sign of movement. My mother was not going to allow things go wrong if she could possibly avoid it, so she decided for me that I was going to find Tony. When I knocked at the door of number 19, Tony's father answered the door. He was a big, bulky, brute of a man, always dressed in a shapeless brown suit, who always managed to look downwards without moving his head. After a brief conversation, limited to a series of monosyllables, I concluded that Tony was still in bed, and was definitely not going out because he had a cold. He was expert at arranging the onset of a cold, usually to avoid going to school, but he could also become fit and well instantly if there was something that he particularly wanted to do. So on this Sunday morning I was on my own, kitted out in my only suit, that my mother had pressed for the occasion, and with a large paper bag containing that pair of brilliant boots individually wrapped in a perfectly clean piece of scrap cotton material. As I arrived at the squadron on the dot of 9.30, the cadets were getting ready for the routine morning parade. I was among the group of recruits in their Sunday best who were asked to stand on one side of the parade to watch proceedings.

The parade took a long time, starting off with the complicated routine of cadets getting into their right places. After the NCOs had satisfied themselves that all was in order, the parade was formally handed over to a warrant officer of some dignity, who later handed the whole parade over to the commanding officer. I had not seen him before. Unlike his adjutant, he was over six feet tall and was very thin, with a pronounced military style. After making a very long and careful inspection of the cadets on parade, with the warrant officer taking suitable notes for further action, he made announcements about the forthcoming events. One of these events was flying at Hendon on the following Saturday. Although this was one of the very activities that Tony had used to recruit me, his name was not included on the flying list. Then there came the announcements for cadet training during the morning and the parade was dismissed just as formally as it had been assembled. There had been no mention of activities for us, but only moments later the warrant officer came over to tell us that we were wanted in the office.

Seven of us assembled back in the foyer area where we had first arrived to join. The walls were still drab but at least we made conversation this time. I was the first to be invited into the adjutant's office, where I was relieved of my first contribution to the squadron funds. The next stop was a visit to the clothing store where I found the warrant officer smiling all over his wicked face.

'Uniform time has come for you, my lad!' he said, by which time his big smile had worn off.

'Thank you, sir,' was all I could manage in reply.

I had never been too thrilled about getting new clothes because there was always an inquest at home to pass judgement on the suitability and colour, and often to apportion blame for ill-considered choices. Even my mother was subject to occasional criticism for expenditure on items that were considered to be excessively costly. The previous day's experience had been a bit of a training course for me, but here I was clutching a bag containing those gleaming boots and not being given too much say in the matter of a uniform.

A pair of brand new trousers came off the shelf first. I grabbed the bundle of thick serge material as it came flying over the table, quite unprepared for its weight and velocity. My nice delicate skin had been used to soft, cotton-based materials and the feel of thick military clothing now worried my nervous system considerably. There was nowhere that offered any privacy, so my first attempt at seeing if I fitted the trousers was made in full view of the other cadets. I was glad that the uniform did not include underclothes, so that the show was limited to the more respectable parts of my body. The tips of my fingers became almost numb when the sharp-edged metal fly buttons had to be forced into their stiff button-holes. I predicted that going for a quick pee might now be a thing of the past. When I returned to the vertical position the general opinion was that they were not the right size, so I had to go through the whole process again. Those who were waiting thought it was all very funny – until their turn came.

The warrant officer had previously told us each to bring with us a pair of braces, black socks and approved boots. We all had these items clutched firmly in our hands, in a variety of packaging. I opened my big mouth to ask if he wanted us to wear all these accessories now. The warrant officer came round to our side of the table and inspected the undersides of the boots, to confirm that the soles were fitted with right number of hostile metal studs, then he made sure that the socks were exactly as he had prescribed. Having investigated the army method of tying leather bootlaces and fortunately, thanks to my father's training, got it right first time, I now had to demonstrate the formal way of tying them to the remaining cadets. Then there was a tunic, with a cloth belt and shiny silver buttons, each stamped with a motif and the letters ATC. It was not new, neither was it a particularly good fit, but then I could not have been one of the standard listed shapes for military human beings. I had difficulty in locating the two hooks into the eyes on my collar. It felt much too tight around my neck and I made the mistake of criticising this tunic. In exchange, I was given another tunic of exactly the same size, almost as if it were a punishment for complaining about the first one. This one was brand new. I was not aware of it at the time, but I was probably the only cadet there who was unaware that new clothing was more aggressive to the skin than re-issued items. I silently wished I could have the first tunic back, but decided that it might not be wise to cause too much inconvenience to the warrant officer. The forage cap was the finishing touch. I was not sure how it was supposed to stay on my head, but I was told that it would if I avoided rapid movements.

As I was first to stand in the stores fully dressed, I was able to enjoy watching the other cadets being subjected to similar treatment. At the end of it all, the others were sent off to do some foot drill. The warrant officer wanted me to wait while he rummaged through some paperwork.

'You in the band?'

'Yes, sir. I joined this week.'

'One pair of gaiters, one white webbing belt and a set of dress cords.'

'Thank you, sir.'

'Wear them now. Let's have a look.'

I guessed that I might have made a mistake in volunteering for the squadron band, as that meant I had the task of cleaning this white webbing equipment. The cloth belt needed to be removed from the tunic to make way for the webbing one when I was on band duties. I had seen my father wearing brown leather gaiters with his khaki uniform for his Home Guard duties and I remember him getting into a bad temper with them, but I had never really understood their real purpose, or the difficulties that they presented. I gathered that I was on the point of finding out. When my pair came across the stores counter I was still mystified, so I asked for help. The warrant officer knew all the tricks of the trade as far as gaiters were concerned. I was invited to stand on the one rather rickety chair, while he manipulated boots, socks and trouser bottoms and made an artistic job of the lot. Then he took them all off and I had to try it for myself. I now understood the technicalities of the affair, but it took some time. Only as I began to realise that the uniform seemed designed to create a planned level of discomfort did the warrant officer make a last inspection and seem satisfied with what he had issued.

I was the only bandsman amongst those who got their uniforms that morning and, because of the extra equipment, was last to leave the stores to join the rest of the recruits. I intended to try hard to make a good impression, so I left the stores with my arms swinging in true military style. What I imagined the other cadets would see was a member of the band in all his glory. I got as far as the sergeant and came to a halt at the side of him. He knew that I was to be taught foot drill. The removal of that white webbing and the handling of a rifle would come later. By midday, all seven of us were in a straight line on the parade ground, where we were exposed to both the hot sun and the sergeant's talents at teaching drill. Two cadets out of the seven were not wearing their uniforms, as they had failed to produce the essential accessories, so they had to return on the following Sunday. I was quite surprised to find that being shouted at to undertake the necessary movements of my feet and arms to comply with designated words of command, clad in that unyieldingly hot and heavy uniform, somehow developed an unknown ability in me to do much better. It was made even more uncomfortable as all the possible routes for ventilation in the uniform had been effectively closed off. Instantly, I began to feel like a real soldier. During the next hour I was persuaded that if I did not concentrate hard to get the saluting, standing still and marching exactly right, I might have a long and unpleasant afternoon ahead of me. I had to be home for Sunday lunch, so I just had to make the effort.

Any hope of enjoying the pleasant walk home was dashed when I was told that my civilian clothes could be collected from the stores later that evening. I did not look forward to the discomfort, but I discovered that all new recruits were expected to go home wearing their uniform, and to wear it for the rest of the day. Later in the week, I found out that it was one of the warrant officer's unwritten rules for new cadets. His rules also demanded that cadets don't run or walk, so marching home was compulsory. The King's uniform had to be respected above all else.

I listened to those rows of studs crunching away on the paving stones. My collar was chafing my neck as I swung my arms to shoulder height, the trousers were being aggressive to my legs and those leg muscles were definitely having problems. What, I wondered, would I do if my cap fell off? I was not certain that I liked all this rough treatment, but I was beginning to accept that, given a little more confidence, I might even be proud of the organisation and its uniform. When I was on my way to college, wearing a bright red blazer and black trousers, I was never aware of people looking at me, although those who lived in our road must have noticed, but now I really felt self-conscious. Now that the government had abolished the black-out requirements, even more people were going to see my new figure passing along the road. The fact that I was now part of the 30 per cent of the population of Great Britain who wore a military uniform did not, at that moment, seem to enter into the matter.

Lunch would already be cooked by now and I might even be late, so there was nothing for it but to face the family comments. As I marched round the corner, within sight of home, still feeling that the warrant officer might be watching from somewhere, I could see my sister sitting on the garden fence. My father had treated the fence with creosote and she was not really supposed to be sitting on it. The sight of her gave me a clue that lunch was not yet on the table. Catching sight of me, Pam ran inside to spread the news then came out again to watch my progress. She must have shrieked quite loudly enough to alert the neighbours. On my arrival at home, my father promptly dragged me into the lounge and made me stand to attention in front of him. With his Home Guard background knowledge, he carried out his own inspection while my sister pranced around in excitement and my mother watched from a safe distance. When he was fully satisfied that all was well I was allowed to take my cap off and hang it in the hall, then I was declared to be acceptable to the family. I was warned that caps were not to be worn inside the house except on isolated occasions of military significance. An unusually restrained lunch followed, with each member of the family sneaking the occasional glance at the newly-clad cadet figure in their midst. My sister asked if I was hot and suggested that I took my tunic off, but my father reminded her that I had volunteered and there was a matter of honour to consider. He would not allow me to be in a partly-dressed state at the table. It was pretty obvious that I was going to be the centre of attention for some time and my father was going to enjoy ruling me with all the force that he could muster.

I wondered what Tony was up to and after lunch I was determined to find out. He might have planned to lumber me with this wonderful ATC idea and then not continue himself. My father did mention that he wanted me to help him with a few jobs but, after I pointed out that it would be most undignified in this smart new uniform, I was allowed to go and see the allegedly ill Tony. I went up to my bedroom, put on my cap and stood in front of the full-length mirror for a few moments. Now if I went and saw Tony while dressed like this, I was likely to score a few social points over him so, before I did anything else, I had to get it just right. I crept into the next bedroom to find out if my father's Home Guard boots were better than mine, but they were nowhere near military perfection, so I abandoned the idea of borrowing them. I set about looking at the small details of my dress ready for the onslaught on Tony. The temperature had risen a little, but there was insufficient breeze to lessen its effect, even if it had been able to gain access through that thick blue serge to get to my skin. I knew that members of the Army were compelled to fight a war while dressed in a similar fashion to this, and I could well be in the same position in a few years' time. When I thought that I had got it all just right, I went back to the mirror. This was my first day inside a military uniform and I was quite impressed with its precision, the highly-polished leather and the white webbing with the sun's rays bouncing off the brass buckles. I stood there stiffly at attention for quite a while, looking at this new beautiful sight. This was just how Tony was going to see me as soon as I could possibly get there. It was not at all comfortable and I was sweating more than I ever remembered, but I decided that I was not going to be beaten by the afternoon temperature. As I marched up the road, there were sounds of lawnmowers and hedge-clippers working away in gardens and all was quietly pleasant in the true style of an outer London suburb on a Sunday afternoon. Even the dogs were laying in the shade, fortunately not wanting to make the effort to bark or to investigate the unusual noise and the new smell of military equipment. There was just the added rhythm of my boots as they produced jolts to my body structure that I found unusual, but curiously satisfying.

I knocked at number 19, took a few paces backwards, forced myself into the position of attention and waited. Tony opened the door and stood there agape until he found his voice. I did not detect any obvious signs of illness, and I presumed that he had developed one of his crafty plots to avoid something or other. It was all falling into place, just as I had planned. I ignored his rapid flow of questions and warned him not to fake a cold in future because it could have some nasty side effects, including not having his name on the list of cadets detailed for flying. I let slip the information that I had joined the band, which seemed to torment him further. In an attempt to recover a little credibility, he invited me to stand in the centre of the lawn and persuaded his parents to imagine what he would look like, too, in a short time. His father had been in the Army and had been discharged through ill health a year or so earlier. He had a miserable disposition but the news that I had beaten Tony to being issued with a uniform appealed to what little humour he had left. I discussed many things with Tony that afternoon, including the offer of help with his school homework, but most of my breath was totally wasted because he was more interested in what his own uniform would look like when he got it. I offered to tell him about the little tricks of the trade with uniforms that I had already learnt, on condition that we went for a walk over the golf course. I knew that the path was fairly clean in good weather, and he agreed to come with me. My real motivation was the chance that we might meet some of Tony's friends so that I could score a few more points, with the bonus of getting those boots worn in before Tony got a pair, so that I could have the last laugh in that as well. After we had walked several miles I was very pleased to get back to number 19. My feet and legs were really hurting now, but I was not going to tell him that. Just before I left Tony, I told him that I needed to go back to the squadron during the evening to recover my suit and shoes. I offered to let him accompany me, in his scruffy civilian clothes, but it was all too much for him and he gently declined. It certainly made my day, and I guessed that after I left Tony may well have had one of his bouts of serious sulking.

At tea-time, I discovered that Pam had been discussing with Donald's sister the stunning style of my nice blue uniform. As the last slice of my mother's home-made cake disappeared, I could hear Donald's voice from the back garden next door. He was very tactful and polite, hinting that he would like to try on my uniform to see how it looked on him, but I steered the conversation gently away. When I told him that I had to return to cadets that evening, he realised that accompanying me would be the perfect excuse to avoid going to church with his mother, as an alternative to the missed afternoon visit to Sunday school. I suggested that if he really felt the need to wear a uniform, his Scout uniform might be appropriate. He did not like that idea: perhaps it was too much bother. I had the trump card and Donald knew it.

By the time that he had walked and I had marched to the squadron, Donald had done some serious thinking about his future plans. He boldly announced that he wanted to leave the Scouts and join the ATC. During the few moments it took to report to the warrant officer, introduce Donald as a new recruit and retrieve my bag of civilian clothes, I detected a change in the warrant officer's mood. I was ordered to wait in his office. I could not think of anything that could be wrong but, to be on the safe side, I came smartly to attention as he approached. He let me stand there for a while, then questioned me about what I had been doing since leaving the squadron at lunchtime. I answered truthfully, but there were disturbing moments of silence between his questions. Eventually, I discovered that he was puzzled by one pair of previously immaculate boots that had since become dirtied by mud and grass cuttings. It was a relief to know what the problem was, and to be aware of his level of observation. I had to admit that I wanted to impress Tony. I got a very stern warning that, in future, I was to walk on hard footpaths if at all possible. Donald had heard all that had been said while he had been waiting, and I gathered that his instant urge to join had waned slightly. However, the lure of a smart uniform was going to be a serious challenge to his scouting activities. I left him at his front door, full of enthusiasm and ready to talk to his mother. If he joined, he might even succeed in finally freeing himself from the family tradition of attending church.

I came face to face with my father as I opened the front door, and he followed me up the stairs and into my bedroom. I was still proudly wearing my uniform, slightly confused by a few of the day's events, but otherwise I felt on top of the world. I had one of those instant flashes of an oncoming disaster when I saw his eyes fall upon the trail of mud from the front door to my bedroom. I started to invent a plausible explanation to help me wriggle out of trouble, but stopped myself to allow him to open the conversation and to determine his current mood. My father was a bit upset to find that I had made my precious boots and the stair carpet dirty. There was only one sure way to bring the situation back to normal and that was to plead enthusiasm and to volunteer to clean the floor and both our two pairs of boots.

When I undressed I gave my feet an inspection: they looked quite normal. I spoke to my father about muscle problems, as he often demonstrated a high degree of common sense. His immediate suggestion was that I get another pair of boots and go for a run every night after doing my homework. I abandoned the conversation at that point, on the basis that it would either cost money, or involve me in an excessive amount of physical effort, or both.

※ ※ ※

My mother had been issued with instructions that within five minutes of arriving home from college on the Monday, I was to be parked on the kitchen stool and left there until two pairs of boots sparkled. I achieved this without any difficulty, but then I found that my father was turning the situation very much to his advantage, since between us we had a huge amount of webbing equipment to be cleaned. We finished off the evening's work by preparing this lot for our next parades, during which time my father's mood became more manageable. There were still a couple of hours of useful time left when my father raised the matter of one set of muscles in poor condition. What I did not know at that moment was that my father had acquired a spare pair of boots. He made sure that I put them on, and then gave me fifteen minutes to run to the house of an office friend of his, and back again. It was a bit of a struggle, but I missed his target by only a minute. He looked really pleased while he announced that on every evening that I did not go to the ATC he would personally ensure that I went for a run.

On the next parade evening, as soon as I arrived home from college I went upstairs to get changed. This was the first occasion when I had to dress myself in my uniform, without help or supervision, and I discovered lots of little imperfections, so I had to make a second attempt. It had taken a lot longer than I had anticipated, but I was determined to be ready well ahead of time. It was lucky that on this particular parade evening I did not need any of the webbing, as that was to be kept for band duties. I arrived at the tea table fully dressed, much to my mother's surprise and concern in case any food spillage should cause a crisis. Tony arrived with the usual indiscreet bang on the front door. I could see that he was not happy about still having to wear his old school clothes, although he had tried to do something about his shoes. We arrived at squadron much earlier than usual, mainly because my mother had considered that her expertise was limited to civilian clothing and she did not want to interfere with military items. That was strictly my father's area of responsibility and he had not arrived home before we left.

I now felt very much a part of the cadet organisation as I marched, with all the military skill that I knew, along the driveway into the headquarters, with Tony trailing along behind. The new thrill did not last as I was picked out from the parade by a corporal who required my presence in his class. I thought that we were going to have an informal chat in front of the rest of the class of young cadets, but my leisurely attitude did not please him. He was not much older than myself and had recently been promoted, and I had innocently presented him with his first golden opportunity to flaunt his new rank. I was now his helpless victim. Standing at ease while in front of his class was definitely not permitted throughout the duration of the lesson, as he delivered a very positive lecture about how not to wear the King's uniform, using me as a human visual aid. I had put a lot of effort into creases which were not all exactly in the right place. However, thanks to the demands of my father, I had at least shone my footwear to the point where it was better than that of many other cadets. He adjusted my cap because he considered it to be at the wrong angle, but there was nothing else of any great concern. Just as I plucked up courage to ask about the regulations, he dismissed the class for their canteen break. I was left standing there, having earned a reprimand for attempting to speak in his class.

After canteen break my task was to find a pair of dirty boots from the stores and demonstrate the method of cleaning them to the rest of the class. Tony was in the class and I was sure that he would remember to broadcast the details to his friends at some convenient time.

Two weeks later, Tony had been issued with a uniform. That dreadful corporal used him as his victim to illustrate how to clean webbing. Tony had to show the class how to spread the white blanco over a pair of gaiters, using an old toothbrush, and how to polish the buckles so that the webbing was not marked. He tried to make fun of his demonstration but the corporal reacted by showing how whitener came off very easily in the rain, allowing it to run over Tony's polished boots. What Tony had not yet discovered was that fitting gaiters was a bit of an art. The side straps were designed to fit tightly into the buckles, an operation that needed both strong and delicate fingers. They also had to be in the right place in relation to boots and trousers and just one little slip in their assembly could very rarely be put right without starting again from scratch. It was one of those military plans guaranteed to test patience when time was most at a premium. I discovered that many devious cadets obtained two sets of trousers, one pair of which were illegally modified to be worn with gaiters and were permanently turned up at the hem to the correct height, which made their fitting much easier. The only real problem after that was making sure it all looked perfect and not getting caught. It was fairly clear that Tony had not yet made the discovery. Although I had, I could not find a spare pair of trousers.

⁂

Complaining about aches and pains had started something off a few years earlier, when I had lots of colds – nothing complicated, just the common type. That was all very well until a few other ailments crept in. I had finished up in hospital after almost a year of painful deafness, but happily came out as good as new. Since then, both my parents had been a bit more careful with those innocent little defects of the human body. Therefore I did not want to set off the family panic button again, so I decided that the little muscle problem needed the help of the ATC, rather than a full-blown inquest with the doctor.

One parade evening I discovered the sports officer. He knew all about ailments in the world of sport, and I chatted to him about the boots that were making life hard for my leg muscles. He lit a cigarette and ran his fingers gently over the offending parts. It was nothing very dramatic, but I felt that this man knew what he was doing. Then he turned me over a few times on the workshop bench while practising his massaging skills. I stood up and it felt better straight away. The problem, he said, was a simple one to solve. My legs only gave trouble when they suddenly had something to do after a lot of relative inactivity. I was pleased about that. The long-term cure was to embark on running, starting slowly at first and then increasing my performance gradually. I was faced with something that I had previously tried to reject, which was was a serious attempt to get fit.

Then he started to explain the other part of the problem to me. I was getting worried now. Boots with metal studs often give trouble when doing drill, especially when coming to attention because this produces a jolt that travels vertically through the body. I had to demonstrate drill movements to him and then he showed me how to come to attention with the impact coming on the ball of the foot first. He made a note of my name. Every Sunday afternoon at 2 p.m. was to be a leg muscle improvement session. I was detailed and it was an order. I had to pass my physical fitness test and he was going to make sure that I did. I talked about leaving parade on Sunday morning with insufficient time to get home and back, and have lunch as well.

'Easy,' he said. 'I will tell your parents to reorganise your lunch-time to the evening.'

I was convinced that there was a plot between the squadron staff and my parents. I was not going to say a word until the day before the first session, just to see if anything was mentioned at home.

I continued my runs on a fixed route, and the sixteen minutes that I started off with was coming down by small degrees. I went for a run on Saturday evening, and had a bath when I got back. My parents had not mentioned anything, so I broached the fact that I would be at the squadron all day on Sunday. Now my mother's normal reaction to a statement like that would have been concern about what to put in the sandwiches, but all she asked was what time I expected to return home. I guessed at 6 p.m. She must have known something.

I went to the squadron as usual on Sunday morning, taking care to carry shorts and plimsolls in a bag in my left hand. I had been trained to have my right hand free while in uniform in case I needed to salute. At 1 p.m. there were ten of us munching our sandwiches. An hour later, we were laying on our backs with our legs pumping, alternating with a few jogs round the hut. What I did not expect was that we should have to do all this in our normal uniform. Several weeks later the theme changed. Instead of the sports officer, the session was run by the warrant officer and the activity changed to drill alternating with running.

My feet were gradually accepting the challenge now. The pains were diminishing, but all this physical activity was important if I wanted to get past my ATC test rather than be consigned to the scrap heap of unfit human beings. The spare pair of boots was now being used, on all days when a formal parade was not scheduled, for a run to the bus, from the station to college, at college and the same on the way back.

4
Winners and losers

A lot of cadets had gathered round the squadron notice board to have a look at a new document that had recently been pinned to it. Routine notices did not normally attract so much attention, so when the crowd had subsided I went to have a look for myself. The date for the annual inspection of the squadron had been fixed for Sunday 6 May 1945, and all cadets were required to be in attendance by 9.30 on that morning. There was a less obvious statement, on the bottom of the same notice, pointing out that excuses for non-attendance were not required and would not be accepted by the commanding officer. In the weeks leading up to the inspection, there was a lot of work to do to make the headquarters ready in time. The timber buildings had been repainted in stages over the course of the previous two months but the work had not been completed. The outside areas had been given some attention despite the problems with obtaining materials, and the grass had been cut at irregular intervals using a rather inefficient domestic lawn-mower that had seen better days. There was no hope at all of doing any more substantial work to the fabric of the buildings. The rest of the notice stated that although normal training would continue on a limited scale, some of the cadets would be employed on improving the areas around the buildings. It was followed by a schedule of cadets ordered to help with work on specific days.

My first date fell during an evening session. I had already warned my mother that I wanted to leave much earlier than usual, so she had adapted her routine to allow for this. As we were going to do some manual work, the warrant officer had asked us to wear old clothes for the occasion. That was a bit difficult for me because my college uniform, my best suit and my cadet uniform definitely did not fall into that category and wartime restrictions meant that I did not have too much in the way of old clothing that still fitted. About all that was left in my wardrobe were the pair of white shorts that I had not worn since my pre-college days and two reasonable sets of underclothes. I decided to consult my mother on the problem and, as I was about the same size as my father, she came up with an instant answer. She would tell my father that I had borrowed some of his old gardening clothes for the evening, and I was given permission to do the unthinkable and rummage through his wardrobe for something suitable.

Unfortunately, my father had been spreading manure on his allotment and his trousers had not been washed since then. There was only one choice. It had to be my father's old shirt and pullover that he had bought before the war started, my raincoat and the pair of short trousers that I had discarded when I started at college and that had not yet been cannibalised for rag. I put them on and looked in the mirror. I supposed that I had seen better-dressed scarecrows, and I would have to suffer the mockery of my fellow cadets when I arrived. My mother reluctantly approved, but then there was another hazard. Pam wanted to accompany me along the road, and I had to dissuade her. Tony was already in sight and was waiting for me to catch him up, and he was properly dressed ready to go on parade, so Pam asked why I was dressed in rags to go to the squadron. I spun her a story that if I turned up looking really untidy, then they would throw me out of the cadets and I would be free to join the Army. I thought that, with a bit of luck, she would open her big mouth on April Fool's Day and make herself look silly when I denied it. When I got to the squadron, I was delighted to find that I was not the only one experiencing difficulties with finding old clothing, so the facetious remarks were distributed fairly among the working party. The sergeant gave us the task of cutting the grass with a scythe, as another cadet had already commandeered the mower. After all, two scarecrows in a large expanse of untidy grassland would hardly look out of place.

On the Saturday before the inspection I set to work cleaning everything that I needed for the following day. The mammoth task was to clean my euphonium and by the time I had completed three hours of intricate work, getting the cleaning rag and polish round all of the tubes, I had suffered a few scratched fingers. Using brass polish inside the house was definitely not allowed unless the weather was bad, but I needed to use the kitchen when it was no longer required for cooking, to clean my belt and gaiters. Then I left them to dry on a rack above the gas stove overnight. That just left the pressing to be done, and by mid-evening, all was complete.

On Sunday morning I woke up a bit earlier than usual, in time to get to the kitchen to retrieve my kit minutes before my mother got going on the breakfast, and to put a few final touches to the euphonium and uniform. My father was listening intently to the radio with such concentration that we all ate our breakfast slowly and in remarkable silence. The news was coming through that the German forces were in a difficult position and there was speculation that they would soon surrender. At this time, the main area of wartime activity was switching to Japan. My attention to the news was interrupted by Tony's arrival, so we set off for the squadron together.

The parade of over a hundred cadets was assembled in a fairly short space of time; as we waited for the inspecting officer to arrive, we played some light music.

He arrived at precisely the right time, parking his bicycle in a secluded position at the rear of the building. After his journey he went inside for a moment, presumably to tidy himself up before being received formally by the commanding officer. He was conducted round to inspect the main parade, before his inspection of the band. From my position I was able to see him speak to the bandmaster and the front rank of trombonists, then, to my surprise, I found him in front of me. The rings round his arm indicated a rank that I had not encountered before, so at first I was quite nervous. However, my nervousness diminished as he asked my name in a reassuring way. He asked about annual camp and about my ambitions in life. I had been briefed to show an interest in joining the RAF, rather than reveal that I had been studying building, so there was little truth in what I said. I was surprised that he managed to talk to every cadet in the squadron and as far as I could hear the conversations, he seemed to ask a different set of questions of everyone he met. At the end of the inspection he spoke at some length about the probable cessation of hostilities with Germany and the continuing war against Japan, which confirmed what I had heard at breakfast time. He was quick to point out that young men would be wanted in the armed forces for many years to come, and our training as cadets was still of national importance. He commented on the outstanding smartness and enthusiasm of the squadron and seemed particularly impressed with the band.

After the formalities of the parade he was ushered into the CO's office and we were sent to the canteen for some welcome, and free, refreshments. After we had taken part in our routine training for the rest of the morning there was a parade in which the CO made a point of thanking us for our efforts and saying that both he and the inspecting officer were very pleased with the squadron. All my polishing and cleaning had been duly recognised, but it might not have happened that way if my parents and the squadron officers had not been very firm in demanding high standards in all that I did. I felt very satisfied with myself that day. Tony and I had planned to go to the cinema that evening and we were both going in the uniforms that we had been asked to wear and that we had worked so hard at. It would be like a mark of loyalty to the squadron.

Adolf Hitler had died almost a week earlier and, by Monday evening, the whole of the country was aware that Germany had surrendered. My father's first intention was to light a bonfire with his Home Guard uniform, until he was tactfully reminded that it was probably illegal to do so as it belonged to the government. Then he wanted to burn his gas mask, but there was a problem with the smell. I did not want to get involved with these issues and I was sure that my mother could handle my father, so I went out to search for Tony. He was missing from home and his sister came to the door. I discovered that his parents had taken him out for the day, probably due to the high level of mischief that developed when he was left alone. Mrs Allen lived three doors away and called me into her house as I wandered back from number 19. She was terribly excited as she had just learned that her husband, who had been a prisoner of war in Germany, was now reported to be safe and well. The ubiquitous answer to any crisis was a cup of tea, and she already had the kettle on. Her excitement waned a little when I turned down her offer, so she opened the kitchen cupboard and produced two glasses of a most peculiar liquid. It smelled awful. It was obviously earmarked for a celebration so I wrongly assumed that it would taste better than it smelled. It burnt my throat and, after a short time, it was not doing my head much good either. She reached for the bottle to top up my glass and I caught sight of the label which told me I was drinking brandy. I instantly decided that I did not like it, but as a polite escape was clearly out of the question, I set about drinking as little as possible while she emptied the remains of the bottle into her own glass.

The dear old lady obviously wanted someone near her to share her joy, and I just happened to be around at that moment. When I eventually got away, I made a brave attempt at walking home in a straight line, but my legs were not co-operating with my brain. I remember using the fence for support and trying to get hold of the door knocker, but I must have landed against the door with a hefty thud. Some time later, I woke up in bed, with the doctor and my parents leaning over me. It was dark outside and the weather was misbehaving, so I must have been in bed for several hours. The doctor asked a few pertinent questions and very quickly established that I had got seriously drunk. I must have fallen asleep again, not waking up until late on Tuesday morning. My head was banging away and there was a horrible taste in my mouth. I tried to gather my thoughts, immediately rejecting the idea of college and breakfast. There was only one thing that I wanted urgently, and that was the toilet. I glanced out of the window and noticed that it was raining very hard, so that reinforced my decision not to go anywhere except back to bed. When my mother eventually came into my room, I had to explain how I got to this state,as there had been a lot of concern about my current state of health. My mother confirmed that it was Tuesday. Within an hour the rain had stopped and a few rays of sunshine were filtering through the gaps between the curtains. I calculated that it must be about midday according to the location of the sun. But if it was midday on Tuesday, why was I hearing father's voice from downstairs? Obviously, something was amiss that needed investigation. As I was beginning to feel a bit better, I decided it was medically safe to wash and put on some clothes, then to make a quiet investigation of the ground floor.

Downstairs, I lurched towards the lounge windows and saw that most of the ladies who lived in the street were erecting tables in the road to prepare for a celebration. The milkman was having difficulty in manoeuvring his horse and cart between the obstacles. The dustman had got his lorry to the end of the road, then had abandoned it there because there was no room to turn round. A few gentle enquiries enabled me to discover that while I had been under the spell of Mrs Allen's brandy, a national holiday had been declared and a party had been hurriedly arranged to celebrate the end of the war with Germany. Asking for cooked food at this hour of the day would not be looked on very kindly, so I sought my mother's permission to raid the larder for bread and cheese. I felt a bit better after that and it was certainly much nicer than going to college.

The feasting really started late in the afternoon with as many culinary niceties as the meagre contents of larders would allow. It was really a day for the younger children, with a few balloons and fireworks that had been stored away for just such an occasion. I noted that residents who were frequently heard arguing with each other over their garden fences were now happily all working together with a common purpose. Everyone was so happy that we were triumphant after six years of war and that we had not been overrun by German forces.

There were some very hurried arrangements during the week to organise a thanksgiving service at the football ground on the following Sunday. It was a two-mile march from the squadron headquarters and, for this distance, the simpler items of music were chosen from our library. The service was formal, with hymns played by the band and a two-minute silence, followed by Johnny Elms playing the *Last Post* and *Reveille* to absolute perfection. Then there was a march past involving a reported thousand service personnel and civilians, with an open invitation to the drill hall for refreshments afterwards. It was usual for the band to put their instruments away safely during these events, and we were last to arrive in the drill hall. Our welcome at the refreshment area was a total and unscheduled surprise to us all. As we entered, there were cheers and applause for our musical performance. We had never been so popular before and I was certainly overwhelmed by it all. After an hour our bandmaster signalled that it was time to depart, but the assembled company had other ideas and were not going to let us leave quite so easily. Their requests for more music kept us entertaining them for another hour. When eventually we got away, amid more rousing cheers, I just felt so great despite having to be late for Sunday lunch.

That was not quite the end of the celebrations for the month. If it had not been for my father and his efficient diary, I might not have known anything about Empire Day on 24 May. This day had been set aside for youth organisations of all kinds to make their presence known, usually by their members wearing their uniform for the day, but it had not always been very well supported over the years. My parents were very proud of all they had in life so during a serious family discussion one evening the subject of Empire Day arose. I was not aware until then that the warrant officer was in the habit of meeting my father from time to time, but it must have been because of a connection at work, as my father was not one for serious socialising. Some time later I realised that the liaison between them was being used to guide my ATC activities, which explained a number of events that had happened to me.

I detected a plot somewhere when my father decided that I should represent the squadron at college on Empire Day, and he would not entertain any further discussion on the subject. When he said something final like that, it always meant that any attempt to question his decision had serious consequences. I thought that it was all very unusual for him to dictate what I should do in the ATC, so I had a word with a number of other cadets on the next parade evening. I discovered that some of their parents had made similar demands. At the end of the evening, the topic was mentioned on parade. Our CO clearly expected us to wear our uniforms during the day as a mark of respect for those who suffered in the war. It was a result, then, not of a particular plot between my father and the warrant officer, but rather some general pressure by parents upon the uniformed youth organisations, following the cessation of hostilities in Europe.

The walk to the bus stop took nearly ten minutes and accurate timing had been necessary in the past to ensure that I met my friends on the way. It was somehow not quite the same as going to college in my college uniform or going to the squadron wearing cadet uniform. I was proud of both sets of clothes, but I did not feel at ease. Perhaps the difference was only that I was within sight of people who did not normally see cadets at that time of the day, or could not relate an ATC uniform with a briefcase full of homework, or perhaps did not appreciate the significance of the date. Whichever it was, the reaction from the remainder of the community was quite interesting. I was the subject of many inquisitive looks. An Act of Parliament decreed that intending passengers for a bus must form and keep a queue. Being truly British, they were conditioned into facing the same way as well. I fell in behind a number of other people just as the Act had intended, but I became very conscious that some were itching to have a good look at the unit details on my shoulder flash, without actually making it too obvious. It was a good game to turn slightly so that whatever they desperately wanted to see was just out of their view, and I discovered that, if I aimed my eyes at theirs, they reluctantly looked for an approaching bus or into their morning newspaper.

During the war years, bus conductors seemed to have developed a turn of wit to keep their passengers happy in times of crisis. On this morning I did not particularly want a jolly and talkative bus conductor, because I would then become the butt of his witty remarks. I hoped that there would be sufficient room in the bus so that I could find a seat upstairs, away from the standing passengers, though that had the disadvantage of requiring extreme care to make a dignified exit on the way down again. A heavy briefcase, studded boots and a sharp turn or rapid deceleration was not the best of combinations for moving around in a crowded bus. Then there was the risk of losing a layer of polish from my toe caps in the struggle to get along the gangway. I was lucky, as the first bus that came took most of the front of the queue, and that left me with a reasonable choice of seat on the one immediately behind it. The bus conductor was one of the old-fashioned, probably ex-service type who tactfully got on with the job of issuing tickets to passengers who were beginning to overload the bus. There was a little glint in his eye and a hint of a smile as he went about his work. When I got into the underground station, I was delighted to hear 'A very good morning sir' from one of the station staff who acknowledged my status. It was an improvement on their usual theme, as I was used to being labelled as one of the mischievous little brats going to college. As the train got closer to London the number of representatives from the cadets and other uniformed youth organisations increased quite considerably, so I did not feel quite so prominent as I had earlier in my journey.

Together with fourteen Army Cadets, six ATC Cadets and a few Sea Cadets and Scouts, I completed the contingent of uniformed students in the class, and we seriously outnumbered those that were left. Our master very tactfully asked about the significance of each of our badges and amended the class register to include our ranks. I had always thought of the Army Cadets as aggressive opposition, but a considerable bond grew up between us during the day, with an exchange of information about our respective units. After the initial shock to the education system, and some military imitations from the minority, I gradually felt that I was being accepted as a normal human being. By the time I had left the last of the morning classes for the dreadful canteen at lunch-time, I had received a surprising number of enquiries about the cadets. There were many who wanted to experience the instant thrill of being in a uniform and many others were quite convinced that they were going to be compulsorily enlisted in the forces and shot at by the enemy. Many were looking for some preliminary training as an aid to self-preservation.

At lunch-time there always was a bit of congestion in the male toilets, but today it was worse. I put the delay down to the difficulty in getting those difficult metal trouser buttons undone and then done up again. The cubicles were designed for the personal needs of one body at a time, so when I spotted a group of four students huddled together, I had the impression that they were intent on causing disruption in some form. With a fair number of cadets about, many of them making recognisable military noises and all needing to obey the call of nature at some time, there was a good chance that a planned joke would be fairly successful and liven up their day. I had just finished a most satisfying piddle, and was starting to adjust my dress, when a group of them forced me to face the wall in a corner, by placing a set of very strong hands on the back of my head and on my waist. My boot studs did not grip at all on the smooth tiled floor, so once my arms had been forced behind my back and I felt the click of a pair of handcuffs lock my wrists together, I was in rather a difficult position to get free. I knew that my cap had been taken and there was a hand in my trouser pocket removing money. That indicated that it was not a practical joke or harmless fun, but a rehearsal for more serious crime. I remember a hefty impact from behind, and then I must have passed out for a while. My next recollection was of being viewed from above by two of the masters. I was still not properly dressed and was embarrassed to note that my dick was still protruding. No one had dealt with that part of my anatomy and it had to wait until my hands were free. Our college had specialist departments for building and engineering, so they borrowed tools to break the handcuffs and applied a small plaster to cover a cut on my face. There was very little other damage to speak of, except for the loss of money and my cap. During the afternoon, and from somewhere unknown, I was presented with a replacement cap, and the Army Cadets in my class had thoughtfully gathered up enough cash to make sure that I had sufficient to get home with. I thanked those who had helped me after that ordeal, but on the way home I was rather more observant than usual. I had not seen who my attackers were, but I had a slight inkling that it might not be too long before someone reached the top of the list of suspects. After all, the college had its known rebellious students.

Within a week, I had paid back the small loans of cash and made two very good Army Cadet friends into the bargain. I noted with some concern that one particular ATC Cadet in the class had kept himself well away from the events and for him that seemed to me to be very much out of character. For most of the time he was quiet and self-contained, but sometimes he had a bout of high spirits. There could have been some link between him and the assault, but I was stumped for ideas for bringing the matter to light. Perhaps it was best left for a while, then something might turn up.

5
My lovely body again

It was another Sunday morning. I admit to having made a lot of noise with the door knocker at number 19 at a rather early hour; when Tony eventually came to the door he was still half asleep. This morning I had promised myself that I was going to get him to the squadron.

'Hello, Tony. I heard that you were very ill!'

He looked surprised.

'No. I'm OK. I feel fine.'

'Oh, I'm pleased about that. Were you going back to bed again, because I did not want to disturb you?'

'No.'

He rubbed his eyes, still looking a bit confused.

'Good. I'll be back in an hour, then. Make sure that you are properly dressed for parade. I've had a tip about flying.'

I left quickly. He watched me go down the road for a moment before he shut the door. The time was 7.15 in the morning, which meant that the hour I had given him was due to expire at 8.15. I knew that Tony would do anything to go flying, except perhaps go on parade on Sunday morning. I wondered if my plot was going to work. It had been raining overnight but it had cleared up and all that was left now was the smell of wet grass and the remains of a few clouds drifting across the sky.

A week earlier I had passed my physical fitness test by doing a long jump to the required standard, and running 200 yards at some dangerous breakneck speed. That was it and I now had the entry on my record card to prove it. The adjutant had queried why I did it in my uniform instead of vest, shorts and plimsolls.

'Sir, it was the result of a bet with two sergeants who thought that I was useless. It cost them a shilling each – and, sir, you will need to make an note about all the other subjects that I've passed in the last month. Can I have my basic badge, please?'

He never even looked up.

'No. You've got one more exam to go. See me next Sunday at nine o'clock.'

'Yes, sir.'

I saluted, though I do not think he noticed. I turned about and marched off, closing the door most carefully behind me.

It was a bit after 8.15 a.m. when Tony indicated his arrival with his usual knock on the door and came inside. The milkman had not been but my mother had made breakfast. Tony looked round the room.

'Why am I so early?'

'Because you've got to go to the squadron with me and I am due there at nine o'clock. The adjutant wants to see me.'

'Why?'

'Don't know. Wasn't told. Come on we're going now.'

Tony was not happy. I was sure that he thought he should still have been sleeping.

While I was in the squadron office the adjutant informed me that there was a good chance I would actually have to join the armed services within the next few years. It might only be a temporary interruption to my chosen employment but, before I could have my basic badge, I was required to take a preliminary ATC medical examination. This was the reason for my having to arrive so early. I found it quite incredible that I had been detailed for a medical without any hint that it was going to happen. If my mother had known in advance there would have considerable fuss at home before I left, but perhaps this type of instant instruction was planned to overcome these parental problems.

It was no more than a couple of hundred yards to the bus stop. There were still very few private cars on the roads, so the sight of a bus just leaving was of little concern to me as the service was quite frequent. I must have attracted a little bit of attention while I waited there, with a small packet of papers in one hand. Standard issue ATC uniforms did not have a designated space for envelopes of the foolscap size, so the only option would have been to fold it repeatedly and stuff it in one of the small breast pockets on the tunic, but this would have resulted in a very crumpled document. I even had the luxury of having a bus warrant for the four miles that I needed to travel to the appointed address. When I presented it to the bus conductor it made me feel rather important. I was now on official government business, complete with an envelope clearly marked 'ON HIS MAJESTY'S SERVICE'. I kept it in my hand, just in view, to tease the nosy parkers.

The doctor's three-storey house rose up above the pavement like a small mansion on the corner of a pleasant avenue. I felt so terribly humble, climbing up the flight of stone steps and then using the great door knocker which created a hollow echo on the other side. I expected the door to be answered by a nice, kind nurse or the doctor himself, but the person I saw could have been the doctor's aged mother. She directed me to a lofty waiting room. I was sure that doctors always arranged that patients were left in the waiting room long enough for their imaginations to run riot. I felt as if I had been sent to be used in a medical experiment or research. There were no sounds of activity from the other side of the surgery door. A notice on the wall stated that he opened on Sunday mornings for cadet examinations only, and I was there alone, without a soul to share the terror of any forthcoming torture. Only a year earlier I had been sent to hospital for them to sort out a painful bout of deafness and nasal problems. There, an irritable doctor had subjected me to some very rough handling before making the decision that I needed a session on the operating table. The thought of a repetition of that experience was not very nice.

When I did get inside the surgery I was relieved to note the absence of any horrifying instruments in the room. When he had finished having a good look and listen from the outside, he then investigated further by inserting something technical into every orifice giving access to my inner workings. He actually got me interested in what he was up to and, as he proceeded with the examination, explained the technicalities of medical science in simple terms that I could understand. I asked if I was medically suitable for the Army or Air Force and the doctor took a long time explaining the basic requirements for military service. He had spoken to the sports officer and found out some background and I was assured that I was quite acceptable for a military career. But then, the real reason for my visit was that I was required to come up to a set standard to be accepted into the ATC, at the time a requirement for my basic badge. If I was good enough for the Army, then I was also good enough for the ATC, and I had nothing to worry about, except that my entry into the armed services was now guaranteed. It was well over an hour before I was released into the outside world. On the way out I had the pleasure of seeing two unknown cadets in the waiting room, looking rather scared.

I arrived home for the formal Sunday roast joint and all its trimmings much later than usual, so I felt duty bound to offer my parents an explanation. I told the story while my mother was in the kitchen, trying to make a spoilt lunch look more attractive. I thought that I might at least have got just a little sympathy. My father thought it was highly amusing and pointed out that I had volunteered to be a cadet and promised that he would make sure that I accepted what was coming to me. He added that he would have been even more pleased if the doctor had added a few injections to his list of cadet activities and I had come home with an arm full of chemicals. He always took great delight in knowing that I had been given a hard time, on the assumption that the experience would be valuable.

During that afternoon I could not work up any enthusiasm for anything that was likely to tax my brain and I noticed that my father was not too active either. Perhaps it was the state of the weather, or just the result of lots of work that had suddenly come to natural end now that war and Empire Day and college examinations were out of the way. My mother noticed that we were both at a loss to know what to do. There was nothing that attracted us. Even the wireless failed to rustle up an interesting programme and I was certainly not going to look for Tony. My mother suggested that we went out for a walk, taking care to be back at tea-time. A ramble over the golf course was suggested, but I knew almost every inch of that route. Then my mother suggested that we went to see if the prisoner-of-war camp was still there. She was tactfully trying to get us out of the house, for reasons best known to herself.

My father came to a decision and announced that he was going for a walk to the small lake where Donald sometimes went fishing and for nature study with the Scouts. It was about a five-mile round trip through pleasant suburban areas and parkland. I thought it was an excellent idea, as it would keep my father out of my way, but he was not having that. I very quickly discovered that I was expected to accompany him, but I wondered why. We started off by traversing the level crossing that I had used as a short-cut to school in the earlier days of the war and where we used to annoy the crew of the steam engine that ferried two coaches of passengers to and fro. We had discovered that by larking about on the railway line we could irritate the fireman and provoke him to throw lumps of coal at us. Naturally we took the coal home to augment our meagre supply. My father was not saying very much, so I decided to make conversation and see what happened.

'Father, did you have to have a medical to get into the Home Guard?'

'No. They just told me that I had to wear a uniform on most evenings when German aircraft were about, look for bombs or any resulting damage and then report it.'

'Didn't you have to go for a medical like I did?'

'It wasn't necessary, because we could do the job whether we were fit or not.'

'Did you have to wear a tin hat, then?'

'Yes, but only as a protection against odd bits of shrapnel.'

I was not having any success in kick-starting a lengthy conversation, so I thought for a while to see if I could think of other ideas to get him going.

'Father, did you know Mr Martin?'

'Yes, he's in my office. Why do you ask?'

'Well I knew a boy called Swill Martin at school.'

'Swill is a funny name. That wasn't his real name, was it?'

'No, but we called him Swill because he was as fat as a pig, and he used to eat up all our left-overs at lunch time.'

'Oh!'

'Did Mr Martin have to be in the Home Guard as well?'

'We all did.'

'So how many did you have on parade each evening?'

39

'About six of us — that was usually enough.'

'But if there were about thirty of you in the office, that meant that you only needed to do a duty every five days, so why did you go on alternate evenings?'

The conversation was well in progress now, so I kept it going.

'Well if there were no raids, we went and played table tennis or went for a drink.'

'That's not what old Swilly told me.'

'What did Swilly tell you, then?'

'He said you had a room by the side of the canal and round the corner from the table tennis room.'

'That's right.'

'Swilly's dad said that the two of you had a couple of girls in there on most nights.'

My father looked embarrassed.

'Look, my ankle is starting to hurt again. I think that we ought to turn round towards home.'

'Well I'm OK.'

'Yes but I don't want to have any days off work with it.'

'What did the girls do, then?'

'They only made the tea.'

'What, just for the two of you?'

My father knew that he had been rumbled, and we were on the shortest route home.

'Look. Whatever you do, don't tell your mother, as she might get the wrong impression.'

'I shouldn't think so. You're in love with her — you must be, because you kiss each other when you go to work and come home again.'

I think that my father knew he had said too much and he was quietly panicking.

'Yes we do like each other, but you're not going to mention it to your mother, otherwise I shall find a good reason to do something about it.'

'You can't do that.'

'Yes, I can. Look, I'm having no more of this discussion about what I did at work. It's secret.'

I could not press him much further so I let the matter drop. I knew now that if ever I was in a difficult spot, I had something to bring up in conversation when my mother was about. The only thing that my father said on that subject before we got home was that if I mentioned it again I would be sent away to a boarding school. I took no notice as I knew that my parents could not afford it, but I would rather comply and conform to my father's wishes anyway.

Tony and Donald came to the door that evening, wanting to know where I had disappeared to during the morning. I told them that I had to go on a confidential errand to London, but I was not allowed to say exactly where. That really got them both guessing and to change the subject I asked Tony about his Sunday morning activities. He was still not very happy about being extracted from his bed at that early hour, but he did think that his early arrival could result in his name being put on the list for flying. Tony changed the topic of conversation to ask what we were going to do now. He suggested that there might be a good film on at the cinema. When we got to the cinema we found that Tony was right, there was a good film on, but there was also a long queue to get in. We agreed that there was no point in waiting so Tony's mind quickly applied itself to finding other forms of amusement. While Donald and I had been seriously discussing the matter, Tony had wandered off somewhere. He reappeared with a big smile and a girl on each arm. Only Tony could have achieved that in the space of ten minutes. Tony was being very polite and made the introductions. Jane asked why Donald was not wearing a uniform, which made Donald look very embarrassed. He had probably not been in this kind of situation before. We paired off, Jane with Tony and Pam with me. The weather was not too warm so, by general agreement, we found suitable refreshment in a local café. During the next few hours we enjoyed a lot of social chat as we shared some food and drinks. By now it was dark and much colder outside and we no longer had enough money for further eating and drinking. Tony discovered that he had not even got sufficient cash for his bus fare so he decided to walk Jane home. Our evening party broke up. Donald, Pam and I went to the bus stop and we made our way home.

I was on my way up the stairs to bed when there was a knock at the door. It was more delicate than Tony's characteristic knock and when I opened the door his father was standing there. Tony had not yet arrived home and he asked if I knew where he was. I could give him no more information than that I had last seen Tony with Jane leaving a café in the High Street. His father let out a grunt of acknowledgement and went away.

Tony was not at the squadron on the next parade and I understood that he had not been home since our evening out. Pam was waiting outside the squadron as I left, asking if I had seen Jane. This was a mystery that I was going to keep well away from. Clearly their respective parents had a real problem to sort out.

6

Off to somewhere unknown

The squadron notice board was primarily used for the routine instructions, and not many cadets really bothered to read them in any detail. It was all very formal and not in the least attractive to the poorly-educated cadets who found that they had difficulty in coping with the official jargon. Nor was it very convenient for the smaller cadets, as it was high up on the wall and they were forced to perform amazing if minor physical feats until they read down far enough to find out if it was to their advantage. A large gathering of cadets around the notice board one evening made me think that there had either been a disaster or there was a forthcoming popular event. Few other notices ever produced such interest, so I went investigating too. I discovered that there was to be an annual camp, at an unknown location, for seven days for some intensive military training. It was quite probable that it would be held on a Royal Air Force establishment, but the current security situation was such that we would not find out very much until we got there.

There was an invitation to put our name on the appended list, with number, rank, surname and initials, in that precise order, and with a request for a contribution of eight shillings. One of the established senior NCOs whispered some of those nice little words in my ear, from which I positively got the message that I should experience all kinds of unpleasantness if my name was not the list before I left that particular spot. Attendance at an annual camp was quite voluntary, of course, but I noticed a lot of very threatening persuasion going on. By the time I wrote my name down, there must have been 80 names above mine on the list.

My parents had to be told the dates of the camp and the news had to be broken carefully, to avoid any alarm. They were usually quite happy for me to embark upon these activities and they trusted me. I was careful to avoid any mention of Tony because his name was naturally associated with mischief, danger and chaos. I had already been detailed to reserve myself a place. For the small sum demanded, my parents would not have to feed or look after me for a whole week. To them it was a most attractive idea, and they openly discussed the advantages of not having me around to annoy my sister and of not having Tony around, with the resulting savings to the family food bill. My mother saw other benefits, and suggested to my father that he no longer had an excuse for delaying the redecoration of my bedroom, and with a slight temporary rearrangement he could even redecorate my sister's room in the same week. He was not impressed with this extra burden and I was quickly dispatched to my bedroom while my parents sorted out their differences.

At breakfast time on the following morning, my mother announced that, after due consideration, I was going to be sent to camp. My mother very rarely came out with statements like that in such a positive way. As my father sat there in silence, I assumed that she had achieved the unusual trick of getting her own way. Now I was reminded to be sure to pay the money at the next parade, out of a temporary increase in my pocket money, and told that sufficient funds would be provided to allow me to maintain equality with the other cadets. I had to agree to wash behind my ears properly every morning in particular, and to undertake all those other activities of a hygienic nature that I sometimes tried to avoid at home.

I reported to the adjutant, to pay the camp fees. I was always very careful to pay my military respects to him and this occasion was no different, except that he was in the middle of adding up a column of figures and I had to wait in his office until he was ready to attend to me. Standing to attention without moving was now a practised art, but I was beginning to feel uncomfortable and could have done with leaving his office for a few moments. Although it would have been polite to ask, I felt that interrupting the mathematical flow was not a good idea. My discomfort was becoming serious and there was nothing for it but to release one of the heftiest farts that it has ever been my misfortune to let fly. I was still standing to attention and he was still adding up. His pen was now at the bottom of the column of figures and he was on the point of looking up when I decided to speak.

'Sir, my profuse apologies for the wind, but it must have been something that I ate before I came out.'

He looked up at me and I looked straight ahead. The tense silence, now accompanied by the appalling smell, was almost unbearable. This was surely going to be rewarded with hours of fatigues or something just as nasty. He stood up and then walked towards his office door.

'You can stand there until the smell has cleared.'

'Yes, sir. I'm very sorry, sir.'

The door closed and I heard his footsteps go across the bare floorboards of the foyer. I heard the noise of cadets in the main parade area and of voices, but nobody entered the office. Later I heard the sounds associated with canteen break, and the footsteps of someone approaching the office. It must have been a cadet because officers wore rubber on their shoes. The door opened but I dare not turn around or move from the position that I had taken up on arrival. Someone was behind me. Slowly the flight-sergeant came within my line of sight.

'Cadet, you're deep in the shit.'

I had to try my best to get out of this predicament.

'I did apologise to the adjutant, flight-sergeant, but I must have eaten something aggressive and there was not the time to excuse myself. I'm sorry, flight-sergeant.'

'That sounds fine but you've brought the adjutant's paperwork to a halt, so you will report to me after final parade.'

'Yes, flight-sergeant.'

'You can go to your class now. Canteen break has finished.'

I left the office and he followed me out. After the final parade that evening, I reported to the flight-sergeant as instructed, having first succeeded in getting a receipt for the eight shillings, and a brief list of essential items that I needed to take to camp.

The flight-sergeant met me inside the adjutant's office and it had to be best behaviour time again.

'The adjutant had a lot of work to do tonight and you have disrupted it. That means that on Saturday afternoon at 2 p.m. you will report here to help the adjutant with his backlog of work and you will not leave until it is done.'

'Yes, flight-sergeant.'

That was a far lighter punishment than I had expected, but I would have to see what Saturday would bring.

When I got home, I studied the information sheet concerning camp. The squadron would supply a waterproof groundsheet, but everything else I needed to wear seemed to be my problem. I had to make sure that I had shirts for use with detachable collars, but no collars were to be taken, and I had to have a pair of shorts. Then there were the necessary underclothes, toilet kit, knife, fork, spoon, unbreakable plate, mug, needle and thread. My father said that he would lend me his Home Guard issue kit bag, with the promise of a severe hiding and no pocket money for a month if I lost it. I noticed that the kit bag was short of a padlock, so on Saturday morning I ventured off to the shops to see what I could get. I explained to the lady behind the counter in the ironmonger's precisely what I wanted and what it was for. She was confused by the fact that I needed a padlock for a military kit bag, as I was quite obviously far too young to join the Army. Her husband came to the counter and both of them cross-examined me about the ATC and my involvement in it. They looked at each other in silence and nodded. There were a few extra items that I needed and while these were being organised, her husband went off and brought back two likely-looking potential cadets. I remembered all the intense persuasion that Tony had inflicted on me, and realised that I might have done a similar good public relations act on the shopkeeper. The two boys were remarkably silent and I imagined that they could be quite a troublesome handful in the right circumstances. The arrangement was that I would call for them on the following morning and take them along to join.

While waiting for the bus back home, I was thinking again about the rumours that had been circulating that cadets were to be drafted in to the Army, without any regard to which of the cadet services they had joined. Then there was that notice about annual camp with no indication of where we might be going, and the intense pressure by the senior cadets to get me to volunteer. I wondered if there was even the slightest chance that information about annual camp might conceal plans to conscript us all into the Army. I might have been too young for fighting like the soldiers did, but I was also aware of the existence of boy soldiers. What a thought! I would have loved to know the truth, but I was not sure who I could ask without tempting someone to give away classified information.

I knew that I was wanted on Saturday afternoon, so at lunch-time I took care about what I was eating, so that I did not cause offence again. I did not have any more precise instructions than to turn up at 2 p.m., and I made sure that I was there on time. The gates were locked and the first person to appear was the flight-sergeant, dressed ready for football match.

'You have upset me, young man.'

'Sorry, flight-sergeant, but how?'

'I expected to see you in your civilian clothes, at which I was going to send you home to put your uniform on, but I see that you have done the right thing.'

'Yes, flight-sergeant.'

'The adjutant will not be here for a while, so you can amuse the local residents with rifle drill until he arrives.'

I went to the stores with him and took possession of one heavy rifle, then he told me to place myself at the entrance to the squadron, with an order to come to attention if anybody walked by. The adjutant arrived after half an hour and I was told to go into his office. Several hours of the afternoon were taken up with checking his accounts and making sure that the cash agreed with them. I was glad that there were no errors and at the end of this the adjutant seemed fairly pleased, but before the rifle was returned to the store and he was ready for home, I was subjected to another lengthy bollocking. My father wanted to know why I had been to the squadron on a Saturday afternoon, and I just told him that I was helping the adjutant with some paperwork prior to camp. I think that he might have believed me.

On Sunday morning I left the house early and took the bus into town. The two brothers were seriously unhappy about joining the ATC and my arrival, in a smart uniform, at the ironmonger's shop did nothing further to convince them. Their parents were instantly aware of the problem. While they politely asked me to wait, I was aware of some shouting and protests going on in the room at the rear. When they emerged again at the door, they were both feeling their ears to check how much damage had been inflicted. On the way to the squadron they were clearly anxious about joining. They were not prepared to talk to their parents about it until they knew more about what was involved. I was almost in trouble too. By the time that I had been to town and back on the bus, the squadron had assembled for parade and I only escaped from more punishment by pleading that I had brought two potential recruits.

I desperately wanted to know more about the possible conscription into the Army that I had heard about. I did not want to make a fool of myself and I concluded that, as I had not formally been told about it, then it was quite likely that none of the other cadets would know either. The answer was to ask one of the officers. As luck would have it, I found the warrant officer in the stores and I decided to ask him. He did not know the answer and thought my fears were unfounded. However, he noted my great enthusiasm to join the Army and told me that if there were any opportunities, he would let my father know. That was just what I had not wanted, and my big mouth could now have landed me in trouble. I dared not ask anyone else for advice in case someone saw the possibility of a practical joke. The other danger now was that my father might find out and become interested in the idea. I would find both of these events quite impossible to deal with, so my best chance was not to mention the matter again.

From this point until departure for camp, all of our Sundays were to be reserved for the preliminary training needed for this great event. I was nominally in the band and had been issued with a euphonium. At my rate of progress I would be nowhere near proficient at it by the time we went to camp, so I was to play the cymbals as a temporary measure. That meant the minimum of band practice and the maximum of learning drill and the camp routines. The space on the notice board which had been occupied by a list of cadets who were to attend camp had now been replaced by a training programme for Sunday mornings. At the bottom of the notice was a very bold reminder that any Sunday absence could result in forfeiting payments and not going to camp.

For the two evenings before departure for camp my bedroom looked remarkably untidy, a situation which my father quickly noticed and demanded rectification. I had laid out every item I needed for camp, in exactly the same order that it appeared on the kit list, now carefully pinned on my wall. Pressing the tunic and trousers took me the best part of an evening, which quite surprised my mother as she considered that clothing was her responsibility. I had asked her on many occasions to leave my uniform for me to deal with but until now it had little effect. From that time my parents kept their distance and looked into my room only often enough to check that all was well. I do not think that they were aware that cadet training over the past few weeks had covered a vast range of domestic subjects.

I had been shaken from a pleasant sleep by my worried mother very early on the Saturday morning, as it was the great day of departure for camp. In those few moments, as I tried to achieve a sufficient level of consciousness, I saw the Home Guard kit bag leaning against the bedroom wall, almost fully packed, as if to remind me of the day's plans. I was never enthusiastic about getting out of bed, but now there was a feeling of urgency developing in the household, so washing, dressing, eating and packing the remaining sundries were dealt with in an unusually efficient way. There was nothing else to do except to go through the front door and be on my way. My mother wanted to kiss me goodbye but I was rather reluctant to oblige in full public view. She got her way, but then my sister wanted a kiss too, so I was forced to comply, to avoid further commotion. I really was glad to get away as fast as I could just then.

The railway station car park had hardly seen a car since the beginning of the war, except perhaps for the occasional taxi or commercial vehicle, and it was certainly seriously under-used. It now played host to a lot of well-organised and mischievous cadets. There were several parents who had accompanied their precious offspring, and who exchanged kisses with them in public amid great cheers and other noises from the remaining cadets. A group of five aged ladies, who had made early visits to the butcher and fishmonger on the other side of the road, were heard discussing the fate of all the assembled young men on the assumption that we were all off to attend to some real warfare. A minor collection of people who should have been passing the spot without concern had stopped to have a look, and the local police constable was observing from a very safe distance. With a few shouted orders we were organised into three ranks, then after a count of bodies and a lot of shuffling of papers, the initial administrative part of the operation was sorted out.

There was no positive indication at this stage as to where or when we were moving. Cadets do not like prolonged periods of inactivity, which are always made a little worse by the rules which compel them not to move their feet while standing at ease. One of the issued items of uniform was a groundsheet which could also be used as a cape. This had to be rolled up very precisely and was worn at the rear, at collar level. The intention was that upon the onset of rain, the cape could be released by pulling a tape hanging at one end. That just happened to be within reach of the rank behind any intended victim, and this caused a suitable diversion. The small stones lodged between the cobbles of the car park also provided suitable harmless ammunition. Cadets quickly realised that being in the rear rank was of some advantage in situations such as this. Eventually there were unusual signs of intense activity amongst the officers, and we were off into the station and on to a train. As we were now being observed by civilian passengers at close range, no further attempts at mischief were practical, even if there had been sufficient room to manoeuvre. I suppose that trying to negotiate cadets between stations in London was rather like driving a herd of cattle. Within an hour we had arrived amongst the steam and bustle of Liverpool Street station with yet more surplus time to wait for instructions. The news soon filtered through that we were off to RAF Woodbridge, located somewhere on the east coast beyond Ipswich. At least I now had a vague reassurance that it was not going to be a draft into the Army.

The squadron had been allocated two complete coaches in the train. The guard had encountered boisterous cadets before so, in the true style of a sergeant-major, he issued very strict instructions about our behaviour on his train. While the train was stationary there were serious fears about the outcome of any disobedience. Once the train was moving through the tunnels underneath the bombed ruins of London and the smoke from the engine was belching past the carriage windows in an effort to escape, there were renewed opportunities to disobey the guard's instructions. My mother had packed me some sandwiches for the journey, just as she did for the family holidays. I was not the only one tucking into their supply of food. Once that was gone the paper bags and food remains became the focus for mischief. I had not known it earlier but there were a few cadets who had not attended camp before, and tradition dictated that they had to suffer the effects of an initiation ceremony. The plan was being instigated by several of the NCOs with many years of experience between them, and whose strength I was unlikely to match. Whoever they chose to undergo the first initiation was not going to have a pleasant time, and I was becoming very anxious about my fate. The pile of surplus unwanted food was carefully collected and put in a heap. Paul Bates was the chosen victim who was required to pick out the bones and eat the rest. He looked horrified, but reluctantly took his time over the task amid cheers from the other cadets. I remembered my mammoth fart at the squadron, and hoped that Paul would not be caught out in a similar way. There were just a few scraps of onion and apple core remaining when Paul decided that he could eat no more, only to find that the conspirators wanted to see their plot through to the end, so he was laid out on his back on the floor and forcibly fed. When Paul broke free he made a very quick dash to the toilet and took a long time returning.

While we were waiting for Paul to return, there was an interlude of singing songs, all with vulgar and sexual themes, that had been passed down the ranks year after year. I was astounded to discover that those NCOs, with their impeccable discipline, outstanding smartness and good family backgrounds, actually brought themselves to sing these common, objectionable songs. Maybe my own education had been lacking somewhere, or perhaps I had been protected from the tougher parts of school life. But now there was a marked slowing down of the train and the guard made a leisurely stroll through the carriage. What innocent little cadets we were, chatting niceties to each other and carefully not occupying any space in excess of the bounds of our allocated seats. I noted that the officers at the end of the carriage had taken no notice of proceedings and had very quickly removed the pile of money that was forming as their winnings at cards grew. As the train came into Chelmsford you could not have wished for a more angelic-looking party of cadets.

Whistles blew and a jolt signified the continuation of our journey. Paul Bates was sulking in the far corner of the carriage, watching progress through rural Essex. I was hoping that the initiations would abate for a while, but a few moments later one of the NCOs was pointing unmistakably at me, and there was no doubt that I was in deep trouble. I felt my face go cold and tingly and my heart begin to thump wildly as I acknowledged that it was really me that they were after this time. At least six of them piled on top of me and it was well beyond my strength to try to struggle. All of my uniform came off, followed by my socks and underclothes, and I was dumped stark naked on one of the tables. Someone had plans to tie me down to the table, and it was while the string was being found that everybody suddenly disappeared into their seats. I looked up from my horizontal position to come face to face with a grizzly guard. He stood in front of me, in all my glorious nakedness, and gave me a first-class telling off. The NCOs explained that I had done it for a bet. Two officers appeared from the depths of their card game and defused the situation, to the train guard's reasonable satisfaction. Finding all my belongings and getting myself dressed again was quite a job. An officer was posted in the centre of the carriage to ensure good behaviour.

The train drew into Melton station and general chaos took over as the party unloaded its kit on to the narrow, timber platform. Further along the platform there was a large two-storey building which housed the waiting room and station offices. On the opposite platform there was a small waiting room and at one end there was a signal box. All the officers and half of the cadets piled into waiting RAF coaches and were on their way to camp. That left 30 cadets under the supervision of Johnny Elms, who was band-sergeant and a very capable musician who played in the local dance band at home. The time for the coach to return for its second consignment of cadets had not been determined, so we had some time to spare. By an overwhelming show of hands, Johnny was persuaded to get his cornet out. He stood on the waiting room table and gave a very good rendering of the hokey-cokey. Cadets are always very quick with such cues, so there was soon a line of 30 cadets prancing along the platform. As confidence increased, the line took its route across the track onto the other platform, around the signal box, over the level crossing and back into the waiting room. The locals going for their shopping had rather a surprise and they stopped and stared at the invading troops upsetting their tranquil existence. On the third trip over the railway tracks the signalman started quoting extracts from the railway rule book, which generated abuse from a couple of cadets in reply, so we decided that it was time to find out if the village had any attractions.

The nice lady in the café seemed to take pity on us and we politely rose to the occasion, and this yielded five cups of tea. We were rather unwilling to go and disturb the village any further, as we were aware of several RAF personnel walking around. More tea was ordered and paid for. Then Johnny Elms came in the door looking for us, as the coach had returned. It was fortunate that the driver's cab of the coach and the goods-cum-passenger space were quite separate because the cornet was out again, with Johnny now playing some anti-German music.

A left-hand lurch and some violent braking brought the coach to a halt and we were let out on to the roadway. There was a large notice to deter unofficial visitors, and a locked gate separating us from two uninterested corporals, one guardroom and a further collection of buildings forming the RAF station. We had taken the RAF by surprise and the officers were negotiating for entry. It was clear that the paperwork was not just as it should have been, and until written authorisation was available, the gates were going to stay very firmly locked with all of the officers and cadets on the outside.

7

First days at camp

The Royal Air Force aerodrome at Woodbridge was stuck out in the middle of the Suffolk countryside and its location suggested planned isolation from the outside world. The long, straight road that led past the camp gates towards Melton was deserted. The edge of the road led directly on to an area of gorse-covered sandy soil, to which nature had added a few clusters of trees and then decided to set them at an angle from the upright to indicate the strength of the easterly wind. Nature had also added some large birds which had probably commuted from their riverside nesting places, having been partly tempted by the remains of RAF food.

We finally arrived inside the camp perimeter fence next to the guardroom. Standing in three ranks inside the gate was not much different to being outside the gate, except that we now felt more secure and hungry than we did earlier. I think that I understood the attitude of the corporals who did not instantly let us into the camp. They showed no signs of having much to do, with the possible exception of cleaning their guardroom, and they must have had plenty of time to think about how they could interpret the King's Regulations to their advantage. It seemed that the camp gates did not open too often and to have unidentified cadet visitors arrive in great numbers presented them with the opportunity to exert the small amount of authority that they had been given.

Hunger must have got the better of the officers as they negotiated an arrangement for us all to be allowed inside the mess to eat. For me, stage one in this operation was to locate my unbreakable plate and cutlery, otherwise known as irons, from the depths of my father's kit bag, and queue up outside the closed double doors of the mess. One of the unofficial rules of the catering staff forbade the opening of the door from the outside. There was a big, poorly-written notice saying so. When the cooks considered that they were ready, we were allowed in to reform the queue inside. The top of the servery was made of well-dented aluminium, full of hot food, in front of a line of wicked-looking individuals whose lives were made suddenly brighter by the arrival of so many junior victims who could be tormented as they hopefully awaited the delivery of food onto their plates. I was happy to see that those with previous camping experience had pushed into the queue ahead of me, as I was now able to observe just how to hold a plate so that food did not glance off it on to the floor. I had an unrehearsed demonstration of that when a ladle full of hard-crusted pie hit the ground with a resounding thud, failing to fall apart. However, I was in a good position to observe the head of the queue and the great game of obtaining food. The most spectacular item was the big lumps of mashed potato that would not leave the ladle in a pre-determined way, so those dispensing it were forced to bang the ladle on the plate, hence the requirement for it to be unbreakable. I soon discovered that going for a meal in the armed services gave me the opportunity to stuff myself with food gluttonously at precise times, even if the means of so doing were very basic.

There is nothing like food temporarily to satisfy a cadet and since the output of noise and the input of food cannot conveniently take place at the same time, the meal had the desired effect despite the spartan conditions. After quite a large input of food, I was left with dirty plates and irons. Following my nose, I discovered the washing-up facility which comprised one vast tank of boiling, soapy water and a similar one of boiling, clean water. All that I needed to do was dip each plate and iron in the respective tanks for the grease to turn to liquid and fall off, but since these items were made of metal, I had to complete the cleaning process before the heat was conducted to my fingertips. Observation of the cadets leaving the washing-up area was quite educational. Some gloomy faces hung over the steaming water, looking for signs of their beloved irons at the bottom of the tank, and there were others who had found that their plates were in now in many pieces. A good collection of cadets suffered from over-heated fingers. All this was accompanied by adverse comments. This was my first encounter with the airmen's mess and I was very careful not to jeopardise my means of effective eating during the remainder of the week.

We quickly returned to the routine of three ranks yet again and were manoeuvred round to the back of the mess and into a queue for entering the stores. Inside, I was scrutinised for size by an aged airman whose duties allowed him to issue me with a bicycle of an appropriate size. It was nothing like the one that my father had bought me earlier in the year, in fact it looked remarkably dangerous and in the very last stages of its useful life. There was no air in the rear tyre and no means of inflating it; the front wheel rim made a horrible grating noise in its progress along the concrete floor. At least I had a bicycle in which the pedals had some mechanical connection to the rear wheel, and handlebars and a saddle that were well-secured to the frame. One cadet ahead of me was complaining, but he was made to understand that lights and bells and other niceties were luxuries that the RAF could not afford. The bicycles, which were issued so that we could get around the camp, were the accepted alternative to using feet. Rather obscure directions were given to enable us to find our billet, so I put my kit bag over my shoulder and made what I considered to be a good attempt at balancing with just one foot touching the ground. Metal pedals and studded boots were not an ideal partnership in these circumstances and after a metallic clatter I found myself in an undignified heap on the road. It was quite clear to me that walking was the best option when loaded up with kit.

The camp road made its junction with a sandy track leading uphill, through the gorse landscape, to a cluster of five nissen huts about a mile from the mess. Our officers had briefed an RAF corporal to oversee our activities during the week. By arrangement with our own NCOs the squadron was split up, with those cadets who were in the band being housed in one hut and the remainder of the squadron in a similar nearby hut. The corporal had decided to brief us before we got any further. We were told that Woodbridge had not hosted cadets before and our status in the RAF was not very clear to him. Although he made a pleasant job of formally welcoming us and said he genuinely hoped that we would enjoy the week living like airman and learning about work in the RAF, he could not keep the sneer off his face, and I got the feeling that someone had off-loaded us onto him. His introduction promised a niceness that was unlikely to last too long. Our next task was to get some bedding and to make sure that we knew about the FFI and morning inspections.

Each cadet's entry to the hut was allowed only after collection of two sheets, three blankets, a pillow and a palliasse from the adjacent store. Careful aim ensured that I did not lose grip of the whole lot while avoiding a collision with the frame of the single outer door. This led to a vestibule that also provided access to a broom cupboard, and through double swing doors, to the main part of the hut. The inside of a nissen hut was yet another new experience. The floor was concrete and the walls were plain brickwork to a height of about three feet. At that point they supported a gloomy half-circular roof of corrugated iron. Electric light bulbs hung from cables attached to the highest point of the roof. Our beds were put at right angles to the side walls, leaving a centre aisle and providing space for several cast iron coke stoves from which the burnt remains had spilled out and dirtied the white painted concrete surround. The smoke from the stoves was directed by a roughly vertical metal pipe to a badly-cut hole through the roof. I had seen cowsheds that looked more inviting than this.

I had been allocated the bed nearest to the far end wall of the hut, where a door and two small windows had been fitted in the brickwork. It was my responsibility to ensure that the door in this end wall was kept locked from the inside and I rested in some comfort with the knowledge that any intruders would need to enter the hut from the other end. I listened to the detailed rigmarole for presenting my bedding for the 6 a.m. inspection. Although 6 a.m. was not my normal waking time at home, I could not imagine getting any reasonable sleep on a mattress and pillow stuffed with irregular stalks of straw. Several attempts were necessary before I got some idea of the precision required for the bed to pass a formal inspection. Having a good night's sleep was going to be quite another story. When the NCOs were satisfied that the bedding in the hut was totally to their satisfaction, they stood us in a line down the centre of the hut to witness our beds and bedding being taken apart so that we could have another go at getting them right.

It was now early evening and someone said it was FFI time. I did not have a clue what FFI was but the NCOs knew and they were not going to give away much information. There seemed to be two groups of cadets: those who knew all about this forthcoming event and those who were destined to find out the hard way. The senior NCO decreed that we wear our shorts, socks, boots and cap, from which I concluded that something seriously physical was going to happen – unless it was just another session of making our beds and laying out our kit for yet further inspection. As soon as we were in an acceptable straight line, suitably attired and in front of our respective beds, the NCO invited a party of adults into the hut, all dressed in white coats and bringing with them items of equipment used by the medical profession. It seemed that FFI, although still unexplained, was a form of medical inspection. After one of those commands that at first I thought I had misheard, we lowered our shorts to our ankles; a glance out of my right eye revealed that others were similarly embarrassed. As the party of medical staff made their slow progress along the line, followed by the more senior of the NCOs, cadets took inquisitive and very embarrassing glances at their neighbours. In due course the party was studying me in great detail. I was asked about my medical history. One listened for noises with a stethoscope while two others lifted my testicles and penis. I heard a few nervous titters from nearby cadets while this was going on, then the fourth member of the party had a good general look around and made notes. I looked on as they continued along the line on the other side of the hut, but was able to observe the ritual in much greater detail. Eventually, there was the usual exchange of courtesies and they left, apparently satisfied with their evening's work.

However, there was more to come. Once our shorts had been rehoisted to their correct level, we were marched to one of the more distant huts where rifles and bayonets were stored. Two padlocks and a steel door were intended to keep out any intruders, although it looked far easier to kick in the corrugated iron wall of the nissen hut. The walls were lined with timber racks designed to accommodate rifles. Each cadet was issued with a rifle, already fitted with a webbing strap and a long menacing bayonet.

The storekeeper-cum-armourer was an RAF flight-sergeant who tried to take us through some rifle drill, but it was nowhere near the standard that he required. My enthusiasm for trying harder was not increased by the fact that I had nothing between my body and the rifle except a pair of shorts. The other difficulty was that about half of the cadets had not had any rifle drill instruction, and many of us had opted for other training when we saw rifles coming out of the stores at the squadron. This was one of my reasons for volunteering for the band. The flight-sergeant did not seem keen on teaching us any more so we were sent back to the billet, but we managed to get some rifle drill tuition from our NCOs before it got dark. The airmen were highly amused by our efforts and suggested that the ATC should be issued with lances and shields instead. After we had suffered that ordeal, what little of the evening remained was our free time, so most of us went off to the NAAFI to spend money on food, or to challenge the airmen to a variety of table games. By 10.30 p.m. even my uncomfortable bed looked good for a night's sleep, but with a variety of unusual noises originating from the many cadets who were still very much awake, and a good selection of dirty jokes, it was almost midnight before their antics had subsided. Just before I finally went to sleep, I discovered that FFI was the military term for 'free from infection'.

I was safely cocooned between the sheets and there was a lot of noise around. There was a clatter and a thud, a cadet shouting for help, and great jollity. I peered out from the bedclothes to investigate. The NCOs were out of bed, half-dressed, and had decided that the rest of the cadets should follow suit. Their method of achieving this was simply to lift one side of the bed, whereupon one semi-conscious cadet was quickly parted from both bed and bedclothes. Some of the metal bed frames came apart during this process. Being at the end of the hut had its advantages and I was able to get out of bed before the tipping party struck. Somewhere near my wrist was a watch indicating 5.45, confirmed by the fact that it was unpleasantly cold and daylight was in short supply. I managed to adopt a vertical position despite my sleepy stupor, and I aimed myself in the direction of the outside door. A 200-yard sprint, dressed in the minimum possible for respectability, was not a very attractive prospect at that hour in the morning, with the wind blowing at me for all it was worth and carrying a wisp of rain with it. The washing facilities were stuck out in a small clearing between some scattered trees and comprised a long line of earthenware sinks fixed to a sawn timber framework, one tap to each and one outlet without a plug. With no hot water and no protection from the elements whatsoever, there was a great urgency to get clean and back to the billet as quickly as possible.

The threatened 6 a.m. inspection, with its background of horror stories for minor imperfections, was a bit of a non-event. As it happened the whole idea had been generated by the NCOs who at the time had not realised how near it was to the start of breakfast at 6.30. So the whole squadron took to its bicycles in the quest for food. I consumed much more food than I normally did at home, but then the hour was earlier and it needed to last longer, though I do not think that these facts came under consideration as I watched it all being piled up on a plate in front of me. When I got back to the billet, I discovered that the squadron was committed to the traditional Sunday morning visit to church. For me, one of the delights of being in the ATC was that I could avoid church on a regular basis, so now I was looking for a good reason to escape.

I had learned that service regulations had been written precisely so that there was always a good reason for doing exactly what our seniors told us to. At my stage in the cadet organisation that included everybody, because discipline and safety were at stake. However, if the regulations were investigated fully, sometimes there was a loophole allowing the system to be exploited. The NCOs were clearly thinking along the same lines. They had already rejected one suggestion that we could plead that we were Jews or Catholics and opt to go to another place of worship in small enough numbers to get lost on the way. Johnny Elms came up with the idea that he had known the vicar previously, and we would not appreciate his sermon, or perhaps the station church might be full up with RAF personnel. A few moments later we saw our RAF corporal arrive and Johnny Elms decided that at least he would have a shot at persuading him towards his point of view. The great pleading was heard in silence; eventually the corporal accepted our view that perhaps this vicar was not the right man to enthuse cadets, so he arranged for us to go to the guardroom where he would try to make other arrangements for our training. We were all delighted that escape might now be possible. In due course there was some discussion at the guardroom as the matter was considered.

The corporal placed himself rather ceremoniously in front of the squadron and announced that the station church was already overcrowded, and there was no transport available to take us to any other local church. Our hopes were rising and I concluded that we had found the elusive loophole in the regulations, but our smiles did not last long. As he continued, he pointed out that our training programme specified religious instruction and that was what he intended that we should have. The church at Sutton was only two miles away across the Suffolk countryside, and the vicar there needed a larger congregation. At this moment our issued bicycles were well out of range, and our attempt at making bright suggestions had already brought its little disaster. It was bad enough travelling the two miles and trying to keep in step, especially knowing that the expected end product was a boring church service. We arrived at this beautiful little church, set in a sleepy village, not yet exhausted by the march but very unwilling to take part in much religion. Just to add to the pain, I had to put some money into the church's coffers as well. I had to look at the appropriate book to follow what was going on, and make reasonable singing noises because the corporal was so dangerously near me that any lack of concentration was going to be noticed. When we eventually got back through the camp gate after the return two-mile slog, I had a further mile to go to get my irons for lunch. It was an awfully long and unnecessary journey just to get out of fifty minutes of attendance at church on the camp.

During the course of the last few years, there had been reports of aircraft not returning from bombing raids over Europe, but it never really occurred to me that some of the aircraft that made it back to England had their last landing at Woodbridge. Our afternoon's activity was to look at the pile of aircraft remains near the end of the main runway and listen to stories of the disasters and the survivors. It was the first time I had been so close to such large aircraft. While the interest of other cadets revolved around the bombing, the fighting and survival, I was thinking how such masses of metal got into the sky in the first place and then succeeded in staying up there for such long periods. Large lumps of fuselage had been shovelled up together, with bits of jagged tail fins poking out, all at peculiar angles. Some of the wings were still connected to their respective fuselages but identifying parts of aircraft, as some cadets were trying to do, was almost impossible. Even more horrifying at this visit was the inspection of an adjacent large shed with shelves holding many personal effects, all very carefully labelled with the number of the aircraft, and hinting at a silent story of airborne death. This visit, which started in great delight as cadets anticipated getting near real aircraft, ended with a stark impression of the horrors and cost of warfare. Sunday afternoon at camp had certainly left its mark.

At home, Sunday evening always passed without sparkling activity, except of course for mischief if it went undetected. I did not think that Woodbridge would offer any improvement over this. The NCOs were busy considering how they could get out to a public house and back without being detected, and how they could find their way. Maps were only available upon special authorisation, and to start out by asking for directions could have jeopardised the entire plan. They all left together, in one large party, leaving cadets without alcoholic drinking experience condemned to an evening of possible boredom. I sat on the edge of my bed and considered putting an acceptable crease in my trousers, but the only available electricity supply was for lighting. There was the possibility that an iron could be heated on a stove in the hut, but that required fetching fuel from the dump without being seen, and then persuading the coal to burn. Of course, once having obtained an iron, I should have to search out a table upon which to operate. The plan was doomed so I had to consider another method. Another cadet who had been to a camp before had had a reasonable amount of success with laying his trousers between the mattress and its cover overnight, but I was warned that any movement during the night could have disastrous results by the following morning. It was worth a try in the absence of any other practical ideas.

It was as I was applying great concentration to cleaning my rifle that I became aware of the noise of excited cadets outside the billet and a great reduction in the numbers inside. In the twilight, I could see figures leaping about like natives at a tribal dance in the jungle. The local rabbits had come out to nibble away for their evening meal, only to find themselves being attacked by a group of cadets who had very little knowledge of the agility of wild animals. It became obvious to all that the rabbits were extremely active, and were certainly not going to wait around while cadets tried to run after them. Little loops of wire set up to catch the rabbits had finished up by trapping the feet of two cadets, whose resulting descent to the ground was rather more violent than they had anticipated.

While the rest of the cadets were exercising the rabbits, two of us had expressed the opinion that the heating in our hut was lacking and during the course of the evening had found a compound containing coke. We investigated and discovered that with a slight modification to the fencing, it was possible to extract the coke. The second problem was where to store it, but the rabbits had the answer to that. We simply needed to dump the coke in not too mountainous heaps near where the rabbits had been. All we needed now was a spare bed and some willing hands for conveying the coke. As it was becoming clear that the battle with the rabbits was all but lost, there were further noises in the distance which heralded the return of the NCOs. On their arrival we exchanged accounts of the evening. They had, by chance, discovered the location of the officers' mess and had carried out a successful raid on its external beer store, so they were now in a moderate state of intoxication. We invited them to have a go at trapping the rabbits but, as nature was now taking its course, the NCOs elected to piddle over the rabbits rather than try staggering after them. A few of the NCOs were taken by the idea of winning more coke, and a determined effort for a short period ensured a stock near at hand.

As darkness threatened and travel over the area of scrub was becoming more hazardous, I decided to resume the chores of cleaning my kit amidst the objectionable personal eruptions resulting from excessive intake of beer. I was very careful not to disturb my pair of trousers under the mattress, but if tomorrow morning was to be punctuated by hangovers, then perhaps any imperfections might not be noticed.

8

All sorts of sports

After our arrival on Saturday and a partially active Sunday, we were assured that there was a training programme for the rest of the week. We never actually saw the programme but it probably existed. Whatever else happened, breakfast was planned for 6.30 a.m., so I needed to be out of my bed by 5.45 at the latest. There was no problem about waking up in time because a cadet in an adjacent bed was a human alarm clock and was heard making intelligible noises soon afterwards. The other persistent noise was the sound of torrential rain banging away on the metal roof of the billet. Having become conscious, the thought of baked beans, eggs and sausages was sufficient to entice me out of bed, but I needed a pair of socks first and they were in my father's kit bag, just out of range. There was nothing for it but to brave the cold concrete floor for a moment, but it was not to be like that. My foot landed in water. Another quick dip into my father's kit bag located my plimsolls, and they would have to do until I investigated the mystery of the wet floor. I could just see a very dim reflection of the sky from what should have been a concrete surface. I really needed more light to see properly but there was none available. It was still dark outside and the rain was driving horizontally and seeping through the gap at the bottom of the badly-fitting door.

Now I could make this darkness operate to my advantage. I reasoned that if I got a towel and a bar of soap, I could have quite an effective wash just outside in the lee of the hut, but I would have to be quick about it before the NCOs woke up. It would also save the trek to the designated washing point, and my boots would not get dirty. That worked nicely, so the next objective was to dress myself ready for breakfast. I was now in a position to go to the other end of the hut to search for the light switch. I soon found the switch, but there was no power. The storm must have upset the electricity supply, so here was a chance to wake the NCOs up and tell them about the problem. While they were attending to that, I needed my cape and the bicycle, then I was off to the airmen's mess for food. There had not been any power there either, but having suffered the same problems over the war years, the cooks had found ways round it.

As I was enjoying my meal the NCOs arrived and decided that they were going to have a serious word with the corporal about the state of the hut. It was unlikely that the programme would now run as planned because of the continuing rain, though it was now nowhere near the earlier torrential conditions. The corporal appeared in the billet not long after we had arrived from breakfast. He and the NCOs made a quick investigation and they discovered for themselves that the rain had blown in under the door. The corporal ordered them to get the place cleaned up. A search produced one bass broom and a bucket, both quite useless for effectively disposing of the water. One cadet suggested wearing sports kit for swimming, football or a kind of hockey using bicycles while our uniforms were drying out. The RAF found more coke for the stoves and better cleaning implements while a practical variation on a game of rugby took place. Conditions were better in the afternoon, and a visit was arranged to the control tower. We had time in the evening to get the billet and our kit in a presentable condition.

On Tuesday, I used the same trick for washing, and two other cadets joined me. Our activities were split between preparing food in the cookhouse and making a visit round the various stores. I think that our main purpose was to see what we could scrounge rather than learn about equipment. Now that the training programme had been disrupted the corporal was in some difficulties, but the rifles had not been seriously used yet. There was not much hope of finding a rifle range, so we took the things apart in the billet, under the corporal's supervision, to find out how they worked, and then put them back together again. He set up the scenario for battle on a dark night. That really meant that we did it all again, blindfolded. Then he thought that we needed some rifle drill. Marching around with the rifle in the slope arms position was getting very painful, and my arm muscles were complaining. I suppose that it was acceptable for fit airmen but I did not appreciate it. There was no point in complaining, as that would have effectively 'volunteered' us for more in our spare time.

Wednesday morning started far too early. I was woken by the noise of one loud, monotonous voice echoing around the nissen hut, and all I heard was a loudspeaker announcing 'End of message'. I was aware that my left arm was remarkably stiff. I moved the bedclothes away from my ear to detect any further developments. There was the usual collection of sleeping noises and some further evidence that I was not the only cadet to have been disturbed. The wind was gently rattling a loose corrugated iron sheet, otherwise the countryside seemed to be relatively at peace. At least there was no rain hammering away on the roof. It was not even time to hear the birds twittering, so I suppose that I must have drifted in and out of consciousness for a while. I was brought back to life again by the same voice saying 'Stand by for broadcast'. Nothing happened except the continuation of the hissing noise. Then another 'Stand by for broadcast' and more of the hissing noise. 'Owing to a number of youths absconding from an approved school, all personnel are to make an immediate inspection of their bicycles and to secure them with a padlock and chain. If bicycles are missing, the guardroom is to be informed at once.' I was considering getting out of bed to comply when a voice from somewhere in the hut aggressively said 'Bollocks!' Then 'End of message', and the hissing ceased. In my view, anyone who wanted to break into the camp and steal the heaps of mechanical rubbish that they described as bicycles was welcome to do so. And how were we supposed to obtain a padlock and chain at this unearthly hour of the morning? My arm was still hurting and the RAF bed did not suit the contours of my body. 'Bollocks' summed it up very nicely.

When the official time came to abandon the warmth of my bed and start rushing around again in lots of nothing much, I looked round the end of the billet where the bicycles had been dumped for the night. They were still in the same untidy pile as we had left them, so there was no chance of an interesting diversion to the day's programme.

Tradition had it that every Wednesday afternoon was earmarked for sports for all those RAF personnel not on essential duties. Our training programme had a similar blank spot after lunch. I did not want to endure any more sports, even if it could be fitted in after anything the RAF might have deemed a higher priority, and I was definitely not interested in team games. At college I made a good job of maintaining the position of a human goal post when the proper equipment was in short supply. However, neither did I like aimless walking and cycling. I had lived in a small town in Dorset for a time and I had a love for the open countryside. It all fell into place when Corporal French was asking round the billet with a similar idea and looking for company. RAF Woodbridge was named after the local village, and Corporal French and I chose to investigate. By now the guardroom was used to the idea that cadets were about and they did not make any problems on the odd occasions when we went out of the station in the evenings, looking for something to entertain us. However, identification was always demanded before we could get back in. One cadet had already discovered that the sandy soil could be scraped away from the line of fence if our re-entry presented difficulties when the gate was locked shut. That led me to think that the camp would probably have been vulnerable if ever an invasion had taken place.

Neither of us was proficient in riding the precarious bicycles in the state in which they had been issued to us, so we started off by taking things carefully. We tried to avoid bumps in the road, and, aware of the lack of brakes, we walked the downhill inclines. We took our first rest at the level crossing at Melton station to look at the river, the birds and the local train. We did not make ourselves too conspicuous when the signalman came out to open the crossing gates, in case he might have remembered Saturday's antics. From here on it was unknown territory, but we carefully chose who we asked for directions to Melton and went for another mile into Woodbridge. The town had a charming old-world atmosphere about it and was quite undisturbed by any military activity along the east coast. Very few people were about and most of the shops were closed because of the weekly early closing day.

We propped our bicycles up against the church wall and went walking to explore further. I soon found out that the local inhabitants wanted to know who we were, and they were very cautious because our uniforms were not exactly like the current RAF pattern, but thankfully they were not in the German style either. For a while, Peter and I parted company to look out for things that interested us, and it was during this very short time that two boys made a definite beeline for me and asked what I was doing in their village. They were most particular about it being their village, as if we were trespassing. They were quick to explain that because they lived near the coast and their father was a policeman, they had been very precisely briefed about strangers. My explanations satisfied them and I continued on my way.

Peter had told me to meet him by the church. I did not see him immediately, but when I found him he was round a corner in a side turning being cross-examined by the same two boys who had intercepted me earlier. The weather was becoming colder as the wind increased in strength and blew, without any significant obstruction, off the North Sea. My stomach reminded me that I could do with more food. I asked the two boys where we could obtain tea and cakes, so they invited Peter and me to go home with them, where they were sure that something could be arranged.

Their house was situated at the end of a terrace, with the front door opening directly on to a narrow footpath. Their father only allowed access through the front door on special occasions, so we were accompanied through the side gate so that our bicycles could be parked away from the footpath. This allowed us entry through the kitchen door. Both of their parents were at home and we were politely introduced to them and made welcome. Their father was one of the old-fashioned brigade of policemen whose eyes roved around without missing a thing. He was probably capable of sorting out the whole village single-handed. He asked us about camp and, in an apparently casual way, carefully guided the conversation towards the Melton station affair of Saturday. The facts were being registered in his memory but to my relief he did not pursue the matter in too much detail. During the course of this conversation the older of the two brothers had left the room. Then, as plates of scrumptious food were being delivered to the table, he reappeared wearing his ATC uniform, and his younger brother appeared later as an Army Cadet. This created a welcome change to the conversation for another hour. Just before we left, the policeman had 'a quiet word' with us to point out that the bicycles were not roadworthy, although he accepted that the RAF had some responsibility in the matter. We were told that if we saw two boys of about our own age in the area with London accents, and who did not seem to be local lads, then the police would be interested. They had escaped from an approved school not far from our camp and had given rise to that disturbing announcement in the billet. I understood now why two cadet sons of a policeman had viewed us with some suspicion.

On the way back to camp, and after passing Melton station, the road went uphill and through a cutting. At the top of the hill I saw a convenient hollow in the bank, so we decided that it was time for a short rest. We dozed for a while, but it could not have been for long. I woke up with a jolt to see my CO and the adjutant standing over me, so I leapt up and saluted, leaving Corporal French innocently asleep. They were both concerned about not having any tyres on their bicycles, and we had three tyres between us. The CO ordered us to swap bicycles, based on the doubtful statement that they had a long way to travel and our bicycles looked better than theirs. They were probably going to Woodbridge or Ipswich for the evening. As the officers rode off downhill, Peter was suddenly awake and admitted that he had feigned sleep and kept an eye on proceedings. Amongst the usual noises of the countryside and a distant steam engine, we heard shouts and the metallic sounds of a crash. Peter and I looked at each other and wondered who was going to take the blame for not explaining that the bicycles did not have any brakes. The bottom of the hill could only have been about 300 yards away. We both agreed that it would be appropriate for us to travel a safe distance in the opposite direction as quickly as possible. The officers were right about the state of the bicycles, and we pushed them most of the way back to camp. That meant that we missed our evening meal. More food would have been acceptable, but we had already eaten and we were not desperate. Peter and I went off to the NAAFI to keep a date with an airman who had threatened to beat me at chess. He failed and I won a series of bets amounting to ten shillings. With four half-crowns jingling in my pocket, we had no problem with buying more food.

The cadets in the NAAFI had been individually told by the NCOs to be back in the billet by 9 p.m., and not to pass the message on to any other cadets. I detected that another master plot was in the offing. The news was breaking that during the afternoon Arthur Thompson had been caught searching several cadets' belongings, looking for money. The extent of the theft was not quite clear as Thompson had already demonstrated that he was an excellent liar but, under some physical pressure, he agreed that he would return the money at the end of camp, and on the condition that the officers were not told about it. The NCOs were not at all happy with cadets waiting until the end of the week for their money, and there could still be some money missing from cadets who had not yet discovered their loss. The NCOs agreed that Thompson could not be trusted and camp was the ideal place to inflict some barrack-room justice. Thompson had a bed in the next billet, and plans were devised for dealing with him that evening. The senior members in Thompson's billet agreed with the plan, as they had already suffered similar problems. They were also happy to assist if necessary.

Just after 11 p.m., when all of the occupants of the billet were supposed to be asleep but were actually wide awake, partly dressed and ready for action, there were sounds outside as if someone was walking around, apparently without going anywhere in particular. Extensive plans for just this situation had been made earlier, including a 'security device' comprising an old frying pan jammed between the door frame and the top of the outside single door, so that as the door opened the pan would fall on the concrete floor. After the footsteps went on for some time the pan fell with much more noise than we had anticipated, and only seconds later the inner double doors swung open. The cadets whose beds were nearest these doors were already in place, standing on their beds and armed with pillows. The intruder was beaten to the ground, but it was not until his hat landed on the floor that we realised that it was the orderly officer on his rounds. By the time he got off the floor and brushed himself down, all the cadets were giving the impression of being asleep in bed. He did not say a word, and he probably thought it was pointless to do anything else except retire gracefully from the billet.

It was now essential to have a delay in proceedings in case the occupants of the guardroom had been told of the attack on the officer and had decided to investigate. Another hour passed before the NCOs considered that it was safe to deal with Thompson. Each of us was briefed and allocated a specific task. Fortunately I had to keep watch on three cadets who were expected to sleep during the raid. If they did interfere, then it was suggested that I could threaten them with similar treatment before the end of the week. Last-minute reminders were given to us as we were leaving our billet.

Peter French made a first-class job of entering the billet without any noise. He had even oiled the door hinges in advance. I was one of the first group to creep in to take up my position. There were a few snoring noises but otherwise it was remarkably quiet. I was not expecting it to be so easy. The few cadets who did rouse from their sleep were ordered to stay under the bedclothes, and they all complied. Behind us was the main force dominated by Johnny Elms who succeeded in stripping off Thompson's bedding and pyjamas and securing him to the bed. Not a word or giggle was being uttered by anybody. This first stage was complete before Thompson had fully realised what was going on, but then he started shouting as three of the larger NCOs sat on top of him. In no time at all a gag was in place and the noise abated. The last good view that I had was of molten boot polish being poured over Thompson's body and private parts, then the remaining dregs of polish were used as face decoration. Thompson struggled, with as much strength as he could muster, but he was unable to free himself from the rope netting that had been acquired from an undisclosed source. The next stage was to evacuate the billet, by a pre-arranged signal, in a specific order, with the last two cadets pulling a rope at either side of the line of beds to demolish the stove pipes as they went. We were carefully counted back to bed and the frying pan was replaced over the outer door.

The rest of the night was quiet and after breakfast there was the usual parade. It was the corporal who first mentioned that a cadet was missing and that one bicycle had gone. Further enquiries by him revealed an untidy bed with a set of kit missing. Both the corporal and the officers asked if Thompson had been seen, but nobody appeared to know the answer. Later during the day, two NCOs produced a quantity of cash that had been found near his bed during the raid, and cadets were being asked to check and report if they noticed any of their cash or belongings missing. The officers must have known more than they were prepared to discuss, as there was no attempt by them to glean any more information. It was also possible that two damaged bicycles, one missing bicycle, three officers who had suffered attacks on their dignity and possible encounters with the civilian and military police were keeping them busy.

Someone must have rediscovered the training programme, as we spent half a day with the fire service in lighting fires and getting experience in putting them out again, and then a few aircraft appeared from somewhere so that flying was also possible.

Friday morning was our last full day at camp. Having upset the organisation without really trying, we wondered what little training delights the RAF were going to think up today to reward us for our nuisance value. I was getting the feel of the place and now I was not sure that I wanted to go home quite so soon. I thought about Tony and how he might have amused himself while I had been away. If he had come to camp he might have been one of the rebels, or at least an excellent victim for a good dose of initiation. Immediately after lunch on Friday our bicycles had to be returned to the stores. The RAF really had a plan for us in the morning, and the corporal came to announce that as we were all going be called up for our National Service at some time in the future, the best thing that he could do was to train us to be better at drill. He said that the parade square was just over a mile away, next to the airmen's mess, and the journey on foot would do us good, so we would not need our bicycles. What he did not clarify was whether we would be able to get back to the billet in time to get our irons and go back for lunch. Someone mentioned it to our NCO but he said that he had the matter under control. After lots of drill and expert correction of the details, we had just twenty minutes before the doors of the mess opened. The corporal had a wicked glint in his eye and he was clearly trying to make sure that we did not get any lunch until we had marched back to our billet. Our NCO had other ideas. He left us for a while and returned with a conspiratorial smile on his face. He had made a deal with the cook and had acquired enough plates and irons for us. We commented on how miserable the corporal looked when he noticed us all at the front of the meal queue.

The time arrived for the return of the bicycles, but they were not going to get their wrecks back without waiting for us to walk to our billet and ride the bicycles back. This seemed to upset the RAF slightly but there was no alternative. We awarded ourselves ten minutes rest, then we lined up our bicycles ready for the scramble to the stores door. Someone was heard to call, 'Race you there!' Someone else said, 'Let's all have a mass start.' The latter suggestion was the more popular. Apart from the difficulty of starting on the sandy surface, it was a tarmac path and downhill all the way to the stores. Each of the cadets had a bicycle so to be fair we needed an independent means of signalling the start. There was no one around to help so we tried tying a weight on a piece of string between two electricity poles and setting light to it. That failed because it burnt through too quickly. Peter French came to the rescue with the idea of spreading some breadcrumbs on the ground; the start would be indicated by the first bird to land to risk sampling the morsel of food. The birds were rather reluctant at first, but it worked and we were off. There were some mechanical failures, mainly because of the age of the chains and sprockets, and a couple of bicycles suffered impact damage with the wall of the stores 'due to the lack of facilities for effective deceleration', as it was later described on the damage report form. The storekeeper was most unhappy with his stock of bicycles being returned in such a decrepit condition, alleging that the cadets had damaged them and were required to pay. However, the cadets were now wise enough to complain in turn with a story of their individual disasters but it was Peter French who put the final touch to the complaints by insisting that he would call the local policeman in Woodbridge to give evidence if necessary. The arrival of our CO helped, especially when he indicated that he was intending to claim against the RAF for negligence in respect of his damaged uniform when he crashed at Melton. Just for good measure, he also pointed out that the cadets would not be paying because they had no money left, and as they did not get paid for going to camp, he could not see a way out for the storekeeper. At that point, all arguments ceased.

The remainder of that day could be construed as punishment, or it might merely have been insurance by the RAF to make sure that we were going to sleep well that night after lots of hard work on the billet and its surroundings. Having cleaned everything to a reasonably satisfactory standard, we were invited to go for a run. The idea appealed to us. We had visions of a local route round the RAF station, having first had the rare opportunity to remove our uniforms and burn off some energy wearing shorts. The storekeeper had other ideas. We had to report to the stores, each put on a set of webbing kit with a pack, and go and sit in the coach parked next to the stores, awaiting a pleasant ride to the North Sea coast. We all climbed out of the coach when it stopped next to a few houses and farm buildings and were left standing in three ranks when it drove off. An NCO had a set of instructions in an envelope. These said that we were to get back to camp in time for an evening meal. The kit was heavy, the heat of the day was not very kind to us inside that uniform. We must have been about six miles from camp and our food was due to be served there in about an hour. We stood in the middle of this country lane, not really admiring the view but cursing our luck. We stopped a chap who was driving a tractor. He had been in the Army and understood our plight perfectly, but the tractor was quite useless in this situation. If we waited, he would see what he could do. Next a cattle truck wanted to get past us. It stopped as we moved aside, and the driver's head appeared from the cab. 'Must be about five tons of yer out there.' The local accent was peculiar but yes, I supposed that altogether we did weigh about five tons. He chatted quietly to the NCO and then told us to get aboard. 'Look lads, it's going to be a bit smelly and hot and uncomfortable for about half a hour, but no one speaks a word during that time and I'll see what I can do.' Then he slung a sheet over the side slats and top of the truck. Now it was dark and stuffy and full of farmyard smells as well. The gearbox was grunting away under the floor, but at least we were moving at a steady speed. Then the lorry came to a halt. There were voices outside and we assumed that the driver had got out. Then he returned. There was a metallic clanking and we started off again. The road surface was terribly uneven now, and we came to a halt again. That peculiar accent was there again. 'No talking, lads. Get out, and mind how you tread as soon as I take the sheet off. The rest of you go with your sergeant, and two help me with the sheet. Best of luck.' That was amazing. I wondered how the truck actually got beside the old wall behind our billet. After the removal of that webbing and a bit of tidying up, we jogged to the mess for food. We were even first in the queue again.

We asked the sergeant to explain when we got back to the billet.

'It was a pure fluke that we found that farmer, and he knew what it was all about. As luck would have it, his fields back on to the RAF station, but he can't get to them because the little bridge over the ditch has collapsed and he is allowed temporary access through the camp gate. As far as I know, the corporal is not aware that we are back, so if we have a rest for an hour and do anything we need ready for tomorrow, then by the time he finds us it will be too late to get involved in anything else.'

'What about this kit, sergeant?'

'That's what will bring him back up here. It's issued on his signature, so that's his problem. If we lose it, it's still his problem because we didn't sign for it.'

9
Going back home

The eighth day at RAF Woodbridge started off with a few variations on the usual routine. There had been yet another successful raid on the beer store at the rear of the officers' mess during the previous evening, now that one of our cadets had mastered the art of lock-picking. That fuelled a limited celebration in the billet, accompanied by a good selection of practical jokes based on all the mischievous things that had been perfected during the week. I awoke with a stomach upset and was not very sure how much breakfast I was going to cope with. Today we were off home. Last night's empty beer bottles had been stuffed into rabbit holes so they would not be found in the dustbins. The length of curtain wire that had dangled between adjacent light fittings to provide a Heath Robinson addition to the heating system had to be removed, as did the nails that had replaced the standard fuses, to allow a dangerous amount of electric current to flow. The whole billet was a hive of activity until it was time for our last expedition to the mess for breakfast. My pocket was now almost empty of money. Some of it had been necessarily spent on polish and blanco for my kit, and on food and drinks in the evenings. I had been able to entertain a few of my cadet friends in the NAAFI and to buy a brooch for my mother, mainly as a result of my winnings from the airmen at draughts and chess. I did not appreciate that I was so good at these board games, but perhaps the occasional challenges to my father had paid dividends. A collective appraisal of our combined finances did not produce very much, so the purchase of even the cheapest luxury on the way home was quite beyond our means.

In due course some transport arrived. I recalled the chaos that ensued on our arrival at Melton and noted that the officers were now taking a deep interest in the way that cadets were being loaded into what they politely called coaches, but in fact looked more like prison vans. Johnny Elms was again in the position of being the senior NCO, and was quickly aware that there was neither visible nor oral communication between the officers, who sat in their traditional place in the front seats with the driver, and the cadets occupying the rear seating area. His trumpet was packed in his kit and out of convenient range, but that did not prevent an outburst of rugby songs, accompanied by movements that later created a bouncing effect on the vehicle. On our way into Woodbridge on those

RAF bicycles on Wednesday afternoon, we had to be very careful riding over the poor surface of the road next to the level crossing at Melton. That, combined with the coach making a sharp left turn that coincided with an emphasised beat in our chorus must have had something to do with us sliding around on the wooden seats. In the course of that left turn there was a thud and screech from underneath the coach, which came to a sudden stop. Someone opened the back doors and we found ourselves in the parking area in front of the station buildings. The driver was looking sadly at the body of the coach that was not now quite parallel with the surface of the road. It seemed unlikely that it would proceed much further without expert attention. Without wishing to be accused of insubordination, he tactfully suggested to our CO that the behaviour of the unsupervised cadets could have been to blame, but our CO was not having that. The exchange of quotations from King's Regulations was not for our ears, so we were quickly directed to wait on the station platform.

The porter was standing some distance away, further along the platform, and the signalman was watching proceedings from the safety of his cabin window. The telegraph bells in the signal box rang delicately, the signalman went inside to reply and the crossing gates were opened. There was the whistle of an approaching steam train, then it came to a halt amid a cloud of steam, and with two empty carriages reserved for us. There was a bit of a free-for-all as we boarded the train and aimed for our chosen seats, but soon the door was slammed shut, whistles blew and the first jolt signified our escape from the RAF at Woodbridge.

The cadets had now reformed themselves into groups that bore no relation to those who had sat together on the forward journey. The NCOs settled themselves into a group at one end of the carriage and the trouble-makers were at the opposite end. I was invited to take my place among the senior cadets, which I took to be a sign of their changed attitude towards me. Most of us were noticeably tired as there was very little conversation taking place. From the carriage window I had occasional glimpses of delightful nautical scenery alternating with the flat Suffolk countryside that I was unlikely to encounter again for some time. I thought about what I was going to tell my parents when I got back home or, perhaps more important, what I was going to leave out. If I had been told about annual camp in all its detail before leaving home, I doubt whether I would have ever considered taking part. Now that it was nearly all over I was glad, in a way, that I had sampled a new and quite different experience. Perhaps I might even change my views about being conscripted into the services.

Somehow, I felt different. It took a lot of thought to discover exactly why and how. One week earlier I had been considered a relative weakling, or perhaps I had for a time been partly isolated from life's rough and tumble by living in Dorset. But during the week I had been subjected to some very harsh discipline inflicted by cadets only a year or two senior to me, and without any chance of escape. Together with other cadets, I had got myself into trouble on several occasions and earned a good rollicking for it, yet we all remained loyal to each other. Perhaps it was just that loyalty that was appreciated by those who invited me into this very seat on the train. I had been coerced into taking part in many practical jokes and devious ventures. Perhaps for the first time in my life I was now an accepted member of a team. I had certainly been organised, and I had survived without my parents for a week, with moderate success. I had been given just a little bit of responsibility, looking after a rifle, though I dared not think what would have happened if I had failed in that task, and I had been trusted to deal with three cadets during the assault on Thompson. On the first day at camp, one cadet had been discovered in an unacceptably unwashed state, to his cost. The result was an involuntary immersion in the unhygienic contents of a static water tank, followed by a severe scrubbing. One great lesson that I learned was never to be dishonest with fellow cadets, and I had seen some harsh justice being inflicted for that crime.

When I first joined the ATC I took instant pride in wearing my uniform, once the slight initial embarrassment had subsided and despite its outstanding discomfort, yet for one week I had worn nothing else during my waking hours. The isolated exception was in the cold and wet before breakfast, when I had to wear my sports kit. At that moment, I was not really sure if I wanted to go home and wear my best suit or school clothes again. There must be an unconscious thrill somewhere that actually made me enjoy pressing an obstinate uniform, bulling boots, cleaning webbing with blanco and polishing all the intricate bits of brass. Certainly something had switched my enthusiasm into a different direction. I had not heard of the progress of the war on the radio and had not seen a newspaper while at camp. Telephones were difficult to find, expensive and unreliable, so I had been almost out of contact with the outside world for a week. On reflection, it had been a jolly good eight shillings worth of food and experience.

The drab scenery surrounding the approach to Liverpool Street was a clue that the carriage windows ought to be shut to keep the smoke from the engine on the outside. The cadets were quickly counted coming off the train, then there was a quick transfer to a local train and an uneventful journey to our local station. A few groups of parents were waiting for their valuable offspring to emerge from the station entrance, but mine were not there. Tony had been waiting for nearly two hours to greet me, so a group of us made our way along the High Street. We had only gone a few yards before we were stopped by a number of people who asked us what it was like at the front line. At first I was confused by that question until I realised that they had presumed that we had come back from war service in Europe. I had to explain very gently that I was a cadet and had just returned from an annual camp at a location that I was not allowed to name. They were quite disappointed.

I had not been allowed to take the front door key with me to camp in case it got lost, so I had to knock at the front door to gain entry. My father answered the door. I suppose that he was relieved that I had not come to any harm and I was still in one piece, but I did feel rather tired. I was not sure that he was too pleased to see Tony trailing behind. My kit was dumped in the hall and I went into the lounge to find my mother wholly absorbed with yet another batch of knitting. The radio was promptly turned off and I was bombarded with questions about how I had fared. It was time for tea and I had not eaten since my early breakfast. My mother allowed herself to be diverted from asking questions and retreated to the kitchen to deal with that little problem.

I think that we all saw Tony as a recurring nuisance that we did not need to endure. After pointed remarks by my parents that there was no spare food waiting to be eaten, Tony got the hint. Once he had gone I was asked to remove my kit from the hall to my bedroom. The room had been decorated and the smell of paint still lingered. My mother had been busy making sure that my civilian clothes were clean and pressed ready for the morning, and then there was that lovely luxurious bed and a real gas fire for heating. I was looking forward to enjoying both very soon, and there was even the possibility that I might go to bed early. How lovely it was to be at home with all its comforts. There was just one thing left to make the day perfect. I sat down at my mother's side and gave her the brooch. We were alone and we had a cuddle for a few moments. She liked the thought that went with that brooch, but she must have wondered about all the sacrifices that I made to get the money together for it. I was pleased that my father had taught me to play draughts.

As the end of July led into August, cadet activities were relatively quiet. I had almost run out of suitable stories to tell parents and friends about camp. There were a few stories that needed to be modified slightly before I told my father and I was always a little suspicious that he might eventually discover the real truth. I had to be even more careful what I told my mother. One great danger was that she did not understand military jargon at all, so she wanted to discuss doubtful matters with my father. Then I found myself in the dangerous position of having to explain something to both of them while avoiding giving away anything that would merit their further investigation. There was no homework left to deal with, and Tony was now away somewhere with his parents.

When all else failed the radio was a great source of enjoyment, until one day we heard the news that an atom bomb had been dropped on the Japanese city of Hiroshima. Only a few days later, Nagasaki was attacked. Later reports about the extent of the damage horrified the nation. Just two little bombs had demolished two entire cities. If warfare were to continue on this scale the end result was unthinkable. But over the radio came reassurance from our politicians that it was a measure of the high level of American technology. The Japanese would be unable to compete, so they would also be unable to continue the war. Just a week later came the news that the war with Japan was over, and more celebrations followed.

10

Problems with music-making

Now that annual camp had been enjoyed and was almost forgotten until next year, and my holidays from college had come to an end for the summer, it was time for more serious things. I had to consider college homework first because I intended to earn a living, using the knowledge acquired through my studies. Also, I dearly wanted to stay with the ATC. Those two issues would take care of most of my evenings and part of the weekends. Tony and Donald would have less call on my time, and attendance at church was right at the bottom of my list of priorities.

Before going to Woodbridge I had been introduced to a euphonium, although I had nowhere near achieved a state of proficiency with it. Under threat of a bad end-of-term report, I had learnt something about music at school. All that really happened in music lessons was that a teacher would bash away at an ancient piano, adding her own vocal noises, and somehow expect us to follow the song enthusiastically, using the accepted words from the score. During a lesson in which we viewed only the rear of the teacher, any harmonious concentration on music was the minimum requirement to prevent the dear lady from turning from the piano and consigning us to attend the headmaster's study for a whack across the behind. At least I learnt the scale of C, and I had a splattering of an idea of how it was written down on the five lines of the stave.

I was lucky that the euphonium could only produce one note at a time, and I could cope with that once I got the hang of organising my lips and tongue. It was then only a case of pumping out the right note at precisely the right time. At this stage my playing lacked finesse, to the occasional concern of the bandmaster. It became a little more complex in the later stages when marching and playing at the same time were required, and I had the additional problem of preventing my lip missing its location on the mouthpiece at every step, while keeping an eye on the music and staying in line. Fine Sunday mornings were the ideal time for the whole squadron to march around the local roads, headed by the band and followed by a squad with rifles and a collection of the more junior recruits. As always, our return to the squadron an hour later brought children from their homes to trail behind, reminiscent of the tale of the Pied Piper. It was a good recruiting medium and we hoped to convince the locals that there was a youth organisation around which was ready to defend the country against aggressive intruders if ever the need arose.

Our assembly point was outside the band store, which meant that we had to march over a small grassed area before reaching the tarmac parade ground and the drive leading to the road. The bass drum on this particular morning had been given to one of the recent recruits who was madly enthusiastic about marching with the band. Our usual moderately built six-foot cadet was an ideal candidate for this role, but he was ill and had not turned up. Our new victim was slightly smaller and had the drum securely fixed so that it would not slip while he was on the march. He needed to see the drum major, whose mace gave the necessary visual instructions, but he could only just see over the top when conditions were exactly right. After only a few steps he managed to trip over on the uneven grass surface and landed like a pile driver in a wrestling match, to hit the ground with a considerable thud. After he had been disentangled from the drum, both had to be temporarily replaced. With that disaster over, the procession of cadets followed the band along the road to the point where there was a right turn before the road went slightly downhill into a lane. The lane, which was just wide enough for two vehicles to pass each other, served a variety of large detached houses, interspersed with the occasional bungalow and vacant plot of land in between them. One of these houses was the residence of our adjutant. On this day, the milkman had his horse and cart parked in the lane while he was inside the house of one of his valued customers. It was quite usual for the milkman to stop there for a cup of tea. The drum major gave the necessary signal and the drum section of the band started with four bars of music as a prelude to one of Sousa's great marches. The collection of sounds that followed included galloping hooves, crates falling from the cart and bottles smashing on the road surface, but no music. The band came to a halt in a very non-military style in time to see the cart negotiating the corner and passing out of sight at quite a dangerous speed, its route marked by a trail of miscellaneous dairy products. Only the quick thinking by our drum major provoked our instant escape from the scene and back to the squadron headquarters before further complications set in.

Some weeks later, the band was asked to assist with a parade in Wembley. During the previous year, our drum major had perfected an impressive display with his mace that was often a greater spectacle than the remainder of the parade. The band had amalgamated with that of another squadron and we had worked hard at chosen items of music for the occasion. On the day, the band was assembled on the main road at the head of an enormous procession. The plan was that the council dignitaries wished to review many of the local organisations, and a base had been established in the shopping area where the mayor was to take the salute. At the other end of the shopping area, a church hall had been reserved for the participants to congregate after the parade. It was one of those rare days when I had the feeling that all was going well. The weather was acceptable and everyone was on form. Behind the band were some of the older members of society who had been in the armed services and who desperately wanted to be a part of the procession, but whose physical ability was not quite up to it. With a slower marching speed for their benefit, the effort required by the band was reduced. On the approach to the saluting base and in the interlude between successive items of music, the drum major embarked on one of his mace-twirling displays in which the mace was thrown high into the air and caught with absolute perfection. Unfortunately, on the second display the mace made contact with two trolleybus wires, resulting in a shower of sparks and necessitating unplanned evasive action by the front rank of trombonists. The mace landed on the road at one side, beyond its operator's convenient reach, and on impact it fell into its many separate components, the several pieces being recovered by some well-meaning onlookers. On arrival at the church hall we found that a small group had gathered, comprising a very embarrassed drum major, the bus inspector intent on reporting the facts surrounding the delay to his trolleybus service, and one little girl innocently offering a collection of miscellaneous parts of the bent and scarred mace. There were some genuinely sympathetic comments to the drum major, and a later gathering of cadets to inspect the damage to our reputation.

After these two incidents, the band was given a severe lecture about the care of band instruments. They had originally been donated to the squadron many years earlier, were squadron property and could not be replaced through official sources. In brief, that meant that all of the small donations received for band engagements in the last six months would have to be spent on two items. The CO also pointed out that both the milkman and the bus company were seeking compensation for the damage caused. We had to promise that any further damage would have to be paid for by the cadets.

The bicycle that my father had acquired for me as a reward for passing my exams was old and heavy. I was fairly sure that one of his friends had no further use for it, and he almost certainly got it for next to nothing as it was unlikely that he had sufficient funds to pay for it. It had a fixed wheel and the front lamp had been converted from an acetylene lamp, and was now served by a dynamo taken from an ancient motor cycle. It had also been fitted with a large and robust bell strapped to the handlebars, which provided a most convenient fitting from which to suspend the euphonium. On my way from home to attend an additional parade one evening the weather was windy, with an overcast sky threatening a good downpour of rain. I turned the corner of the lane, now known to us as 'milkman's folly', to be caught by a gust of wind which blew my cap sideways. In an effort to set it more securely on my head, I lost control of the bicycle and landed on the side of the road, almost falling into the ditch. I had not incurred any personal damage, but my uniform was now unacceptably dirty and it needed minor attention before continuing.

At band practice, I sat down in my usual fashion, at which point I discovered that I had collected a few bruises. Then I noted, to my horror, that the euphonium had suffered an obvious dent. The bandmaster saw it too, and I was ordered into his office to account for the damage. Despite my plea that the weather had been a major cause of the accident he decided that I had not been sufficiently careful, and he left to consult the CO about the matter. Ten minutes later I found myself standing to attention in the CO's office, trying to think how best I might explain or ease the situation. He did not waste any time in assessing the matter. He pointed out that despite his previous instructions about the care of band equipment, I had chosen not to walk, which he considered to be the safest means of travel in the circumstances. He also took the opportunity to review my progress in training and to inspect my uniform. The latter was still showing signs of my encounter with the road surface and he was not at all pleased. I was the first cadet who had caused damage since his threat of a few weeks ago and I was ordered to report to the warrant officer for jankers.

I had heard of jankers while I was at camp. I knew that it was some form of punishment but I had not actually discovered exactly what it was. As I knocked on the door of the warrant officer's office I was sure that I was going to find out very quickly. I had to be careful not to incur any more penalties, so my explanation for being brought in front of him had to be presented in a formal, military way. As I told him that the CO had sent me there for jankers, his eyes lit up. I had never seen him so look pleased before. His face quickly hardened as he handed me a greatcoat, a rifle and a set of webbing equipment already packed to capacity. My punishment was to be on guard duty, wearing this lot, at the gate for 25 minutes, followed by five minutes running round the parade ground with the rifle over my head. These activities were to alternate for the rest of the evening, and I was to report to him at 10 p.m. It was not too long before my arms were aching from holding the rifle, and being restricted in my movements by the heavy greatcoat. The chap in the house on the opposite side of the road spotted me, then went to get his wife, and together they drew the curtains aside to have a longer and better look. Two very nice-looking young ladies riding past on their bicycles nearly collided with each other when they both became curious about the apparent sentry.

I was beginning to realise that I looked a bit of a twit wearing everything from the stores that could be worn, but then I guessed it was the CO's intent that I should. I then had to endure visits from other cadets while they were having their canteen break. They were hoping to see me make some unauthorised movements while at attention. Soon it began to rain, lightly at first but then turning into a heavy downpour. The chap across the road and his wife took more occasional looks from the comfort of their home. I was getting hotter and wetter and slowly discovering what jankers really meant. I saw most of the cadets leave at the end of the evening, but my duty ended at 10 p.m. My watch was hidden under my greatcoat and there was no chance of looking at it. Nor was I able to ask the time. Eventually I had a message that I was expected in the CO's office before I left for home. I stood in front of him, in a thoroughly drenched state, to discover that he had not quite finished with me. Stage two of the punishment required me to report to the warrant officer, in the same kit, half an hour before parade and similarly on the following two parade nights prepared to be on guard until 10 p.m., with every item of kit and the rifle spotlessly clean. I did not dare tell my parents what had happened that evening, as it would probably have meant a good hiding, so I also had to threaten Tony not to say anything. Neither was I in any position to escape the CO's orders because that would definitely have got back to my father. If I were asked I should have to suggest that I volunteered to help out in the stores and I was wearing the kit as an experiment, as this was the accepted way of conveying it in accordance with the regulations. It was lucky for me that the truth never reached as far as home. On the next evening of my continued punishment I was forced to stay in position near the roadway for only half the evening, but again long enough to miss the visit to the canteen. I had a number of enquiries from concerned cadets about what it was like. I could not work out whether I was becoming their hero or whether they were making emergency plans to escape a similar fate if they ever found themselves in conflict with the squadron staff. Surprisingly, there were also a few cadets who offered some sympathetic words and wanted to try it out for themselves. Whatever other effects that this event had, I did think that it was an interesting experience, and something to remember if I ever got some stripes on my sleeve. It could also be useful if ever I damaged a band instrument again because I now had a short list of volunteers for jankers.

11

More volunteering

Examination time at college was approaching once again and I was looking forward to the exams being all over for another year. There was just a chance that my parents might be able to afford a family holiday at some time during the summer. The favourite venue would be in Dorset near the coast, where my mother's close relations now owned an hotel and the cost would not be prohibitive. No announcement had yet been made but that was not unusual, because once my sister was aware of a forthcoming holiday she made our lives a misery by her excitement in the preceding weeks and was almost beyond control on the days before departure.

Arriving at college one Monday morning I found that a message had been left with my form master for me to report to the headmaster's office. That usually meant that you had to prepare your brain or your bottom for a good hammering, though I could not bring any recent misdemeanours to mind. When I arrived outside his door, at the appointed time, I was a little relieved to see six other students waiting in the corridor who had been similarly summoned. It was not clear to any of us what common factor dictated that we should all report together. We synchronised the time and at precisely the prescribed moment knocked on the door and entered. There were seven vacant chairs arranged around his desk and we were instantly beckoned to sit down, and being asked to sit down was always a good omen. Another sign of our good fortune came when he preceded his address with one of his infrequent smiles. Then, in that penetrating voice of many teachers, he told us how pleasant it was to have representatives of the cadet forces in the college on Empire Day. But that was almost a year ago and I wondered why he'd raised the matter now. Because of his friendly introduction, he couldn't have known that we had all been pressured to turn up for Empire Day. He said had been so impressed with us that he had written to our respective COs and told them so. If nothing else that was a good start, especially as in my case at least he seemed to have forgotten the list of infractions and punishments chalked up against my name. For some time now, he said, he had been considering the formation of a cadet unit within the college. He had spoken to many people about it, but the only organisation from whom he had received a positive reaction was the Army Cadet Force.

He had already approached our COs and had obtained their approval for us to become the recruiters and the founder members of a cadet unit based at the college. If we agreed, then here was our opportunity and he invited our comments. None of the seven of us wanted to speak up first, but someone summoned the courage and pointed out that he was fully committed already and really could not afford the extra time. I followed that by asking when this new cadet unit would meet, silently hoping that it might have taken the place of the history and religious instruction lessons that I hated so much. The headmaster consulted the college timetable and told us that all of our exams would be over within four weeks. After that he would allow us a day to think about the idea. He wanted to arrange things so that basic training could be started then and continue for the rest of the term. From September onwards the whole college would be involved, on a compulsory basis, on one or two days per week after the end of lessons.

Paul and David, two Army Cadets, both said that they were definitely interested. I said that I would be prepared to help with starting the unit, but would probably be unable to continue into next term because of my involvement with the ATC. We all agreed that the whole matter should be put aside until the exams were over. We really needed some more time to think about it. On that basis, the headmaster suggested that we meet again at a time that he would arrange.

During the lunch break next day I caught up with Paul and David. Although they had volunteered, they admitted that it was all a bit of a novelty to them. They had joined the Army Cadets only four months previously so their experience was fairly limited. However, their main interest seemed to be in anything that was explosive. From that discussion I concluded that if only the three of us were positively interested, then I would be in a rather good position at college and one that could only work to my advantage.

Several weeks later, having fought my way through the exams and gone through the traditional self-torture of comparing my answers with those of my classmates on the journey home, I finally got around to thinking about cadets. Eventually I mentioned the matter to my mother, only to discover that both my parents had known of the proposal since the middle of the previous year and they had already discussed it. My mother did not mind too much but she felt duty bound to have another word with my father to confirm his approval. With the imminent arrival of the holiday season, and a forthcoming reappraisal at the beginning of the next term, she could not see any immediate problems.

At an agreed time Paul, David and I met in a little room that was once a stationery store and which had been very boldly relabelled as the 'Cadet office'. Inside were a few chairs and one solitary large table with an ancient typewriter on it. We found sufficient paper to embark on an investigation into the workings of this machine. David, who said that he knew all about typewriters, got the job of persuading it to type something intelligible. Paul and I said that we would try to produce a summary of subjects suitable for the basic training of cadets, so that David could type it up later. All of Paul's ideas revolved around the use of guns of various kinds and the resulting explosions and destruction, none of which activities were likely to be acceptable in the college, even if qualified instructors were available. I thought that I might be able to teach the simple movements of foot drill, using the roadway around the college, but I could see that we were not going to get very far without expert help. I guessed that somewhere there must be a syllabus of training of some kind and I wondered why the headmaster was asking us when he probably had the information ready at hand. After an hour or so, the headmaster came in to see how we were getting on. I explained the problems, also pointing out that David had succeeded in correctly typing his name and address once in the last hour. However, as we were all keen to see the college cadet force succeed, we thought it might be worthwhile to fill in several weeks of our college holiday with something of a military nature.

The headmaster really hated to mention it at this stage in proceedings, but he wanted us to understand that the regulations did not permit us to be in two cadet units at the same time. However, he and our COs fully understood the position and by a gentlemen's agreement the official interpretation of the situation was to be that we were 'on detachment' for a period until the beginning of next term. He had heard what we said about needing expert help and it was a matter that had concerned him very seriously. He had already enlisted the help of a local Army unit who were prepared to train us for a week. If we agreed, and once we had paid our dues and had the paperwork in order, we were to report to the college office a week on Friday, in the morning. After that we were expected to be available and take some active part in the cadet unit, and that really meant through the holidays and until the beginning of the next term.

We met in the college foyer on the appointed day to see what was in store for us. The office typist presented me with a slip of paper giving the address of the local Army unit, so we set off to find it. I did not know this patch of London very well as I only visited the area to attend college. First stop was the café in the High Street to ask for directions and only incidentally to spend some pocket money. Once we eventually found our objective, we went in through a gateway and found a collection of buildings surrounding a central parade square. It was all very quiet and peaceful, which made me feel hesitant about making any noise. A blackboard was propped up against a doorway. The chalked message invited any visitors to venture inside where there was a good choice of unmarked doors. One door led to an unoccupied office. Another was a cleaner's cupboard and a third led to a workshop area. From somewhere in the workshop there was the faint noise of work in progress. Our investigations led us to a sergeant involved in the assembly of a rifle. We waited for a moment at a safe distance while he cursed its designer. The sergeant was a plumpish little man with a ruddy complexion and a permanent smile. He spoke with a soft, pure Irish accent that brought to mind the Blarney Stone, and he was an absolute delight to listen to. Eventually he stood up from the workbench and strutted like a cockerel towards the door. He took us to the rear of the building, into a large office with a couple of desks which looked lost in that vast space. He found two more chairs from the adjacent office and invited us to sit down. Although he had known we were coming, he needed to speak to someone else about us. The telephone was remarkably inefficient. He joggled the receiver rest repeatedly before getting the operator to reply and then it took him a long time to get a connection to the correct distant number. Irish impatience started show during the next few calls, but finally and with a great sigh of relief he resolved the details. He went to a small security box fixed to the wall and took a bunch of keys from it, of which one fitted a door leading to a vast stores area which held everything from dustbins and tools to uniforms and beds. Just inside was a single small desk, with papers and forms placed meticulously square with its edges. The only imperfection was the gleaming linoleum floor that had been dented by studded boots. All of the door handles, the metal strip along the edge of the counter and even the waste bins were highly polished and only someone with nerves of steel would have dared to touch anything. It was all very secure with heavy wire mesh around the serving counter and the window openings, and with massive padlocks on some of the cupboards.

We were there to be issued with uniforms for the week. I had been through all this before, except that this time everything was a khaki colour instead of blue. However, I was surprised when along with the badges he issued a needle and thread and expected me to sew them on before I was allowed to take the kit out of his store. I thanked my lucky stars that I had watched how my mother always pinned items accurately before sewing them on, so the final result was acceptable. Meanwhile, David had got himself into a hopeless mess. Sewing was a new experience for him. Not having used a needle before, he tried pushing the sharp end, thus making unwanted perforations in the end of one particular finger. I had gained two sore fingers trying to persuade the badge and split pin into a forage cap, only to find that the cap was of the wrong size, so the whole process, and the accompanying pain, had to be endured for a second time. It was a classic case of the body being required to fit the uniform, rather than the other way round. Another two hours of sewing and fitting passed before all three of us were in a sufficiently acceptable state of dress to warrant a second opinion. The sergeant was discovered amongst his stores and was not the least bit interested in whether anything fitted. His prime concern was that he had a clear signature for the items with which that he had parted. I remembered the problems that I had in keeping my trousers pressed at annual camp, so I asked for a spare pair of trousers. It was an unexpected pleasure to get them without any further questions being asked. We packed all our newly-issued kit in a large kit bag and thought about going home.

The one outstanding question that I almost forgot to ask was when and where we were expected to go. Even as I thought about it, a well-filled envelope was stuffed into my right hand. I knew that buried in the dense formal text would be the details that we really needed. I interpreted for the other two. Our instructions were simply to report to Waterloo station on Saturday week and then travel by the first available train to our destination. This gave us sufficient time to sort out what we really needed to take with us.

On the following day the three of us arrived at college with all the various items of clothing, fittings and personal items we needed for the week. We had set the day aside to compare notes and collectively to start the long job of cleaning and pressing. The room soon took on the aroma of steamy woollen cloth, hot boot polish and greasy blanco. Next we had to unlock the mysteries of putting a set of webbing together and of cleaning the regimental badges without leaving traces of brass cleaner in the crevices. I had discovered that what I called a needle and cotton set was described on my list as a 'housewife'. When I thought about it, that was a logical description. By mid-afternoon I considered that we had broken the back of the job, so we laid out our kit on tables, locked the room and left for home by the rear door, early and undetected.

We agreed that we would arrive extra early at college on the following Wednesday to review our day's progress and still have time to attend the few odd classes that were being held before the end of term. On the way from home, I pondered all this effort we were making and the uncertainty of what was going to happen during the next week. When I arrived at college I found the room unlocked and David, dressed in his uniform, awaiting my arrival. His civilian clothes formed an untidy pile at the end of one of the tables and were ready to be put in a bag. My instant reaction was to query whether one of us had got the departure day wrong, but there was no doubt about that. It was just that on their way home he had agreed with Paul that they would both wear their uniforms at college, complete with full kit, for three days to see what effect it might have on other students. And there was always the thrill of pretending that it was the real Army. They had even stuffed blankets in their large packs to add to the effect. I surveyed their previous day's efforts and left them to join their respective classes.

On Friday, they were still just as enthusiastic and, when I arrived, their military imaginations were running riot. They had tried out some drill and there were clear signs that they wanted to shoot someone. I had been trained to be early, as wartime conditions had sometimes upset my journey to college. I was twenty minutes early, and I had been persuaded to be the third cadet in uniform. Dressing myself without a mirror was a long process. It was an awful job to get the webbing exactly right but at least I had David to give a hand. My late arrival in the classroom persuaded the class to embark on a cheer that caused a few moments delay to their progress. Sitting at a desk meant removing a pack, and the sight of a loose pack on the floor was an invitation for others to investigate. I offered them all a chance to join. Some leapt at the idea and others kept a safe distance, perhaps not wanting to be seen as soldiers. I caused quite a disruption to each of my classes that day and masters were having some difficulty in starting lessons on time. I had attracted a small gang of enthusiasts around me, all asking about the Army. If this was the typical level of enthusiasm, then the college cadet force would have a lot of members at the beginning of the next term.

I still did not know very much about Paul and David so I had briefed them about what I wanted them to do on Saturday morning. The most important points were that they should behave themselves and be on time. I had considered that being properly dressed for the occasion and bringing something to eat were slightly less important, although during the course of Friday evening I was not happy that I had that exactly right. I had to remind myself about railway tickets and taking the paperwork with me. I had unofficially been nominated as the senior of the three by the headmaster, who probably only considered my length of cadet service, but I did not have any stripes or any other obvious signs of seniority. I was a bit taller than the other two and may have looked older.

12

A first taste of the Army

On Saturday morning I woke at an unreasonably early hour. I had gone to sleep late on Friday, thinking about the plans for the next day. Was there something that I might have forgotten in the packing process? This was a totally new venture for me and I knew that the Army generated more discipline than all the other services put together. I concluded that the only way to make sure that everything was right was to check it all over again — or was it? I looked at my watch and discovered that it was just after 5.30 a.m. I got out of bed and went for a wash, being as quiet as possible so that I did not wake my parents. I crept back into the bedroom and started dressing. Absolutely everything was khaki. The white shorts and black boots added the odd dash of colour but that was it. A glimmer of daylight was easing its way between the curtains and outside the birds were twittering. I pulled the curtains apart and saw someone's cat creep across the lawn. I went downstairs and made myself a cup of tea. It was a very rare occurrence for me to make tea, especially at this hour in the morning. I thought it would be a nice gesture to make some for my parents. They might appreciate it. Having put on all of my kit, it was a bit of a balancing act to edge round the bend of the stairs holding two cups of tea, but I made it. My mother and father were still asleep but an almost disastrous slip on the edge of the carpet caused the spoon to rattle in the saucer and my mother woke with a start. I made the briefest of explanations and returned to the ground floor. A slice of bacon, an egg and a large chunk of bread were already waiting to be consumed for breakfast. My mother came downstairs as I was getting stuck into the food and volunteered to take charge of her kitchen. At my present rate of eating, I now had at least an hour and a half in which to do nothing. My mother must have got the impression that I had been up all night.

Waterloo station at eight o'clock on a Saturday heralded the morning rush hour for the office workers, each meticulously clad in a city suit, with briefcase in one hand and umbrella in the other, ready for half a day's professional labour before enjoying the major part of the weekend. I had already been to the booking office to buy tickets for the three of us — thankfully paid for out of public funds — and there was still half an hour to wait before the time that I had agreed to meet Paul and David. I strolled around at our meeting point for some time and watched the mass of people passing by. I picked out a few characters in the crowd and wondered what they did for a living. Most people took the shortest route to the entrance of the underground station, looking as if they knew precisely where they were going. Some were obviously occasional travellers, identifiable by their constant search for signs and their hesitant progress. Some looked very positively in my direction, while others appeared to take no notice whatsoever. I imagined that those who looked seriously could have been interested in the cadet forces. When I realised that people were looking at me I started to get that subconscious idea that something was out of place, although people were far too polite to interfere. I went to the toilets to find a mirror and take a hurried look. I found the mirror but there seemed to be nothing amiss. I concluded that I was probably the most intriguing sight of the morning and appeared to them to be too young to be a real soldier.

I knew that I had said 8.30, but by 8.20 there was still no sign of the other two cadets. I thought that they would have at least allowed themselves some extra time for any odd upsets to the train service. I was getting a little concerned, even though, as I tried to convince myself, time was not very critical to the completion of our journey. I suppose that I must have been looking around anxiously because suddenly I attracted the attention of a policeman who maybe had nothing else to do except look for the unusual. When I saw him approaching me I had the sudden urge, perhaps brought on by subconscious panic, to dodge round the side of the bookstall. However, I took control of my nervous system, realising that such a move would generate even more suspicion. The policeman strolled up to me, in a very casual way, and then stood towering over me as he asked a string of innocent questions to confirm what I was proposing to do for the rest of the day. After each question there was a pause long enough to allow the response to travel up to his brain and back again. I was sure that I had given him the right answers and he seemed satisfied. But then he bent down and quietly delivered a message into my ear to the effect that if he saw me again with a cap badge which had not been polished properly, he would be delighted to arrest me for taking insufficient care with the King's uniform. I was just about to take my cap off to have a look when he delivered the second message that if he saw me with my cap off, he would be delighted to do me for being improperly dressed. So I was in another 'no win' situation. I did not know too much about the law so I did nothing but politely thank him for his valued comments and silently hope that he would hurry up and go away.

Amongst the crowds, I could see Paul watching from a very safe distance. As the policeman left to embark on another investigation Paul arrived, accompanied by a worried-looking mother. That gave me an excuse to leave Paul for a moment and do something about my badge. A penny in the slot in the WC gave me all the privacy that I needed to remove the extra polish from the crevices of the badge and then give it a quick clean to put all the shine back. Secretly, I was glad that the policeman had used his expert powers of observation: his little 'words in the ear' could have saved me from something more serious later in the day. In those few moments that I was away David had also turned up, in time to witness Paul going through the tortures of being violently kissed by his loving mother, in full public view, before being surrendered to my doubtful care. I managed to avoid Paul's questions about my encounter with the policeman long enough to allow the matter to be forgotten. My aim was now to find a vacant third-class compartment in the train. That gave me the choice of a window seat, and we staked our claim for space for our kit on the luggage rack. If I had thought about it earlier, I could have left that badge-cleaning problem and dealt with it in the toilet at the end of the corridor of the train, thus saving one valuable penny.

Until the train started on its journey, there was nothing much to do except watch the general activity on the station and look at Paul and David doing the same thing. David's cap was on the seat. It should have been on his head. His badge was dirty, just like mine had been earlier. David had not properly polished the buckle on his belt either. I was not very polite as I told him about it and he was about to swear roundly at me, but he stopped in time. It was quite clear that the Army Cadet unit to which he belonged was not very particular about these things. He reluctantly spread the contents of his kitbag over the seat and floor to reveal an enormous collection of largely useless items from which he plucked a brush and rag and brass cleaner. A flurry of passengers coming into the compartment were quite amused to see David trying to get all his belongings into some semblance of order so that they could sit down, at the same time trying to win my approval for his efforts at cleaning. It was quite obvious that one particular lady had held a disciplinary position in the services. She showed all the signs of having been a difficult old battle-axe in her earlier years. She watched David do the necessary cleaning. Once she moved to say something but then stopped herself. Now and then David flashed a feeble smile in the direction of other passengers so as not to ignore her totally, but it was not really successful. Perhaps he was hoping for a little sympathy. Paul and I did not want to get too involved so we tried to avoid eye contact with other passengers.

After an hour and a half of sitting still, David's relief was transparent when, with yet another application of the brakes, the train stopped at a station and he saw that its name matched the destination on the tickets. I knew that he was going to be much happier once he was released from the inquisitive scrutiny of the other occupants of the carriage. We unloaded ourselves on to a platform built of timber planks, perched up on the side of a steep embankment, with a small shelter connecting it to a covered stairway leading down to a road. At road level, we were intercepted by one of the station staff who appeared to be very helpful, despite the fact that he wanted to know a lot more about us. He knew all about the camp and its permanent characters. When I pulled out a sketch map of the area and asked him to confirm the directions, he took me back up to platform level for a good view of the surrounding area. With one arm over my shoulder he pulled me closer to him, using his other arm to indicate the general direction of the lane as it wound its way past the church and the few cottages. From the wavering of his first finger I got the message that the camp was way over the brow of a distant hill. I asked about transport. The local buses were not quite as frequent as they were in London and only ran past the camp on Wednesdays and Fridays. The man that owned the only village taxi had died two weeks earlier and nobody had been found to replace him. I learned that it was customary for the sergeant-major to meet the afternoon train and march his troops the two miles uphill because that provided a convenient opportunity for him to do some dubious bargaining with food and cigarette supplies in the village shop. When the chance arose during annual camp weeks, there was an arrangement whereby several erring cadets from the camp would be detailed to accompany him for apparent fitness training, but in effect provided him with some additional capacity in their kit for whatever needed conveying.

By the time I got back to Paul and David at road level, I had decided that this particular sergeant-major was to be avoided at all costs. I had to make sure that we made enough progress to camp to avoid meeting him on the way and, if he was there on our arrival, to make ourselves so busy that he would choose other unfortunate cadets for that return journey to the station. David was sitting on top of his kit under the canopy of the station entrance, looking quite unhappy with life. I interrupted his grumbling about the lack of a High Street to ask where Paul had gone. He waved his arm in a southerly direction and grunted a word that I did not understand. Paul had crossed the road and had tried to climb up a small bank of earth to peer through a gap in the hedge, in an effort to watch the natural activities of farm animals. I arrived at the very moment that he lost his balance and fell backwards, to finish up with his large pack wedged in the ditch and with him laying on his back on top of it. While he was stuck in that undignified position, with David now looking on and having recovered his sense of humour, I took the opportunity to break the news that once he got himself vertical and tidy, he was going to march all the way to camp without stopping. David was not laughing any more. I relayed the messages about the lack of transport and the ways of the sergeant-major. It was going to be tough on his little feet going through that beautiful countryside, but he was a cadet and he was not going to have any choice in the matter.

It was such a picturesque little village: a rambling collection of houses and cottages marked out the road, some with their front doors within feet of the roadway and others, with well-kept front gardens, set much further back. The church, public house and general shop were all conveniently next to each other near the crossroads. Every building in the village was surrounded by a beautiful display of flowers, and some had window boxes. My mother would have been delighted to see all this. The arms of the signpost had been removed for security reasons and the wrought iron railings had gone to provide metal for war purposes. Paul wanted to go in to the shop but just before he got to the door he noticed a number of customers wearing khaki clothing. He came to a dead stop and decided to abandon that idea.

Once we had gone through the village and crossed the main road, the lane sloped gently upwards as it meandered between the hedges. It was pleasant enough, but was nothing very exciting or out of the ordinary, so I concentrated my thoughts on what I imagined was to come. David and Paul looked as if they were also intent on getting to camp as quickly as possible. We were making good progress, approaching the highest point on our route. On our right was a wooded area and that tempted me to suggest a stop to review progress and give me the chance to transfer any scraps of food from my kit to my stomach. I had not eaten since my very early breakfast, so the feeding process was well overdue.

A mound of earth amongst the trees provided us with a vantage point from where we had a good view of the surrounding countryside. It was in the shade and beyond sight of the road. I could not see any signs of the camp and hoped that it was not too far away. In the other direction I could see the church amongst the trees, and a wisp of smoke from an engine indicated the line of the railway. David wasted no time in finding a good supply of filled sandwiches and soon gave the impression that he had set himself a challenge to consume a known quantity of food in a limited time. Fortunately, he was far enough away from his parents to avoid incurring any criticism from them. Paul's progress through his supply of food was much slower. He at least had sufficient training to lay it out in picnic fashion. We had been resting there for some time before we heard the sound of voices and many pairs of boots making contact with the road surface. In keeping with the habits of most animals at times of impending danger, we kept quiet, watched and listened. These moments of enforced silence offered little to interest David so he glanced downwards, to discover that one of the natural lumps of ground which had provided such comfortable seating also housed a nest of ants. The ants were attracted to the food droppings and his observations indicated that they also liked the hairy cloth of which his uniform was made. David had grown up in the inner suburbs of London and was not experienced in the ways of the countryside. His dealings with animals were probably limited to giving the local cat a hefty kick when he considered it to be in the wrong place. To contend with the occupants of an ants' nest required a technique for which he had not been trained. I mentioned to him that one of the best ways of disposing of ants was to pour boiling water over them. In his minor panic, he took several seconds to realise that the idea was not very practical. Paul hinted that he might be able to shake them off. We laughed at his dancing performance as he tried out this method, which ended in failure. Then he suggested that David try squashing them to death but instantly had to retract his remarks when he realised what a mess this would make of his uniform.

By now David was quite convinced that he was the subject of a series of practical jokes, made worse by the increasing collection of crawling insects and the sheer difficulty of getting rid of them. He announced that he was going to try to persuade them to leave by smoking them out, rather like a story that he had heard about controlling bees. For David this was an outstanding brainwave, but I wondered exactly how he was going to produce sufficient smoke for the exercise. I did not have to wait for very long to find out, as he produced a box of matches and a half-empty and rather squashed packet containing a few cheap cigarettes. The professional demonstration of lighting up and blowing smoke over the affected areas of clothing led me to conclude that he was a secret smoker. I knew that young smokers valued their cigarettes very much when pocket money was in short supply, so the disposal of the ants must have been a high priority to him. The scheme took a good time and was reasonably successful, except that David had convinced himself that the last of the insects had not yet been located, and in all the isolated spots of roughness in his clothing there just had to be another ant.

After the ant crisis had passed, we made ourselves tidy and continued our journey. Within 400 yards, the road went downhill slightly then turned sharply left, where a large notice on the corner of a high fence declaring this land to be government property. A pair of impressive double gates stood open and, from here, the road surface was of loose gravel, well rutted by heavy vehicles. A few yards further on there was a barrier across the road in a gap between some very high and secure fencing. Inside the fenced area, and on the same basic layout that I had seen at Woodbridge, there was a large timber hut from where a number of young soldiers carefully watched our every move.

I had not yet acquired any great skill in giving orders, but I managed to convey a positive message to Paul and David to wait outside the fenced area until I had formally reported in. I discovered that the organisation was not working at all well and I had effectively taken one sergeant by surprise, separating him from his beloved cup of tea. I managed to gain the attention of one bright young soldier who was armed with a clipboard and a sheaf of paperwork, and discovered that Cadets Paul Holmes, David Wilson and myself had been allocated tent number 26. I had not lived in a tent before, except for a miserable little specimen that my parents had bought me at a time in my life when they considered that I might join the Cubs. That was only erected in our back garden at home if it was sunny, and I was certainly prohibited from using it overnight or if ever there was the slightest hint of rain. Its major disadvantage was that I was often blamed when it was in the way, particularly when the grass needed cutting or my sister tripped over the guy lines.

I beckoned to Paul and David to join me. Tent 26 was not hard to find. It was one in a long straight line of similar tents, all made from a depressing green-brown heavy-duty canvas with very substantial guy lines, and with regulation-sized posts identifying the tents. It was fitted out with six rather unstable camp beds, their thin supports having made minor ruts in the area of dying grass. Two small cupboards had been placed at one end of the tent, both crammed full with blankets. There was an assembly of slatted timber boarding on the floor, put there so that we could approach our beds above the level of the mud, if ever it got that bad. An electric light bulb dangled on a wire from the ridge of the tent, somehow connected to the power supply via a switch which I could not find, and two lines of cord ran from one end to the other, for the purpose of hanging up our clothes. I had a wicked urge to mention ants to David but thought better of it. We dumped the heaviest and removable part of our webbing kit on our chosen beds.

A voice outside the tent was shouting for someone who was in charge and I was nosy enough to wonder who would appear. It was the young soldier, still with his clipboard and paperwork, who was doing all the shouting. I did not consider myself to be in charge but, in his view, there was nobody of greater seniority in number 26, so it was me that he was looking for. He told me that if I got my party to the mess tent within the next few minutes, we would just be in time for a meal. The mess tent was very similar in appearance to our little number 26, but was the size of a marquee. There were lots of trestle tables with matching benches and at the far end a collection of willing ladies, clad in their white aprons, were ready with cheerful smiles and lots of food. It was only half an hour earlier that we had polished off the remains of our own food supply, but we extracted a good quantity of tea from a massive urn. On a side table there was a good supply of fruit that looked very tempting. I saw the apples first, but there were a few oranges amongst them. Since the beginning of the war oranges had been seen only occasionally and now David had got hold of one. He had started sinking his teeth into it when I stopped him. He did not know that the peel had to come off first, so I took an orange myself and showed him how to do it, and how to avoid the juice escaping before he started eating.

That orange was excellent. I had now had sufficient food to last comfortably until the next major meal. In comparison with the only other camp that I had attended, at least it was sufficiently compact that the 'bed to food' distance was a mere two-minute march, and the washing and toilet facilities were well-screened from the elements by a maze of brick walls. The washing area did not have a roof, from which I assumed that the logical brains of the Army had worked out that their troops went there to get wet in any event. The large timber hut near the entrance was the only other permanent structure in the whole complex and it was from there that the administrative instructions were issued.

I had guided Paul and David back to our tent and had decided that, in the absence of any other instructions, I would get my bed made with the blankets in good time so that they would not be dampened by the evening air. If any more sheets and pillows turned up, then that would be a bonus. I was surprised to discover that Paul was not used to making his own bed at home, so he needed some help getting things just right. Although he was glad of the help, he was rather self-conscious that such a simple job had beaten him. During this time, I noticed an increased level in the sounds of activity. Investigation revealed that an army lorry full of bedding had arrived, complete with two cadets who seemed to be there as helpers. One of these cadets started marching like a clockwork soldier, from tent to tent, in a series of straight lines, making halts and turns very strictly in accordance with the drill manual. My opinion of the Army Cadet Force was beginning to change for the better. He was travelling in my direction, so I elected to wait where I was to see what developed. Within a few moments he arrived in front of me outside number 26, finishing with a tremendous thud of his foot on the ground which must have given the worms a bit of a headache for miles around. In a Scottish accent, he announced himself by number, rank and surname, and politely asked me if I could help him with unloading the lorry, using delightful and accurate phraseology which could have been taken from the army publications. Having delivered his request, he remained stiffly at attention awaiting my reply. I was impressed. This little cadet was probably one of those folk whose entire aim in life was to march around like a soldier. He was rather small and seemed very young to be a cadet, but perhaps the rules about the age for joining were different north of the border. However, what he had in discipline, he lacked in his standards of dress. I took this moment to be my golden opportunity to be bold and positive and sort him out.

I told him in a very quiet voice that I had never seen such precise drill before. He did not even smile. It could have been that he was not permitted to smile when standing to attention. Then I walked round him slowly looking for major imperfections. I found that nothing was pressed very well, but I also found his trousers hanging out of his gaiters at the back. I told him all about that in a loud voice. It was a bit inconvenient to pursue the matter now because there was work to be done, but I told him to come back looking a bit smarter before the next meal. David could not be found so, for the next hour, Paul and I helped to unload the lorry.

Paul was getting worried as he had noticed that both David and his kit were missing. I thought about it but could not think of a completely logical explanation. I discussed the matter with Paul but after half an hour it was still a mystery. We agreed to go to the hut next to the main gate and ask there. He was on their list – Cadet Wilson, D, tent 26, 1.50 p.m. – and he remembered a cadet with a pale complexion, about fourteen or fifteen years old, joining the ranks that the NCOs were assembling. He was likely to be back in time for the evening meal. Back in the tent, I gently reminded Paul about the story that I had been told by the stationmaster earlier in the day.

During the afternoon the cadet with the Scottish accent appeared outside the tent, this time looking more like a cut-out from the recruiting literature. I had another slow and deliberate walk round to see if he had missed anything. He had certainly done a good job on his uniform since I had last seen him. I told him that I was pleased with his efforts and he could go now. Nothing happened, he just stood there. Then I tried to make conversation, and he still stood to attention in silence. Paul succeeded in attracting my attention. He had learnt that there are two important sets of words to be used in these situations. One was to give him permission to speak, and the other was to shout 'dismiss'. I actually ordered him to speak, then I discovered that he had been allocated tent 26. I had to dismiss him before he moved anywhere. Paul made him welcome, but his level of discipline was phenomenal. I had never seen anyone checking that the camp bed was clean underneath and then using a ruler to measure the lines on a blanket to make sure that they were exactly in the centre of the bed. I noticed a little card on his kit with the name 'McKenna A C'. He proudly announced that if I gave my permission, the cadets could call him Alistair, otherwise he would only answer to Cadet McKenna. He apologised for his earlier appearance in a slovenly uniform, but he assured me that it was the result of working off the back of the lorry. He was obviously going to set a standard that would be very hard to follow.

Our amazement with this cadet was interrupted by the arrival of the missing David Wilson who burst in and dumped himself and his kit on the bed. Paul and Alistair made little eye-to-eye signs to each other, got hold of David and heaved him out of the tent. I decided that I would keep well clear of whatever their plan was for a while, and I amused myself with an army training manual. I shall never know exactly what Paul said to him but, at some time later, Alistair invited me outside.

The three of them stood in a line with David in the middle. Both Paul and Alistair quickly excused themselves when they saw two other cadets arriving at the tent, and I presumed that they intended to get them organised. That conveniently left David and me alone. David looked very unhappy and had a little tear beginning to roll down his cheek. I realised that I was probably in at the start of a real serious personnel problem for the first time ever, and only I was in the position of trying initially to sort it out. I asked David where he had been and another tear rolled and I watched while he swallowed hard.

'Well, one of the blokes came into the tent when you were helping with the lorry and I was laying on my bed thinking about bunking off somewhere. I explained to him that I was tired after travelling, but he took no real notice, so I told him to push off and bother someone else, so he did. Just after that, the sergeant-major came in and ordered me to report to the gate, so I got bundled into a squad with three other soldiers.'

He fished in his pocket and brought out a handkerchief that had not seen soap and water for a long time and wiped his eyes.

'The bastard made us run all the way down to the village just like you said he might, then when we got to the crossroads, we had to wait for one bloke to run on the spot for a while 'cos his cap was not on straight. Then we had to stand still outside the railway station for ages to wait for the train, with all the village gaping at us, then when he was ready he made us march all the way back to camp. I'm just bloody well knackered, and I think I've got a blister.'

It was time to tell him a few facts about the Army.

'Wilson, there are some things that you ought to know, and the first is that we don't have blokes. They are cadets or soldiers or officers and they each have a rank, and when you want to talk to me or anyone else on formal matters between now and your next visit to Waterloo station, you will stand to attention unless you are told otherwise. That also means that wiping tears off your face is not permitted as your arms will be at your side. If you had done what you were told in the first place, life might have been much easier.'

'Yes, cadet.'

While I was in the mood, I spent a good half hour telling him his fortune for not being very smart and tidy, and I caught up with several reminders about indiscipline.

By now some more cadets had arrived with the party from the station and two of them had been allocated to tent 26. Paul and Alistair had organised them, so there was nothing further for me to do except to note their names and to introduce myself. Some time after tea, I managed to get McKenna on his own as I wanted to find out more about him. He was only just old enough, by two days, to be a cadet. His father had persuaded the local Army Cadet CO to get him a uniform and send him off to camp. He had been hanging around the unit for months waiting for the appointed day to come. His father was in the Army, which went a long way to explain his behaviour. He had a brother and sister at home who were both younger than him, and the household was run on very strict military lines, except that his mother allowed some relaxation of the regime when his father was away. Because of all this there were times when he had considered leaving home, but there were serious practical difficulties so he had looked towards the cadets for help. Unfortunately, on his arrival earlier in the day he found that his father had a temporary posting to this camp as the very sergeant-major whom we were all beginning to fear. I was getting quite concerned in case his father took a special interest in what he was doing, as this could result in some awkward moments. I thought about this a lot afterwards and started trying to find ways of putting David Wilson in the firing line for any criticisms that might develop.

13
Training for soldiers

Sunday morning at 4.30 was the first horrid shock to my system. My usual waking time on a Sunday was around 8 a.m. and I had not slept very well on that bed with its irritating contours, not helped by a background of miscellaneous country noises that continued throughout the night. If I discounted the time I spent trying to get comfortable – and tipping the whole bed sideways twice – I guessed that I might have managed three hours sleep at the most. The Army seemed to have a policy of waking up the larks, so the larks got the reputation for disturbing the rest of the nation. Somebody, possibly a fanatical musician or else doing it as a dare, had got himself dressed and played a few bars of music which roughly resembled *Reveille*. Cadets in a nearby tent happened to be sufficiently awake before the noise started to enjoy themselves for a moment with the singing of some very rude words to those few bars. The words must have been crude because they were followed by lots of laughter and nothing else could be that highly amusing at such an hour. From that point onwards, any attempt at staying in bed was quite impossible. I feared that I might get caught beneath the clothes and suffer some unknown punishment.

I took my first morning look at the inside of the tent, most of it just visible with the aid of the one electric lamp that was emitting light with the power of a glow worm. Through my two bleary eyes I saw McKenna leap out of his bed as if he had been fired from a catapult. I sat up to survey the scene. The remaining four occupants were giving off snoring sounds, but soon woke after McKenna shook their beds. They did not seem willing to emerge from beneath the blankets into the gloom, so I got McKenna to take further action while I persuaded myself that I ought to hurry and get myself vertical. I now witnessed what I took to be a development of that harsh army training that McKenna had experienced at home. He dragged Ian out of the tent, feet first, on to the wet grass outside, having rotated him twice on the journey and leaving behind a trail of bedding. By the time Ian was outside, the rest were prepared to yield to his instructions without any serious delay. Even David wanted to comply.

I did not have to think too hard what to do next as there was sufficient shouting going on to determine our next activity. McKenna had been well briefed and, in the interests of survival in this hostile atmosphere, I elected to follow his example. I did not have to drive the other cadets for they were getting the same message. Outside, in the dark, I could just see an enormous number of bodies standing in three ranks, clad only in white plimsolls and shorts. I had hold of a towel and a bar of soap for this specific occasion. The designated place for the morning wash was on the other side of the camp, and the only way to keep warm was to run there, with a flicker of a distant light as a target point. It was just like the conditions at Woodbridge all over again, except that it was more severe.

The door of the wash house was guarded by a group of soldiers who watched as towels were deposited on a line of timber tables and made sure that every cadet washed under an icy cold shower of water. A hot water system was installed but I saw a small notice requiring it to be inoperative during cadet camps to conserve fuel. Any attempt to avoid passing under the shower was soon detected and the errant cadet was sent round once again for an increased dose of the same treatment. The building must have been purposely built too small for all the troops who were going to use it, so that they were forced either to form queues or to arrange better organisation. I worked out that getting to the wash house first was an advantage if I wanted to avoid the discomfort of waiting outside. As I came out by the rear exit of the shower block, rapidly grabbing my relatively warm towel, I had my name noted. There were a few cadets, and Ian Skinner from my tent was one of them, whose names were selected from the list and were being diverted into an adjoining building by the NCOs. I had been with him and he had not made any attempt to avoid the experience of the ice-cold washing, in fact I was of the opinion that he braved it quite well. I wondered what was going on in that building, but I was certainly not going to stay around to find out, for that could have been really dangerous. Ian eventually turned up and told us that someone had decided that his hair was too long and quite unacceptable for the Army, so he was forcibly persuaded to sit on a chair while the whole lot had been stripped off. We really should not have done so, but we all laughed at his new image. He was not quite sure what his parents or his school mates were going to say about it, but I think that he must have seen the funny side of the episode eventually and resigned himself to the fact that it would grow again, albeit slowly.

The camp routine was arranged in such a way that, after the regulation cold shower, there was an inspection by the camp NCO which required meticulous attention to detail and cleanliness of the tent and surrounding area. If everything was perfect, permission was given to the inmates of the tent to march to breakfast. We were lucky that McKenna knew what his father would demand, as he had to comply strictly with these rules at home, so we nominated him to supervise this task, with each cadet in the tent being responsible for a particular item. McKenna found a piece of timber with a diagram on it showing the only approved layout for our kit. He showed how our bedding, clothing and kit had to be laid out with unbelievable accuracy, to comply with one of the mysterious and baffling customs of the armed services. When the moment of inspection came, I noted that all was well and we left for the mess tent, but on the way I witnessed many cadets who had not come up to the required standard and were starting again from the basic principles of bed-making. Quite a number of cadets were stroking the remains of their growth of hair.

The last of the early morning tortures took effect if a cadet was discovered leaving the table without consuming all the food on his plate. This was considered to be a criminal waste of food that was already in short supply. I saw three cadets get caught for this. Their penalty was to keep the outside toilets clean for a day or until other defaulters could be found to carry on with the job, so the message was only to accept food from the kitchen if you were going to eat it.

At 7.15 a.m. the whole camp was in lined up in three ranks, on parade, on one of the vast expanses of tarmac in the area. I was not really on form for the occasion. I had a good tummy full of their nice breakfast, but I was already feeling the effects of the shortage of sleep and that dreadful early start. We had to stand still for an awfully long time but I became a little more interested when the officers arrived on parade. At least that would indicate that the preliminaries were over. Drill was on the programme for Sunday morning. I was convinced that the Army had chosen marching as its main form of transport on the basis that footwear and human effort were cheaper than lorries or railway trains. I had expected to see some signs of religious training, not that I wanted it, but its absence did strike me as a bit peculiar after the performance in getting us to church at Woodbridge. The most striking change from my cadet service with the ATC was the language used for drill. The NCO in charge gave out a long bellow of warning, followed by a kind of hiccup upon which everyone moved. Most of the cadets seemed to know what was coming next and acted accordingly, but I found that if I staved off the tiredness, I could follow the rest with a minimal delay. In the ATC I often listened for the first part of the word 'Atten...' before the '...shun' came, but in the Army, the first part was not there. On the march, it sometimes became necessary when recruits were on parade for an NCO in the ATC to shout out 'left' and 'right' to keep the troops in step. In the Army, it had become two unintelligible words of differing pitches, and in the course of time and with a good ear for music it was not too difficult to follow.

We had just one break, when the NAAFI van turned up, for tea and wads. Those with money in their pockets were in great demand to lend what they could so that others could get a cup of tea. Most wanted to transfer their weight from their beloved studded boots to the seat of their trousers, but were prevented from doing so by the state of the parade ground. For the rest of the morning we were split up into groups of a dozen or so to learn about basic survival. I welcomed the idea that at least I was going to gain some technical knowledge out of this camp, and survival could be very useful to me. By 11.30, lunch was ready. In my view, this was a most unreasonable hour for lunch, but then the Army operated some hours ahead of any other civilised organisation, and breakfast time had been just as unreasonable. I had now been awake for seven hours so I was ready for a good input of food. I was most disappointed to find that lunch was only a snack and it was the tradition to stoke up at breakfast and eat well in the early evening. I had a good chance of keeping going until around 4.30 when I would expect dinner to be announced. The basics of survival and another little dose of the tedious drill filled up the rest of the afternoon session.

By dinner time I was starving. Having collected all I thought I could eat without incurring penalties for failing to eat what I had taken, I sat down next to Alistair McKenna to try to devour the lot. I had been persuaded to have good manners at the table as a result of the standards set by my parents, and McKenna had been educated to the same standards but, for fear of the consequences, neither of us spoke until both our plates were clean. There did not appear to be any guidance from the NCOs about what we were supposed to do in the evening. When I mentioned the point to McKenna, he had some very positive ideas starting off with cleaning everything, and finishing with sleep when the electricity supply became disconnected at 9 p.m. I thought he might have been saying that to impress other cadets at the table, but then I remembered his home background and decided that he could be very serious about it.

I suggested to McKenna that despite his limited service as a cadet, he was the expert in all those personal skills that are needed to avoid disciplinary troubles at camp, so I invited him to supervise the cadets for the evening in preparation for the following morning. He appreciated that extra responsibility and said that he wanted to see all of us in the tent after dinner. On the way back to the tent I told the other four cadets that I had nominated McKenna to be in charge for the evening, and I wanted us all to aim at the same standards as that morning. In those few moments he had made suitable plans for the evening. He lined us up outside the tent and gave each of the other four a positive job to be completed within the hour. That left McKenna and myself. He said that, as I had nominated him to be in charge for the evening, he wanted to talk seriously to me about a few matters then, after an hour had passed, we would both see what progress had been made inside the tent.

He asked me to change into my sports kit plus a pair of boots and then took me some distance away from the tent so our conversation could not be overheard. He reminded me of my decision and insisted that, if he was in charge, then I would stand to attention if he spoke to me; the reverse would apply when I was in charge. He walked around me to have a good look at what little I was wearing. He found nine blades of grass on the heel of my boots and when I began to illustrate that it was impractical on a grass camping area, he gave me a reprimand for speaking. Of course, he was right, but it was a bit of a shock. He suggested that I read the cadet drill manual ready for the following day, and to make sure that I knew the drill orders. As a last recommendation, he said that if we caught a cadet doing nothing, then we ought to find something physical for him to do. He put it over to me very clearly and with terrific force. When this expert bollocking came to an end he stood there for a moment and stared straight into my eyes with a horrid look of spite, then marched away. I could not see where he went and I felt rather stupid standing in that scanty area of grass. I was not very inclined to move from the position of attention because I was sure to be criticised if I did. Time is very difficult to judge, but I must have been there for two or three minutes. When he came back he graciously allowed me to accompany him on an inspection of our tent. I was happier to see that the bedding and most uniform items were laid out ready for the morning. I admitted to being a little concerned. After all, if the tent was in such an advanced state of perfection, then I could not see how we were going to sleep the night without destroying all the good work. When McKenna was ready, I queried this point with him. He ordered two of us outside, and told us to go to a nearby tent to collect six sleeping bags. They were going to be laid on the ground, slept in and removed before the visit to the showers in the morning. After what must have been well over an hour of being with McKenna, I was now wondering if he should have been totally in charge instead of me.

When we woke the following morning, to another dose of whatever piece of music it was, followed by noises of shouting to drive away the possibility of any further sleep, it all worked perfectly. We were near to the head of the queue for everything because, thanks to McKenna, we were now so well organised. A little temporary stiffness due to laying on an uneven surface was highly preferable to having to mess around in a sleepy stupor at some unearthly hour, preparing kit for an inspection.

Today's morning programme was the challenge of becoming familiar with a rifle. I had seen it all before and I did not particularly like the idea of being reunited with a rifle. At my very first encounter, when I had to manoeuvre the confounded thing — with agonising precision — between the ground and my shoulder and back again for an apparently ceremonial purpose, I considered that it was unreasonably heavy. It might have been acceptable to a fully trained and fit soldier, bristling with powerful arm muscles, whose life depended upon it in battle, but as a cadet I was far short of those qualities. As far as I was concerned, it had to be treated with as little loving care as I could get away with. This particular one was a .303 and my task was to take it to pieces, try to understand how it worked and then hope that it was in a fit state to fire a bullet after I had reassembled it. When we had all done that twice the instructor seemed rather at a loss to know what to do next, so he gave us a few moments break while he went off in the direction of the mess tent. He returned with a supply of thick canvas bags and a ball of string. Just to prove that we had really understood the previous lesson, for our next task we each had a bag tied firmly over our head so that we could not see, and then we had to take the rifle apart again and reassemble it. This was also something that I had done before, but this bag had the dust of agricultural grain embedded in its weave, which provided the incentive to get on with the job and be free of the smell and dirt as soon as possible. Once the rifle had been assembled to his satisfaction, the instructor took the opportunity of inflicting a session of rifle drill upon us. After a talk about bullets and safety, the morning's lesson came to an end, well ahead of schedule. We urgently needed to go back to the showers to get rid of the awful smell and remove the dust out from what little of our hair the Army had not claimed as theirs.

McKenna had briefed me about reading the manual for drill. That afternoon there was to be another session of drill and we were all threatened with being in charge of a small squad of cadets for about fifteen minutes or so. The slightest errors persuaded an overseeing senior NCO to enunciate his sarcastic remarks in the loudest voice possible to embarrass the poor cadet who was struggling to cope. Soon it was my turn to shout out orders to six inexperienced cadets. I managed to arrive in front of them with due ceremony but I felt very uneasy, standing out there alone with the whole squad looking at me. I was having a problem controlling my nerves and could not think of what I was supposed to say or do next. It seemed an awfully long time to be standing there being so indecisive, but in reality it could have been an acceptably short interval. Once I crossed the hurdle of giving a few simple orders with the squad in one position, I tried my hand at moving them around the parade ground. I initially became quite confused as my right was their left and vice versa. However, by the end of my allotted fifteen minutes I was much more confident about this new venture and would liked to have had longer at it. I had received some prompting but had not been shouted at in the way that some cadets had, so I concluded that I had done reasonably well for my first attempt.

Long before the afternoon training was over I was told to report to the sergeant-major in the camp office. My brain was in a flurry of violent activity as I tried to establish the reason for this order. I even tried to convince myself that it could be one of those practical jokes. I trod very warily as I looked for the door leading into the office of that dreaded man. In my search I came across the toilet door and instantly felt the urge to relieve myself and pluck up some courage at the same time. I found an adjacent door bearing the title 'Sergeant-Major N C McKenna' on a very well polished brass plate. I knocked on the door. There was no response whatsoever from inside. If I knocked again and he was in his office then it might appear that I was discourteous in some way, but neither could I stand there knocking repeatedly if he was absent. I wondered what to do. I must have almost deserved a medal for the strain of all the tension that was building up. Perhaps he did not hear my knock. I could not put my ear to the door or spy through the keyhole in case it suddenly opened. Then it did suddenly open. The man himself was standing there, glaring at me with his beady eyes, and with his arm adorned with enough badges to dispel any doubts about his status. He went back and stood at the side of his fully-upholstered chair, then beckoned me in. I saw one of those awful lines on the floor at the regulation distance from his desk, and I eased my boots towards it and landed one great thud where many sets of similar boots had been before. In a moment of near panic I almost saluted but just stopped myself in time. I remember having the presence of mind to announce my name. I dared not look anywhere but straight ahead, but in these few moments I saw sufficient of his face to make me wish that there could have been a distance of several miles between us. If this was the great McKenna, then it explained the actions of his little son. He had this unnerving habit of being just out of my sight while rustling a few papers on a side table, and of purposely keeping me in suspense. Eventually he sat down at his desk and made movements that indicated some intense brain activity. Words were possibly being collected together, ready for an important speech.

He started his oration by reviewing my activities at college and at this camp to date. Until then I had not been aware that my college activities were quite so well known to him. He had related the facts with a fair degree of accuracy, starting off with one little problem at Empire Day and continuing to the point where I had volunteered to attend at this camp. He was very eager to know how his own son was fitting in to the camp routine. I had to be very careful not to say anything that could lead to further and perhaps more difficult explanations, so I restricted my comments to praising his efforts so far. I was becoming quite bored by all this until he imparted the information that there were two cadets at the camp who had been identified as those who had attacked me at college some months earlier and who had since misbehaved in other ways. My next surprise was that I had earned a particularly good report so far in my training activities. I dared not mention that it was his son who had guided me towards the increased efficiency for which I was now receiving the credit. At that point, he came to a sudden halt. He got up from his chair and walked round me several times. I felt a movement around my waist and it was clear that the back buckles on my belt were being examined for cleanliness. On the next circular tour, he almost pushed two pieces of khaki cloth into my face. I did not realise the significance of that motion until he made the announcement that I was now a lance-corporal, and I was in danger of losing those miserable insignificant stripes if I did not do something about the two erring cadets. I could have his son as an aide, because it appeared to him that we had worked together well as a team in organising our tent.

I felt some relief at not being in trouble, and from the delivery of his address it was obvious that his staff were keeping him well informed. I did not agree that a stripe on my arm was miserable and insignificant, but I was certainly not in a position to challenge his words. He had lumbered his son and me with meting out justice on those two cadets. I had no clear idea who they were or exactly what I was supposed to do with them. Perhaps, between the two of us, we could devise some way of making them very sorry for attacking me at college, but it really needed someone with a good working knowledge of practical jokes. My thoughts quickly jumped back to the sergeant-major. I was still looking at a fixed point on the wall, rooted to the spot by an immobile set of boots parked with their toes touching that line on the floor. He walked slowly round the office, stopping again at that side table and not saying a word. On the second circuit when I saw that occasional side view of his face, I was aware that he was deep in thought. At about the midpoint of the fourth circuit his footsteps ceased. His face must have been only a few inches from my left ear. Unaccustomed gentle words flowed, from which I understood that I was to go to tent 30 immediately after lunch on the following day and install myself as the cadet in charge. Other cadets would arrive during that evening. He had already issued the necessary orders for the move. He had now finished with me and I could go. My about-turn and my marching from the room had to be perfect.

I was alone in the tent with the stripes and the 'housewife'. Again I followed my mother's trick of pinning adornments to the garment first, studied them carefully to check if they were right, and then finally, and with great care, sewed the stripes in place. It took many attempts before I was satisfied with the result. I felt quite proud of myself. I went to find Alistair. He saw me coming and placed himself well outside the tent. He noticed the stripes immediately and for him it was the permanent end of our conversations using Christian names. I wanted his help and there was a covered concrete area at the back of the camp offices. We would go there. I wanted a few tips and some more drill instruction. Alistair's eyes sparkled.

'Cadet McKenna. Imagine that you have three stripes on your arm until dinner time. Get going.'

'Yes, Corporal.'

'And don't miss anything.'

'Yes, Corporal.'

I thought that I knew all about dressing myself, but he found a few imperfections that were quickly put right. He had been good at drill since an early age and I had a lot of catching up to do. There was no rest for a few hours, during which I learnt a lot of the tricks of the trade. This session was going to be invaluable for dealing with two particular inmates of tent 30. McKenna was going to make sure that we incorporated all these small improvements when we marched to dinner. If I was not up to standard, then we would avoid the mess and keep going until I did get it right. He was in charge until our evening meal, but I had failed to tell him exactly when that was and McKenna was playing on that point. Reading the regulations to the letter was another of his acquired talents. At least we succeeded in getting there before the serving of food had ceased.

14
Two offenders

Tuesday was not going to be one of my favourite days. To start with, shooting was on the programme and it was going to be my first encounter with real live bullets.

After I had suffered the daily torture of getting out of my nice warm bed and taking part in yet another forced morning run, I was intercepted by two bulky soldiers near the exit of the shower block. I was asked if I was the one whose name was listed on the notice board under the heading of promotions, and I was happy to confirm that it was. This was to be my first whole day with one stripe on my uniform, with all the power that it bestowed on me, and within the hour it would be there for all to see. But I detected that a wicked plot was developing. The two soldiers, probably lance-corporals themselves, exchanged nods and winks and, before I could gather my thoughts together, they were each well in control of one of my arms and had a very firm hold on me. I started to panic and tried to wriggle free but the grip on my arms became tighter and I started to feel pain. What I really needed was to use those heavy boots on my feet to land a kick, but they had thought of that and there was no chance. Cadets were looking at me from all angles, hoping to be there for the kill, but at least I was still in an upright position as they dragged me backwards into a hut and dumped me in a sitting position on to a timber bench. I was theirs and they bluntly informed me of a tradition that an NCO had to look different in sports kit as well as in uniform. My face went cold with fright as the door was locked shut. Time had run out for thinking about the alternatives. There did not seem to be any move to remove my shorts, so I guessed that that part of my anatomy was safe. I might have been in line for a beating, except that there would have been a penalty if the assailants were caught, so that was also unlikely. One of them congratulated me as 'another little super-bastard with one stripe'. He offered me the option of sitting there and co-operating, or trying to be difficult and being forcibly restrained. Whatever it was, was coming to me anyway, so I chose the former option. 'Wise man,' he said, 'Very wise man.' I heard a metallic snipping noise, and then I knew that I had been condemned to a haircut. A mass of hair was soon falling in front of my face, over my bare body and on to the floor. I had assumed that I merely had to have a very short 'back and sides', but a second phase continued with a pair of cold clippers crossing my scalp. I started to protest but was told that this stage was merely the tidying up process so that it did not look too bad. When it all came to a stop my arms were released. My fingers were just able to feel the delicate stubble. It was no use doing anything about it now, but I threatened to complain. I was reminded that it is usual for new NCOs to ask for a haircut when promoted and they both said that they definitely remembered me pleading for a short haircut to win a bet with someone. I had been a cadet when I arrived and I had now been promoted to lance-corporal, and keen NCOs always have to keep up appearances. If anybody wanted to claim more of my hair, they would have great difficulty in finding any, and I was assured that the rest was safe. I was given a wallop on the behind and told to run to retrieve my towel and get back to the tent, while the next victim was heard yelling for mercy outside the door. I was not used to the cold air passing over my scalp as I ran back, and was thankful that for most of the day it would be partly covered by a cap. It would not grow long enough before I came within sight of my parents at the end of the week and I was sure that my father would have a fit. Mirrors were only fitted in the showers, so it seemed that I would have to wait until later to see the damage.

After breakfast, and with no comments having been made about my shortage of hair, we were bundled into a lorry and taken off to the rifle range. As I was under training I did not have to concentrate on the routine of loading the rifle. Every action was preceded by an order and then meticulously checked by the range officer before the routine continued, so I could not do very much which might be unsafe or seriously wrong. Every bullet was counted and checked, and so were the empty cartridges. I hated the sheer discomfort of my torso being perched on top of two ammunition pouches full of everything except ammunition, a large webbing pack on my back packed to a regulation weight and a uniform which began to take on the characteristics of a straightjacket. It may have given a good public image, or even a thrill to an enthusiastic Army recruit, but it was of very little practical use in this situation. Amongst all this congestion of kit and clothing, I was expected to make slow, careful and accurate aim that would eventually result in a phenomenal explosion right next to my ear and a violent jolt to my bony shoulder. It was all rather wasted effort: the bullet did not land on the target and I could not imagine how I could ever become master of this infernal weapon. If only rifles could have been invented that would kill off the enemy without inflicting any pain or making big banging noises for the attacker. However, some encouragement was forthcoming and the instructor persuaded me to rearrange the layout of my body so I stood a much better chance of success. After that, I did manage to get several shots somewhere near the outer rings of the target.

I had fired off my quota of ammunition and was idly watching another cadet laying at my side having severe difficulties. It was taking him a long time to understand what he was supposed to be doing. The instructor had been trying to help but he was still not making any progress and was becoming impatient. I saw the cadet close his eyes and wave the rifle around before he gave the trigger an almighty jerk that sent the bullet way off course. That must have been the last straw for the instructor because he landed this little cadet a hefty kick in the balls, picked him off the ground by his belt and dumped him some distance away from the firing point and out of harm's way.

The end of the morning's session at shooting did not come soon enough. My ears were ringing from the noise and I now had a shoulder, two arms and a scalp that did not feel normal. I knew that the food van was going to be around very shortly, so I was looking forward to a feast. The food van came late. There was a choice of sandwiches with jam in them or sandwiches with a quarter-inch slab of stale cheese. Somewhere there must have been an evil soldier on the production line who was afflicted with either a dose of jankers or a pet hate of cadets. We were impolitely told to eat them up, as they would otherwise go for pig swill, then the pigs might get ill and there would be no bacon ration. That comment was typical of army logic. Fizzy lemonade and tea were advertised but both were cold and had been modified from the original specification. It was lucky that I had a man-sized breakfast, otherwise I might not have survived until now. I had a flash of inspiration and told the range officer that I been ordered by the sergeant-major to sort out tent 30 during the afternoon. He was unable to verify my story, but the mention of a sergeant-major persuaded him to give me the benefit of the doubt. At least I would not be required to endure shooting practice any more during that day.

I had been given a diagram indicating the way back to camp and the main road could be seen from the gates of the range area. It seemed a very simple matter but I soon realised that although the diagram might have been crystal clear to its writer, it was not to me, and it did not show the distance involved. Webbing equipment on my back containing all the useless military junk was not helping one little bit, and I had a long way to go. At the next road junction there was not even a clue to indicate the possible location of the camp. The signpost had not been replaced after its removal, for security reasons, during the war, which left me with a choice of three routes unless I chose to stay where I was until someone came past. Trying to survey the area from a higher vantage point had left me tangled up with a unreasonably prickly hedge on a bank of earth. Then I heard the noise of an engine in the distance. At first I thought it might have been a tractor, but the rate at which the noise was developing soon suggested a lorry. I first spotted the roof of the vehicle above the winding hedge line, and I decided that leaping around in the road might cause the driver to stop. Such an unusual practice is quite safe in the college gymnasium, but in jumping down to road level

I found my head at the same level as my feet, having been made seriously unstable by frictionless boots and a heavy pack. I soon found myself in the middle of the road, complete with a few new minor bruises. I discovered that the thick uniform and webbing kit was quite protective of the human body. The driver had no option but to stop. His head appeared out of the cab window.

'Arse over bollocks, are yer?' he enquired.

I did not think that I needed to reply immediately, as I returned myself to an upright position. Through his laughter, he asked if I needed a lift. Lorry drivers have a lonely existence while working and the sight of someone in a uniform and in trouble switches on their feelings of compassion. Conversation was somewhat difficult with the noise of the engine and the rattle of the aged bodywork, but we managed to communicate through smiles and sign language and shouting while the engine was not labouring too hard. I was certainly very happy to see the camp gates in the distance and I thanked him for leaving his planned route.

I found tent 30 and my aim was to ensure that McKenna and myself were well established before anyone else arrived. As I was wearing most of the clothing and kit that I had at camp, the principal items to transfer were bedding and a few personal items. That left me with the best part of an afternoon and no positive job after the first hour, but I remembered hearing that cadets with nothing to do are attractive prey for those with stripes and wicked minds. There was very little inside the tent that needed any attention, so I stood there wondering exactly what I was going to do next. I could have assumed the horizontal position on one of the beds, but there was the danger of being discovered, and that would certainly have produced painful results. I could have taken some relaxation outside the tent, but that would have made me even more vulnerable to the keenness of the camp staff. I had to think carefully how I was going to deal with the two new troublesome cadets when they arrived, but the process of logical thinking was not an approved and identifiable activity for cadets and there was nowhere suitable where anyone could do this in relative safety. Perhaps I should not have come away from the rifle range quite so fast, but it was too late to do anything about that now. There seemed to be only one sensible answer, and that was to put myself outside the camp for a while. The gate was well guarded, but if I did get stopped and I had a good authentic reason for leaving, then I might not have too much difficulty.

I decided that I would head for the direction of the wood where we had rested on our day of arrival. It was out of sight of the camp, not too far away and I could do whatever I needed without any interruption. The camp gate was open so I tried to look as if I was really intent on getting somewhere, and marched out without creating any suspicion. When I got near the wood I discovered, to my horror, that it was occupied by a party of cadets who were using the area for some kind of warfare training. They all seemed to be very much involved in what they were

108

doing, and my arrival in the area would not have been a good idea. I went round the edge of the wood and found the ideal spot where I could sit amongst the bushes and have a good view of their activities.

I had come here to think about what to do with those two cadets. I thought back to my one and only camp at Woodbridge, but I considered that the standard forms of harassment and punishment used on that occasion were impractical. In any case, I only had one stripe and it would be unreasonable to condemn them before they did anything wrong, although I would have been well satisfied to repay them for attacking me at college. They might be quite thrilled at having to do some physical activities, or being given a job so they could escape from cadet training. I decided that one of the few ways of having my own back was to keep very strictly to military discipline. I might have to wait a long time for them to make a wrong move, but there was a good chance that it would happen eventually. I concluded that I would have to reconsider the matter when I saw them and had spoken to McKenna. With his home background, he could well have some interesting ideas.

Re-entry into the camp was just as easy as leaving it, and the lack of attention by those on the gate meant that I did not have to explain my actions. I could see from this distance that McKenna was outside tent 30 with two small cadets. As I got nearer to them, they both looked a little surprised about seeing me, and I guessed that a stripe on my arm did not please them too much. One just said, 'Hello,' out of his chubby smiling face. Here was my first opportunity to make myself unpopular. He got a reprimand as I pointed out that the correct procedure was to announce his name, and anything else to be said after that had to finish with the word 'corporal'. I did not want to know their first names, but their surnames were Kay and Heffernan. I made them both practise that a couple of times until I was satisfied that the message had registered, then I insisted that they had another go with their heels nearer together and their arms at their sides. They both looked a bit untidy and their training so far had not made much difference to them, but in the circumstances it was not going to be good enough for me. I ordered them to get organised and to report to me after the evening meal.

I did not see them in the mess tent at dinner but that did not strike me as unusual. When I returned to the tent I observed that they had tidied their beds but it was not very impressive and they were nowhere to be seen. By 7 p.m., McKenna and I had finished our chores for the evening and we were starting to wonder why they had not yet appeared. Within the next ten minutes, an NCO arrived from the camp office to tell me that the local policeman had called in for his usual cup of tea. He had come past the village inn on the way where the local farmers often gathered for their evening pint, and he had watched their pub games versus a party of cadets. He thought that it might be a good idea if they were rescued before they or the licensee got into any serious trouble. When I got to the camp office, I was amongst a group of corporals who were detailed to identify the culprits.

When the truck arrived it contained six cadets. I recognised my two and promptly declared that I was not happy about looking after them during their state of drunkenness. My lifestyle at home had never brought me into contact with a drunk before, let alone having to deal with two of them, but it was made clear to me that they were definitely not going anywhere near the camp office. The only alternative was to get them to the tent to which they had been allocated. At least they could stand almost vertically without assistance. With the added supervision of one other NCO, I was able to conduct them to the tent, albeit in a rather haphazard way. The only possible thing that I could think of doing with them was to get them into bed and try to sort out the complications in the morning. It quickly became a question of whether it was more convenient to undress them first and then dump them in bed, or whether to dump them near their beds and then try undressing them. I consulted McKenna on the matter, but he was as green as I was in this situation. Things came to a head when Heffernan realised that his bladder was well overloaded, but fortunately some quick thinking and brute force directed the fluid out of harm's way. Learning from our first experience at this game, we dumped Kay somewhere near the toilets and kept him there while nature took its anticipated course. Eventually we had two cadets in bed, neither of whom seemed too inclined to cause any further problems until the morning.

I was thinking about getting undressed, ready for bed. Here was an answer to one problem. I took McKenna outside the tent, out of earshot of the others. It was a rare for me to catch McKenna without his cap on and I gave him a good ticking off. He leapt to attention and wanted to retrieve his cap but I was not having that for a while. But that was not what I took him out there for. I had lost the bulk of my hair that morning in an initiation for being promoted. It was that brisk feel of fresh air blowing across my scalp that brought the flash of an idea. I suggested to McKenna that Kay and Heffernan might be suitable candidates for bald heads. I told him to go and search out the haircut team and bring them to me.

McKenna also needed to enlist his father's help and to drop a hint that the adult staff ought to look the other way. The two temporary barbers were found and I offered them a sixpence per bald head. Was it to be now or in the morning? A decision had to be made. We agreed that it would not be a good idea to shear these particular sheep this evening because they would not realise what was happening. It would have a better effect on them in the morning, and we might get a better audience. They might also be late for training, with possible hangovers, so all we had to do tonight was to advertise the event.

There was absolutely no sign of a haircutting ceremony when I came through the showers and I was almost disappointed. When I arrived back at my tent to change into my uniform, I encountered the stench of vomit. McKenna had got back from the showers first and was surveying the scene, not knowing what to do next. There was a tent inspection due at any moment and I had to think how to handle the problem. It was far too late to get the two cadets out of bed and cleaning was going to take ages. I told McKenna that we should both meet the inspecting officer outside the tent and ask his advice on the action to take, based on the theory that we were all troubled by the same problem and with a common enemy of two erring cadets. Luckily we were near the start of his rounds and we only had a few moments to wait. I saluted and must have shaken my nervous system into silence long enough to allow McKenna to do the explaining. He was superb. He delivered a speech with such logic and tact that I would never have dared to interrupt. The officer commanded his sergeant to avoid our tent at all costs and they had a confidential discussion out of my hearing. I gathered that they already knew the background to the matter and I was told to take whatever time I needed to deal with the two offending cadets. With that kind of licence, I went off to breakfast with McKenna and took the opportunity on the way to thank him for dealing with the inspecting officer so effectively.

Once the advancement in rank had been confirmed by the removal of practically all of my hair, I was allowed in the area of the mess reserved for the cadet NCOs. As I looked I realised that all the NCOs had either had similar treatment or had voluntarily gone to the barbers to avoid it. The camp sergeant-major had told them all before they left for camp that this was a tradition of his regiment. The NCOs were all completely happy that it labelled them as members of an elite cadet force and could instantly recognise each other as such. Whatever they thought about it, I was going to be deeply embarrassed when I got home. Over the breakfast table, I told the story of my two drunken cadets and their earlier attack on me at college, to see if it would generate any comments on how I should deal with them. It was all treated as a great laugh with many impractical ideas, but nothing that was really of any use. McKenna met me outside the mess tent, and let me know that he was really looking forward to getting back to tent 30. In his orderly life, he had not met this kind of problem before, but then I saw the haircut team watching from a safe distance. I did not know how, but guessed that all was well.

We arrived at our tent and surveyed the chaos. The haircut team were near at hand and ready to pounce. Both of the offending bodies were still horizontal in their beds, not yet wanting to be seen to be awake. We heaved away on one side of their beds, aiming them in the general direction of their own vomit. The result was instant and effective. I held the face of one of them down in the mess by gently treading on his head long enough to make him realise that it was not going to be one of his most exciting days. When I released the pressure I noted that the arrangement of stud marks looked quite artistic. Heffernan decided that he would use his fists on me, but I was thankful that physical training activities at college had included some experience of boxing and my blow landed first. While they were still in the state of undress, I reminded them about the crime of self-inflicted injury to avoid military duties, of failing to comply with the standing orders for the morning activities and their lack of loyalty to me in keeping the tent tidy. The haircut team struck then. There was not a single thread of hair showing by the time they had finished. They yelled and cried and wanted to run away and they threatened all kinds of things. I gave them an hour to get themselves washed and dressed, to remove all traces of vomit from the grass and to prepare their beds and kit for my inspection.

I noticed that McKenna had disappeared since I started being rough with Heffernan and Kay, so I went out to find him. I located him rearranging the little timber pegs which held the tent numbers. I thought that was a clever move, as our tent now had a different number and the vacant tent at the end of the line was now number 30. McKenna had reasoned that whatever cleaning was done, the smell would still be there.

At the end of the hour we returned to the tent to see if matters had improved. They both considered that their efforts were satisfactory but I could see many items that needed further attention. I wanted the job completed to perfection and I told them so. Given another hour and a lot of prompting by McKenna, they had reached a reasonable standard. I could see the messy patch on the grass and the smell was still awful but not quite so strong. I considered that the time was right to announce that they were in my tent because they had been identified as my attackers at college on Empire Day two months previously and I had since been witness to their further misconduct. Now I could feel my confidence growing as I saw the rapid change in the expressions on their faces as the full significance of my words registered. I had all the evidence that I needed to inflict some form of punishment and I could now 'throw the book at them', with the backing of the morning's inspecting officer and his staff. It was only 10 a.m. and I could have two full hours of wicked enjoyment out of watching these two paying for their misdemeanours before they got anywhere near a supply of food. Their first task was the removal of the contents of the tent to its newly-relabelled position. That would require them to lay out their kit all over again. In the meantime, McKenna had spoken to his father and discovered that the armoury contained an awful lot of rifles that needed to be cleaned. All that remained was for us to supervise the work and then criticise it so that it had to be done a second or third time.

The task of moving the contents of the tent was undertaken with reasonable diligence and with some degree of caution as they could have been thinking about the results of their actions if it were not completed to my satisfaction. What I was really looking forward to was their task in the armoury. Officially, the rules about security decreed that an armoury had to be a room that did not have an outside wall, and consequently it had to be without windows and the door had to be kept locked. I got McKenna to take them over to the guardroom and armoury, and he returned some time later to tell me that they were now at work. From this point, McKenna's father had taken an active interest in the two cadets and their rifle cleaning. It seemed that food was taken in to them at regular intervals and they had a bed, so the bulk of their kit remained in my tent. I was really satisfied that justice was being properly inflicted upon them.

15
Off home

It had been raining during the night and the feel of the air outside the tent suggested more rain to come. It was Saturday. I hoped that later in the day I would be away from the army camp and enjoying the comfort of home. There were not always too many delights in being at a cadet camp, but one of the joys was that I only needed to carry the items that appeared on the official list. It was just a case of putting on a uniform once again and stuffing everything else unceremoniously into whichever piece of webbing kit would accept it. For many cadets, another advantage was getting away from their parents. The enthusiasm for pressing uniforms and polishing brassware and boots was beginning to lose its place on my list of priorities. My mother would have to sort out the debris when I got home.

A glance at my watch indicated that it was still too early to fall out of bed, so I must have dozed off for a while. Then I was conscious of being prodded. McKenna was standing at the side of the bed to wake me up. He and Paul Holmes each had a very firm grip on David Wilson who was standing between them. It did not take too much wit to detect that something was seriously wrong. I rubbed my eyes. When they came into focus properly, I noticed that Wilson did not look like he normally did. There were a few reddish patches on his face, which I did not remember seeing before, and he looked as if he was not liking being clamped between McKenna and Holmes. It was far too early to deal with problems like this. I told them both to stay with Wilson until after breakfast, and then I would deal with whatever the problem was.

At the breakfast table the NCO who had been the wielder of the scissors and clippers some days earlier took me on one side to say that a cadet from my tent had let his mates down on the previous evening. The message that I was receiving was that he had had to intervene to stop a fracas and he expected me to sort out my cadet, otherwise I would be going home with more than my hair missing. I was not at all sure what he had in mind but it was certainly a threat that I was not going to ignore. When I arrived back at my tent I saw Wilson standing outside, waiting for me. I could not see McKenna or Holmes. It was unusual for them not to be too far away, but perhaps they had tactfully retreated.

Wilson stood there almost motionless. His very watery eyes and the set of his face indicated that he was on the point of bursting into tears. The story that gently unfolded was that on the previous evening he had got involved with a party of cadets who were playing cards. Although he had not been aware of it at first, he discovered that they were playing for money. By the time he realised, it was too late to back out. Wilson never had much money at the best of times and the game relieved him of all he had. His only immediate escape from difficulties was to convince the other players that he would go to his tent and get some more, but what he in fact did was to discover an unoccupied tent and steal from the clothing of another cadet. Unfortunately for him, the cadet from whom he stole was also in the party playing cards. During the latter part of the evening Wilson was found out and the cadets set about him with their fists. That still left him in the predicament of owing money. From that little story, I concluded that what the three of us might be going home without was our money.

Wilson was crying quite openly now and my attempts to stop him did not have much effect, so I sent him off into the tent while I thought about the matter. There was now a crisis developing and my best ally was McKenna. I looked round for him but both he and Holmes were missing. It was no use looking for them, so I decided to finish packing my kit. This also enabled me to keep an eye on Wilson. About half an hour must have passed before McKenna and Holmes appeared, accompanied by McKenna's father. It was now quite clear that he had taken charge of the situation and he took Wilson off to his office. McKenna, Holmes and I kept well out of the way while we observed the movements of quite a collection of cadets to and from the guardroom, as we carried on clearing out the tent and returning the equipment to the stores.

McKenna and I were asked to go to the office where, having gone through the usual courtesies, we learnt that gambling among cadets was illegal. The result was that McKenna's father had decreed that all of the money that had changed hands had to go back to its original owners. Wilson seemed to have recovered his money and he turned to smile at me, only to receive a reprimand for moving. On the condition that we had properly tidied up our tent, we were now free to go home.

Eventually, there was a flurry of activity. An army lorry arrived and was loaded up with kit and a good number of the cadets involved in the card school. Then more lorries turned up to take cadets to Salisbury. There were just a few things to do before we left. There was the unknown fate of Heffernan and Kay whom I was likely to meet at college when the holidays were over. McKenna suggested that his father had years of experience and was quite capable of dealing with that kind of situation, so they were unlikely to reappear at college. Wilson wanted to talk to me rather urgently, so we found an area behind the guardroom where we would not be disturbed. He wanted to thank me for getting him out of the scrape that had resulted from the card game, and for sorting out all the other little troubles he had got into during the week. Then I wanted to exchange addresses with McKenna. We had become really good friends during the week and I wanted to keep contact with him. McKenna saw this as a formal occasion and would not relax to get a pencil and paper out of his pocket unless I ordered him to do so. McKenna was like that, but I would be interested to see how he behaved when he was not wearing a uniform.

I had checked that Holmes and Wilson were ready to leave but then made the mistake of pausing to take a last look at the camp before we went through the gate. The sergeant-major was standing there with five soldiers, looking for his weekly victims for a march to the station. We were caught and told that there was unlikely to be a lorry going in our direction. The soldiers were also aware that it would be several hours before the next train left for London. I suppose that, in the circumstances, marching was the quickest and most efficient way to get to the station, but it was also the most uncomfortable method if kit was ill-fitting, and mine was in this category.

Fortunately it was downhill for most of the way, but that did not relieve the agony of carrying kit at marching speed non-stop for an hour. The only very slight relief was a brief delay as we crossed the main road, and there was no chance of slackening the pace on the incline up to the station. Then we even had to undergo an inspection and a warning for the need for perfect discipline until we got home, before we were allowed into the station. I had also learnt the penalty for not putting my kit on correctly. I would remember that: it hurt.

Enquiries revealed that the next train to London would not leave for nearly two hours. Worse than that was the fact that we were getting hungry. We searched our pockets for money and I was surprised to see a collection of ten shilling notes come out of Wilson's pocket. He seemed inadvertently to have rather overstated the amount with which he started before the card game and, as they were trying hard to extract themselves from trouble, the other players were not prepared to get into an argument about the amount involved. So Wilson was sent to go and buy some food with his ill-gotten gains. He returned with a bag of sandwiches and three bottles of beer. He said that the man round the back of the pub recommended it. What I knew about beer was fairly limited but I should have preferred tea or lemonade. When he had drunk half of the bottle I called a halt and diverted his attention to the food.

At long last a sign of steam in the distance was followed by the screech of brakes and we were on our way back to London. At Waterloo, Wilson's parents were waiting for him. His mother took instant fright at the state of his face and the ritual kissing of her dear little son revealed the smell of beer. I let him explain as best he could, but it did not show the signs of being accepted. His father looked quite annoyed and he dealt him a couple of hefty wallops in full view of the queues of intending passengers and in total disregard for the need for good publicity. I parted company with Paul and looked forward to our next encounter at the beginning of the next term.

I headed for the underground and the second train to arrive took me all the way to my local station, then it was another twenty minutes by foot to get home. What a lovely sight that house of ours was! Knocking on the door brought no reply. I knocked again, then I saw a note on the side window. My parents had gone to see Mr and Mrs Bishop for the evening and I was to go there. That was only another ten minutes' walk and I was invited in to be greeted by a beautiful appetising aroma from the kitchen. It smelled like real food, most unlike the contents of the big camp kitchen containers that I been accustomed to during the week. I dumped my kit in the hall, took my cap off and walked in. In retrospect, the news about my shortage of hair ought to have been broken more gently. My mother went potty, saying that I looked like a convict. My mother had a standard set of sayings and phrases that she trotted out on such occasions, without ever thinking about the consequences or the need to be tactful. My father glared at the offending sight and threatened to complain to the headmaster, until I managed to persuade him that it was my problem, my hair and by the time he had complained, the holidays would be over and it would have grown again. I wanted to keep my father and the headmaster away from each other as much as possible, as I had already experienced the way matters went out of my control when these two forces got together. Mrs Bishop tried to divert the conversation away from hair by pointing out that I looked awfully hot in that uniform and I ought to take it off. It was awfully hot, but I still had some pride, backed up by a dose of discipline, and there was no chance that Mrs Bishop was going to see the dirty shirt underneath. My mother and father would have gone potty all over again if that had been revealed. I just said that I was not allowed to remove my uniform. The regulations and the sergeant-major said so. Mr Bishop was in the same Home Guard unit as my father and seemed to be the only person with a clear and logical brain in operation at that moment. He suggested that I joined them all for a meal and sorted out the stories of camp afterwards. The nature of the smell now emanating from the kitchen had changed somewhat, indicating to me that burning was taking the place of cooking. That conveniently moved the chaos to the kitchen.

The next week was comparatively uneventful. Donald came and knocked on the door, and so did Tony. They both sat there listening to my stories from camp. Tony said that he wanted to join the Army and have one of the short haircuts that I had recently made popular, and Donald told him that the ATC was much better.

One afternoon they had an argument about it which developed into a fight and my mother threw them both out of the house. It was bad luck on Tony because before my scalping at camp he had voluntarily been on a visit to the barber and had a haircut to match mine and he had already been thrown out of his house for that reason. To make matters worse, it was raining. My sister got told to buzz off more times than I care to remember. She wanted me to put on my uniform and pose for her to take a photograph of me, using a camera that she had acquired. I was not going to do it but I told her that, if I did agree, she had to accept that I was senior to her in rank and she would have to do what I told her. My mother heard what I said to her and disapproved. Pam never got her photograph that day.

One morning, the postman pushed a larger than usual packet through the letter box. All deliveries by the postman were put behind the clock over the fireplace for my father to deal with when he came home. But this one had my name on it. My mother had never met this situation before but she insisted that my father was there when it was opened. When my father arrived after work I protested that the mail was addressed to me. If he was going to open my letters, then I thought that it was only fair that I should see his. There was another argument in which I was told that I was not going to be allowed to go to the ATC until I apologised. I got hold of the letter and it contained my college report. The results were above average, so my father relented slightly. I also found a note in it from the headmaster asking me if I could come to college two days early to help to get the college cadet force going. Now this was just what I wanted. I carefully arranged with Donald to move my khaki uniform into his house, then I took just a few of my essentials as well. All I had to do then was to tell my father that I was considering leaving home to join the Army as it was so interesting.

On the Saturday afternoon, my father discovered that my Army Cadet uniform was missing and so was I. All I had done was go and see Donald for the afternoon. I had also persuaded Tony to knock on my parents' door during that time and ask if I was in. Then I went to see Tony and got Donald to call and ask if I was in. Of course, I arrived for tea a little late but I discovered afterwards that it caused quite a panic. I did not have too much trouble getting my own letters after that.

On one particular Thursday morning the postman called with a letter for my parents that caused them great concern. They passed it between themselves, without saying anything, over the breakfast table. I guessed that something had gone wrong in the family. My father was very nearly late in leaving for the office and my mother was near to shedding a tear or two. When I got home from college my mother announced that there was something important that Pam and I ought to know. She had needed time to plan what to say, then she broke the news that my uncle had suddenly become very ill. All of his near relatives were expected to go and see him as soon as possible. That meant a trip to the other side of London. Friday would be quite out of the question, but my father had agreed to Saturday. My father had to go to the office on Saturday morning but he wanted to join us later in the day. The train to both destinations went in the same direction so we were all to travel together for the bulk of the journey. The task of organising ourselves took on great urgency. I took the view that I was presentable but My father did not agree. My best suit had not been pressed to his satisfaction and my shoes were caked in mud after I had embarked on a minor mischievous plot on the golf course on some earlier occasion. My father and I went up to my room to see what could be done. There were not too many clothes in my cupboard and certainly none that he considered suitable for the family to see. He was really getting impatient, as there was a chance that he would be late for work, and I was prepared to settle for anything to avoid any deterioration in his temper. I stood in silence, as far away from him as possible, until he calmed down a little and only then did he decide that the only dress he would accept was my cadet uniform. I am not sure whether I was horrified or proud to hear that news, and I was not sure what the regulations said. Whatever I thought about it, there was no point in arguing. I now had a delightful choice. Was it to be blue or khaki? I did not have too long to decide. I chose khaki because there would be fewer complications if something went wrong, and anyway it just happened to have been cleaned recently.

When I went downstairs and was ready to leave, my mother did not immediately understand it, but she quickly spotted My father's mood and decided to accept what she saw. I understood that my uniform was to be worn on days of authorised cadet activities only, but the chance had to be taken. Without really being able to say why, I felt slightly out of place until I arrived at my uncle's bedside to discover that four of my cousins were also in a cadet organisation of some kind. We congregated in their large garden to exchange comments for as long as possible, while the older members of the family concentrated their minds on the state of uncle's illness.

My father arrived early in the afternoon and did not mention the matter again until we all arrived home late in the evening. It was then that he decided to have one of those pointed and serious talks with me in the privacy of my bedroom. He laboriously inspected the contents of my wardrobe, only to discover that it was in the usual shambles. His bout of bad temper resurfaced as he proceeded from one unacceptable item of clothing to another. In the process of my being committed to bed for the night, my nice clean white ATC webbing belt became a convenient weapon for him to use to attack my khaki-clad backside.

When I left on Sunday morning to go on parade, there was a positive stiffness when I tried to march. I had been seen on Saturday and the fact had been reported, so I found myself in front of the warrant officer who asked for a very detailed account of the matter, particularly as I had appeared as an Army Cadet. I was not prepared to take all of the blame for this one, after all it had been my father who made the final decision in the matter, and my CO who had approved my involvement with two cadet units. I mentioned that I would have willingly stayed at home in preference to being in the company of a horde of elderly relations. I remembered that there was a provision somewhere in the regulations for attending funerals in uniform, although not in the period before death took place. I offered that excuse, but the bit of the regulation I did not know about said it was necessary to get permission first to wear a black armband. The warrant officer decided that he would verify the information, and would speak to me later. I was extremely lucky. The matter was not mentioned to me again, although I suspect that someone, somewhere was criticised.

16
Autumn term

Two weeks before college was due to start I had a 10 a.m. visit from Tony. I thought that it was unusually early in the morning for him, but he always seemed to behave in very unpredictable ways. He invited me to go for a walk and he was not going to tell me our destination. There was nothing else really important that I wanted to do and Tony's mischievous jaunts were often a good laugh, usually at Tony's expense. I accompanied Tony to the end of the road and we turned left towards the parade of shops. Tony stopped on the pavement and said that he would get some extra pocket money from his parents if he could prove that he could spend what money he had carefully on useful things, and I was here to be a witness to what he bought. We wrote down the names of all the shops, then Tony wanted to be blindfolded with his one and only filthy old handkerchief. Then he would use a pin to pick out a shop from the list. As Tony was manipulating the pin, I was able to turn the paper round and select where the pin went. I did not get it quite right and it landed on the line dividing Brown the chemist's from the barber's shop. Tony looked confused as he returned the handkerchief to his pocket, but I insisted that he spent half of his available money in each. There was more choice in the chemist's so he went there first and searched the display cabinet for something useful. The lady assistant was quite amused when I told her the background to the venture. Now that the manufacturing industry was getting itself established again, there was a new variety of hair cream on sale. To promote the new product, it was being sold at a lower price, so Tony jumped at the idea. The barber's shop was our next call, and the barber got going as he was instructed. Sadly, Tony did not think about his previous purchase until the barber had nearly finished cutting. What Tony wanted was a shaven head in the same style that I had affected when I returned from camp. But I suddenly ceased to become his friend any more when the two purchases were seen not to be compatible. My original prediction was right: it was a good laugh, especially when Donald and I ensured that all the cadets and his schoolfriends knew about it.

One morning a letter with my name boldly inscribed on the envelope dropped through the door. I very rarely had letters but I had won the battle with my father about who opened them. By the typed address, with my title as 'Mr', it looked more commercial than sociable. I opened it with slight nervousness. It must be important, but who would have a need to write to me? All was quickly revealed. It was from the headmaster at college.

My dear Michael,
I have just had a note from the Commanding Officer of the summer camp that you went to, and he was very pleased with your efforts. I would like to talk to you about it, so perhaps you will call in and see me in my office on the Thursday and Friday in the week immediately before college opens for next term, if indeed you are available. I now have approval to start a cadet unit at the college, so please bring any notes with you that would be useful. I also want you to meet a new member of my staff who is interested in this project.
Yours sincerely,

This was a surprise. Students were very firmly on surname terms with the college staff. The headmaster had persuaded me to go to this camp because he had seen several of us on Empire Day as possible candidates to start a cadet unit at college. This rather nice letter seemed to be the second stage of the headmaster's attempt to get the unit going. As far as I could see, I now had the choice of remaining with the Air Training Corps and attending during the evenings and on Sunday mornings, or joining the Army Cadets at college with training on one day a week during term time and occasional weekends. I was now holding a valuable trump card. Each had its advantages. The ATC offered more technical training and flying and, if I ever had to go into the services for a long period, I was sure that the Royal Air Force would appreciate my ATC background and offer me a more comfortable existence. On the other hand, the ACF at college might allow me to keep one stripe on my arm, but I was not sure that their training offered much more than drill and warfare at ground level, and it did leave a big social gap during college holidays. I was not very keen on explosives of any kind, and I had already experienced enough of Hitler's armoury. That did not leave any good points in favour of the ACF apart from that one stripe, but then there were also signs that I might have to go into the Army eventually anyway.

I wondered if my best course of action was to write a note to my headmaster to tell him that I was not interested, but it could also be very difficult if he decided to make a cadet unit compulsory in the same way that other colleges were doing. I thought about consulting my father but quickly rejected that idea, because he would perhaps like the arrangement to work in his favour, and I wanted this to be my own personal decision. After a few days of contemplating and then writing down a list of pros and cons, I eventually decided that the headmaster had to be faced. I would have a list of questions to ask him and two whole days at college to consider the matter. Whatever was said, I promised myself that I would take a week thinking it over before I made a final choice. I wrote all this down in the form of a programme and put it in the top pocket of my uniform jacket where it would be safe.

The holidays did not encourage me to get out of bed very early but this Thursday was an important day for my headmaster and almost a trial run for me for the next term. My sister's first words every morning after waking were ringing in my ears, 'What shall I wear today, mummy?' and today I was thinking along the same lines. I had the choice of a good suit, my red college jacket and dark trousers, an ATC uniform that would have been quite inappropriate at college and my ACF uniform that I supposed would have indicated my loyalty to the college. After serious contemplation during my daily immersion in soapy water, I chose the latter. It did seem the best thing to do, and time was not of the essence. Being at camp had taught me to have everything clean for the morning and I reflected on how that little bit of training had made a noticeable difference.

There were not too many people on the tube and seats were easy to find. The train had hardly moved when I felt a hand on my knee. At the side of me was a teenage girl looking straight into my eyes and wearing a smile that was really meant for me. It was my first positive encounter with the opposite sex and I could not avoid blushing. She must have noticed my embarrassment as her arm found its way across my back. If I ignored her I would look silly in front of the other passengers, so I extended my arm to complete the cuddle. We had not spoken a word until she broke the silence by saying that she absolutely loved a young man in uniform and she really could not resist. Not a boy, nor a cadet, nor even a lance-corporal! This huge compliment to my ego could not be ignored. Only the armrest between the seats prevented closer contact. The man wearing a trilby hat on the opposite seat had politely lifted his morning paper up so that we did not have eye contact but, of course, glimpses were possible when he turned the page. It was not easy at first, but I managed a smile, and our arms achieved a much firmer grip on each other.

'Where are you off to?' she enquired in a beautiful soft voice. The accent was not a local one.

'College.'

'But why in uniform during the holidays?'

'The headmaster wants to start off a cadet unit, so I thought it would be correct to wear it.'

'You will be getting off in four stops?'

'Yes. But how did you know?'

'Oh, ever so easy really. I just stood behind you at the booking office and asked for the same ticket as you did.'

'But where are you going?'

'I just wanted to follow you because you looked so smart.'

I was rather taken aback. We exchanged smiles again. The man opposite turned over a page and our eyes met before he quickly put up the paper barrier again.

'So what are you going to do when I get off?'

'I'm getting off the train too. Then we could talk about meeting again somewhere.'

Several stations later the doors opened and she was making a better job at holding hands than I was as we walked along the platform. We spent a few moments admiring each other under the canopy of the station entrance. Then we chatted about little things. Her name was Betty. She was nice, really nice. We walked arm in arm along the road to college and, after a basic kiss and cuddle at the gate, we had to part company but we had made plans to meet on the next day. The college only allowed boys to be educated there. The girls' school was some distance away, so the opposite sexes never really had the chance to gather at the gate to select their potential partners, as was the case at some establishments. There was a delicate little wave of the hand before we were out of sight of each other.

This rather sudden encounter did little to prepare me further for my visit to the headmaster. I felt hot and confused and happy all at the same time. Life was becoming complicated! At college I looked in the mirror to check that there were no signs of lipstick and all was well, then I took a brief look at yesterday's notes. My thoughts about what to say to the headmaster were now confused by the desire to meet Betty again. Having lots of cadets at college, all clad in their regulation khaki, and me in my civilian clothes because I wanted to stay in the ATC, could put me at a disadvantage. If Betty lived somewhere near the station where she got on the train it might be very convenient, but I wondered if most cadets might live far enough away not make too much difference, except that khaki was the colour that sparked the attraction. I then had to decide between being a cadet at college, with a khaki uniform and having Betty, or staying in the ATC in a better-looking blue uniform and not having Betty, unless the headmaster could arrange for the rules to be bent.

I was still not very sure about what I was going to say as I knocked on the headmaster's office door. My welcome was truly friendly. He wanted to know what I thought about the camp and the training activities there, details of how I got on with the other cadets and whether I had learnt anything which was of some use to my future. I was careful not to speak of it in glowing terms because I might have wished to follow the interview by asking for a trial period before I finally decided what to do. I grew a bit suspicious of his motives when he began to ask about how Heffernan and Kay had enjoyed the camp, and he seemed to know more about McKenna than he let on. When he had exhausted his enquiries, he asked if I would formally become a member of a cadet unit at college. He tactfully pointed out that I had had some valuable experience that would go a long way towards the task of getting the unit going. There were, of course, other students in cadet forces but their qualities were unknown to him. I still had that one stripe on my arm that would have been to my credit if I had agreed, but I pointed out that I was not really sure. I took the plunge and asked if there was any possibility of remaining in the ATC at the same time. He did not take very kindly to the request. I knew what the regulations said, and so did he. He asked what my views would be if he were to make the cadet force at college compulsory. At least I had briefly considered this possibility, and I told him that that brought us back to my previous comment about being in both the ATC and ACF. I was now sure that he was trying to force me into the college cadets and he realised then that I was prepared to bargain with him. He asked me to go upstairs and meet the new officer, and give him a hand for the rest of the day. I suspected that this might be the next stage of his recruiting plan.

This door bore the college badge, with the words 'Cadet Office' printed boldly below it. An officer was sitting at an old desk that had been taken from one of the classrooms. As I entered, he stood up and was extending his arm to shake hands when I came to attention, saluted and announced my name. He did not seem quite sure what to do with his extended arm. I knew the correct procedure as I had remembered the ways of the great McKenna. It was his move. I was going to stay very precisely at attention until he did something about it. Offering my arm to shake his hand was all right for gentlemen but not for cadets. He was wearing his best uniform and quite clearly wanted to make an impression on someone in authority. There was only one little pip on each shoulder, neither of which was straight, but the rest did not look too bad. He must have been appointed fairly recently and could have been sent straight from his interview board to the college office without meeting a drill instructor on the way. What bothered me was that he looked such a prat. He was only about tewnty years old and had untidy threads of blond hair dangling from beneath his cap. Eventually he used his Oxford accent and recalled the contents of the military textbook to retrieve the situation. I was asked to sit at the desk opposite him. He introduced himself using his Christian name and a lengthy double-barrelled surname. When the rest of the cadets got to hear of this there would be lots of witty variations. I quoted an extract from the regulations that required me to address him as 'sir', and this could have upset him more than I expected. He already had a job for me and I was set to work in the adjacent room, now to be known as the 'Cadet stores'. All I had to do was break open the piles of boxes and packets, count what had arrived and put the contents in some semblance of order.

At lunch-time, I was lost amongst the piles of chairs and orderly lines of folding tables that awaited the deluge of students due on Monday. The two kitchen staff had been told about the cadet unit and the sight of me in a uniform brought them to the same table to ask a lot of questions. In return I got an extra portion of apple and blackberry pie which was most welcome. I wanted to keep up good relations with the kitchen staff as this could be of some advantage during the rest of the term. Our new officer, the headmaster and some teachers were locked in serious conversation during the whole of their meal and it continued during the supply of numerous cups of tea. Now I had always found it very surprising that often, while I was not even thinking about anything in particular, the answer to an awkward problem that had troubled me for days suddenly arrived in my head. I left to go back to the store and found it open with no one in sight and the keys laying on the desk. The officer was not very careful, and having a prat around could be useful.

The first stage of the plot was to try to acquire a spare uniform in my size, so I had to make the paperwork for the deliveries of uniforms disagree slightly with what I actually had. A couple of hours spent trying to organise items by type and then into individual sizes did not take any special effort as I found it so easy to make genuine errors. As I thought about my plot, the details were becoming clearer. The new officer came back from lunch much later than I had anticipated.

'Sir. I found your keys laying on the table, so I put them in the drawer of your desk for safety.'

'Thank you.'

That might have given the impression that I was honest. I would have hated it if anything had been found to be missing.

I left college at the usual time that afternoon, thinking more about Betty than anything else. A love affair was a distinct possibility and the time would come when our respective parents had to be presented with the facts. My friends would take every opportunity to mock and there would not be a lot of spare time left in the week. When I got home that afternoon my mother soon noticed something unusual about me, but she merely asked if I was feeling all right. In our family, that alone could have been enough to start off an enquiry.

Before I left home for college on Friday morning I had already told my parents about my involvement with the cadets at college, and I took great care to tell my mother that I might stay late to finish off some work that needed to be done before the next term started. If I met Betty that afternoon, at least I now had a good excuse to prevent me from getting into trouble when I got home. It was lucky that my parents did not usually worry too much about me as I had managed to look after myself to their satisfaction on many occasions in the past.

There was a seat on the footpath outside the college gates and as I came out of the door I saw Betty waiting there for me, as she had promised. Before I reached her, I felt an inward thrill. We embraced, kissed, smiled and wanted each other so positively.

'Where are we going now?' I asked.

'Home.'

'But whose home?'

'You're coming to meet my mum and dad, then we will have something to eat.'

'What then?'

'Don't know. I'll think of something.'

That sounded as if it had been organised quite well. Just a few minutes' walk from the station was a lovely detached house that must have been built just before the war. It had a much nicer front garden than ours. It had been kept so beautifully. There was a large black Daimler in the driveway, quite old but it looked just as good as when it came out of the showroom. Betty had her own key to the front door, which led into a palatial entrance hall. I hesitated and carefully asked Betty about wearing my boots inside the house. There was no problem. Her two older brothers had been allowed to do it and a cleaning lady came in every few days to sort out those little matters anyway. Two brothers, a cleaning lady and a big Daimler. This was something that had been kept quiet until now.

'Meet daddy,' she said, as a large man came out of one of the adjoining rooms. He was of medium height and build, and with a red face as if he had been on a diet of gin.

'Daddy works for the government, but even I am not allowed to know exactly what he does.'

We shook hands. I was still conscious of my boots on his floor but he ignored them so I assumed that it was an acceptable fact of life. A few moments later her mother came in. What a charming lady she was.

I was offered food and we sat around the dining table. It was ten times better that my mother's cooking. My best manners were absolutely essential here. Everything around me was so beautiful and being their guest was really enjoyable but I still could not work out why my luck had suddenly changed. It was a bit like one of those fairy stories. Her parents chatted to me and asked me all kinds of things without really being obtrusive, while at the same time I learnt a great deal about Betty. During the conversation, I discovered that Betty had two twin brothers who had been killed during their war service. They had left home as soon as they were old enough to join up and that was the last that she had seen of them. While her parents were out of the room, she admitted that she was supposed to go to the shops yesterday morning, but she saw me getting off the bus and going into the station. When she saw me in that uniform, she had a sudden impulse to talk to me.

At 6.30 p.m. I indicated that I ought to be going home. Betty and I exchanged addresses and her father insisted on taking me home in the Daimler. I persuaded him to drop me off at the end of the road, because it would have been tactful not to surprise my parents just yet. A Daimler outside our house, driven by a government official, would have nearly hit the headlines in the local paper. My mother and father instantly detected that something was amiss when they found that I could not manage another meal. I made the excuse that the kitchen lady at college had left me lots of sandwiches. They gave the impression of being satisfied with that excuse, but I could not be certain. Tony had called for me to go to ATC and had left when he discovered that I was not yet home. It was too late now to get ready.

The journey to college on Monday morning was uneventful and routine. The beginning of what should have been a concerted effort at teaching by the staff and learning by the pupils, turned out to be administrative chaos with additional signs of hopeless bungling. When the time came to return home I had achieved nothing except a chat to our young officer on the subject of cadets. The headmaster did not want to know as he was fully involved in either trying to sort out the chaos or adding to it. That left me with the ideal opportunity to carry out stage two of my plot. I needed an extra uniform. The prospective cadets had to be kitted out and those who were most enthusiastic had already been knocking on the door. A new cadet with a bag of uniform leaving college would not appear to be out of the ordinary, so one innocent cadet was persuaded to take a uniform out of college and then hand it back to me on the station platform. He had not signed for it, so the records were right. I had to make payment in kind by formally issuing a uniform to him on the following day so that he had the thrill of wearing it on the way home to show his parents. My second uniform was now available for me to wear to go and see Betty, and would not be threatened by the possibility of surrendering the original one if I left the college cadet unit.

I had a message from Betty during the week. She wanted me to go out for the day with her on Saturday. I sat down to do some homework one evening and, as always happened when I wanted to be able to concentrate, Tony arrived. Nothing seemed to have gone wrong at the office, and my father was in a reasonably jolly frame of mind. The time was just right to break the news about Betty. I was debating whether Tony's presence was a problem but if he went into one of his excitable moods it was possible that my father would moderate his comments. I looked straight at Tony.

'I had a good stroke of luck last week.'

'What was that?'

'I met a very nice girl.'

I felt my face going red. Tony was stunned into momentary silence. I did not dare look in the direction of my father but I knew that he would be sitting there quietly with a book in front of him, not now reading the words but listening to our conversation. The air was electric. Someone had to speak. Good old Tony.

'What's her name then?'

'Betty.'

'Where did you meet her?'

'On the tube going to college.'

'When are you going to meet her next?'

That was the question that I was waiting for.

'She has asked me to go and see her on Saturday.'

'Can I come?'

'No. You might make the Daimler dirty.'

'What Daimler?'

'Her father has got a Daimler. Her parents are ever so nice. They've got an absolutely posh house.'

Well, that was most of the details out of the way. I could see that Tony was thinking up the next round of questions. I dared myself to look at my father. He looked fairly normal, so I carried on.

'Dad. Can I bring her round to see you at the weekend if you're in?'

My father was considering. My mother was starting to panic.

'Aren't you are a bit young for this kind of thing?'

'Well, at what age did you and Mother get going, then?'

Tony giggled.

'That's got nothing to do with it.'

'I know that. I just wanted to know when you did it.'

'Did what?'

My father was on the defensive now.

'Well, started loving of course.'

'I'll have to see.'

'OK. If I get a chance, I'll bring her in.'

I formed the opinion that my father was not managing the conversation very well at this point. 'I'll have to see' often meant that he was temporarily stuck for an answer, or wanted to consult my mother on the matter. I had broken the ice. The conversation with Tony, through sheer necessity, had to be directed towards homework now. Tony always had these problems and when I had explained, yet again, the simplest manoeuvring of numbers to answer a question, he went back home. My father did not mention Betty again but my mother was worried about the house being untidy. Suppose the neighbours were to see a big car outside and an unknown girl arriving, what on earth would they think? When my mother went to church on Sunday evening, there would be plenty to explain to the neighbours then.

From the very first hint of daylight on Saturday morning I was thinking about Betty. To get to the bus stop, I needed to pass Tony's house. It was worth knocking on the door to tell him that his presence was very much appreciated when I broke the news to my parents. But I also had the great desire to make the point that I had found a first class girl friend and had a smart khaki uniform with a stripe on the arm, all of which had been out of his reach so far. He was rather put out by this. But he often saw Donald, and I had not even suggested severing our social links. I did see the danger that my spare time might now be under pressure. I had to find time to fit in two cadet units, college homework, Betty and occasional visits to the relations. I got to Betty's house and we set off to see a few of her collection of aunts and uncles. Her father was out in the car so we walked most of the way. By tea-time we had arrived back at my house. I took Betty in and she appeared to meet with my mother's approval. My father was out. He had left early to go to see his office friends, so that made life a little bit easier. We did not stay too long. My mother could never engage in interesting conversation, so I took Betty home. My father was still not in when I got home, but my mother was sure to tell him the news when he did arrive.

Thursday was now earmarked as the day when we stayed on at college for an extra two hours for cadet training. Not many cadets had uniforms yet but numbers were growing. The headmaster was still insisting that he wanted the unit to be compulsory for all, but there were a few who did not agree. The age-old process of calling the register in the classroom had now been replaced by a system involving lining up in three ranks and the same formalities had been extended to the last ten minutes of our lunch period. The bell at the end of classes now indicated a quick dash to the cadet office. One day, when I got there, Heffernan was waiting for me and I sensed trouble. He wanted to know why I was in uniform out walking with a girl and was leading the matter towards a fight. I had experienced problems with Heffernan before and I resented the fact that he was now intruding into my social activities. He moved closer to me and grabbed me by the belt. I raised my knee to get him to release it and then I aimed a hefty kick. He fell backwards against the opposite wall. I had scored a direct hit on the inside of his leg: a matter that the officer later investigated, coming to the conclusion that I was acting reasonably in self-defence. It did not end there. Heffernan's parents wrote in to complain that he was being set upon, but then so had I been by Heffernan. Fortunately for me, there were students and cadets from camp who supported my comments. Heffernan was not seen again at college, and delicate enquiries indicated that he might have been expelled.

The CO of the ATC had been conferring with the headmaster at college. I had been told by both of them that the matter of my involvement in both cadet units needed to be resolved amicably. I had been with the ATC originally and that was where my main military interest still lay. But being a cadet at college had produced a problem and the headmaster was being pressed by his superiors to have a compulsory Army Cadet unit. Other colleges had most successful cadet units and he was not one to miss out. On Fridays it seemed that almost every young man in our town, between the ages of fourteen and seventeen, climbed into a uniform of some kind. On that day of the week, seeing young men going to college in civilian dress was rare.

This was all very well for the armed services and the educators, but both sides had failed to take into account the excesses of homework, girlfriends and other family and leisure activities, and had failed to consider properly anything during the college holidays except for annual training camps. My father demanded that I sat down one evening to think about it, not that I really wanted to have my father involved at all, but he might have been in a position to apply some pressure to the powers that be. My ideas were already very clear. I wanted the mid-week evenings for ATC and homework. I wanted the weekends for Betty and the family events, and any special ATC parades. As for college cadets, if they could not fit it in during college hours then I was not going to attend. During the holidays the ATC and the college cadets and Betty could have whatever time I had available. Now if I was needed for something particular for cadets at college, I would go in uniform. It seemed to be a reasonable compromise, so I asked my father to draft out those comments and sent them off to the two competing parties.

My CO caught up with me one evening at the ATC, just after he had received my father's missive pointing out that I was the most important person in the decision-making process. If he wanted to give permission to the college for me to parade there, then he must respect my conditions. He said that it all seemed very reasonable and he would talk to the headmaster along those lines. When I got to college the headmaster was holding a copy of my father's letter. He tried to force my hand but I dropped the hint that my father was one of the people who indirectly paid his wages and I could always transfer to another college. That letter from my father clinched the deal and I had what I wanted. As for the regulations, my father had discussed the matter with my CO and the loop-hole was to classify my college activities as being carried out 'on detachment'.

No sooner had this arrangement been put into effect than there was a sudden and unexplained disappearance of our ATC CO. All kinds of rumours were circulating. Nothing was ever confirmed but the rest of the squadron staff probably knew some of the facts and were unwilling to discuss the matter. Then the band were informally invited by our bandmaster to transfer to another local squadron. Most of us had to travel further but the new squadron did have the advantage of a better bus service that stopped near the entrance. The squadron huts were set at the rear of an old 1800s style school complete with a playground, lots of classrooms and a large area suitable for sports. The caretaker was a retired Army bandsman, now very scruffy in his later years but dedicated to helping cadets. There was no ceremony about the move that later included the transfer of the remaining band equipment. As a result of the two bands coming together, the musicians now numbered about 50, plus a few knowledgeable helpers who had been in the services. For the first time, we now had several clarinet and saxophone players to add to the brass band to which we had been accustomed. We also had some experts to help with tuition. We had been practising hard at some of the well-known marches, together with a selection of simple and delightful melodies that our bandmaster had composed. We even engaged the services of a group of individuals who made a recording of the band.

Christmas was not too far off. Everybody wanted it to be a good one and, now that hostilities had ceased, there was a slightly better choice of food. We gathered together one evening for band practice, to discover that the bandmaster had distributed music for carols. During the week before Christmas we visited the railway stations, public houses and clubs. The revenue paid for repairs to the band instruments, and some of it some was earmarked for an excellent feast at the squadron headquarters on the last night. It was all really worthwhile. We had money, more recruits and lots of publicity.

I still had lots of hard work to do for my exams at college. I was really keen to get a good report and find a suitable job. Betty helped by dragging me away from all this, mainly during the weekends, and provided a social interlude to relieve the pressure of studying. At Christmas most of the relations arrived, thankfully not all at once. The house was extremely busy and my mother, as always, spent most of the holiday in the kitchen while the rest of us kept well clear of the cooking, but helped with the washing up. My father invited his friends in for a drink and my sister, now seven years old, had a party to cater for all her giggling friends – which

I avoided like the plague. Our festivities at home, by popular demand, included the introduction of Betty and her parents to all the relations and the photographing of me in a uniform of their choice. For the family album they also wanted a picture of my father in his Home Guard uniform but they had all missed this treat by several months.

17
The second year of peace

It was January. The thrill of receiving Christmas presents was over. Mine were mainly clothing accessories, but there were a few pound notes from those relations who could not work out whether I was still in nappies or was now in long trousers. I looked again at all the festive cards that had dropped through the letter box. Tony had not sent me one and I did not suppose that he had even thought about it. Now was time to update my address book and read the pleasant little messages on the cards before they were consigned to the dustbin with the rest of the useless paraphernalia. This January was just as gloomy as any other. It was that time of the year when I left home not long after daybreak and left college just in time to see the last of the daylight. How I wished for the sun and warmer weather.

I had not seen very much of Tony except for our several encounters when we met at the squadron. Tony did not like the cold weather and only went out when he really had to. Donald went missing from the squadron as well. He had been ill and the doctor was a frequent visitor at his house. He had been kept away from school and was being well occupied with the counting and consuming of pills. I was not supposed to know what was wrong with him and I do not think that Donald knew too much about it either. A daily visit to his bedside could often be very depressing. He looked all right but he did not seem to have any enthusiam or strength. The doctor had forbidden him to get out of bed, except for the bare necessities. I found a few books in my father's library, and a few magazines of my own, that I left by his bedside that might have interested him, but I was not sure that he read them.

The weather was unbearably cold. I was glad to be able to go to the squadron, well wrapped up in that nice thick uniform and greatcoat, but the disadvantage was that marching on snow and ice was very hazardous. More than five inches of snow required a change from wet to dry socks at intervals, and that was rather impractical. A new pair of wellington boots, gladly presented by a distant auntie at Christmas, while being much better in keeping the snow at bay did not keep my feet very warm and were not approved dress with a uniform.

I was under increasing pressure to do my homework every evening, so my attendance at the squadron had not been very good. It was no surprise to discover that the Commanding Officer wanted to see me when I arrived for parade one evening following several periods of non-attendance. It is natural to fear the worst on such occasions but I was put at ease when he asked me to sit down. He was glad to have my help as band librarian and was aware of the good reports that followed my efforts in helping with the cadet corps at college. But the important decision he wanted from me was whether I was going to attend annual camp this year. There were several things that I had to consider, including the arrangements for starting my first job and earning some money. I thought that I deserved a few weeks off after leaving college, and camp took place in the middle of July, so I committed myself to the idea. He looked pleased. He opened the drawer of his desk and brought out two sets of corporal's stripes. They were to be mine on condition that I was going to camp. Perhaps the CO was offering these to me as a kind of insurance to make sure that he had my services for some time to come. When I stood up to salute the stripes were still on his desk and he had not actually given them to me. I wondered if something was wrong. I glanced down and they were still laying there, with his hand nowhere near them. As I was plucking up courage to say something, he asked me to leave. I made a little extra effort at an about-turn and closed the door behind me.

Several of my close cadet friends were very inquisitive about what the CO needed me for, and I had difficulty in not telling them the truth. I brushed aside their questions by saying that it was about my attendance and they seemed satisfied. Canteen break came and went and it must have been obvious to the more senior cadets that something was afoot. Amongst the routine announcements at final parade was the news that the squadron now had another corporal. A little tingle of excitement played havoc with my concentration as I stood to attention, waiting for his order for me to come marching out from my place in the rear rank of the parade to be presented with the stripes that had taunted me since the early evening. I did not listen too intently to all the nice things he said about me while I was standing there, but my mind did lean a little towards the effect that it was going to have on Tony. I was so proud to march back to the rear rank, at the same time trying so desperately not to show my intense joy. Two of my friends were already corporals and they were there to congratulate me as soon as we were dismissed. Before leaving I was ushered into the warrant officer's office. First I was offered his good wishes in my new appointment. Then he gave me some friendly advice that on no account should I be on social terms with cadets while on duty, as they had to respect my new rank, and I was not to have cadet friends while I was in uniform. I was looking forward to the time when Tony would see my stripes for the first time.

I was aware that I had a big smile on my face when I arrived home that evening, and it could have been no more than 60 seconds before my parents were preparing to have a minor celebration. My mother was in a bit of a dilemma as soon as she realised that the job of sewing the stripes onto my uniform was quite clearly coming her way. Perhaps she had forgotten that I had managed to cope with a little bit of sewing myself when I had been promoted in the college cadets while I was at their camp. On Saturday morning, after breakfast was finished and the washing up was done, we made a concentrated effort to get those stripes exactly in the prescribed place on the sleeve of my uniform. In my mother's view, I was not entitled to have a say in the matter but after I had criticised her work twice she disappeared into the kitchen in not too happy a mood. My own attempts at pinning the stripes in position were equally unsuccessful but luckily it was not too long before Betty arrived. She quickly saw the answer, reminding me about the spare Army Cadet uniform that I had upstairs. When I brought it home from college it already had some stripes on it. My mother immediately had a surge of renewed enthusiasm once she realised that there was a sample to work from and with a little help from Betty she made a first class job. The effort was well worth it. When I put on the jacket for a final inspection, I got a big kiss from Betty. Those two stripes looked great.

There was a knock at the door. It was Tony. Possibly someone had told him of my promotion, and he might have arrived to investigate. He stepped inside and I could see that he was put out.

'Are those things on your jacket really yours?'

'Yes.'

'When did that happen?'

'Last night when you were absent again.'

'Oh.'

Tony was stuck for words. Betty was beginning to see the funny side of our conversation and decided to intervene.

'Look here, Tony. I have just helped to sew on those stripes and they actually indicate that this corporal is senior to you, so you will have to respect his rank like you do with the other NCOs.'

Tony looked more surprised than he usually did.

'So, tomorrow morning you will report to the corporal here at nine o'clock and then go off to the squadron. Make sure that your trousers are pressed this time.'

Tony was beginning to wish that he had not called and after a short space of time he left. We heard that familiar knock at the door of Donald's house, and he was invited in.

Betty and I went to the pictures that evening and we had a bit of a laugh over Tony. Betty predicted that Tony would turn up on Sunday. I told Betty that she would make a smashing corporal if only girls were allowed in the cadets. We stopped for a cup of coffee on the way home, if only to get out of the cold wind for a while.

By five minutes to nine on the following morning, Tony had arrived. He did not know quite what to do. I took the opportunity to have a look at the state of his trousers and they were acceptable. While I had Tony to myself for a few moments, I reassured him that he must really be somewhere near the top of the list for promotion. Then I pushed it a bit further and pointed out that if he stopped being such a little nuisance he might have been a corporal long ago. I did not really mean to upset him, but I could see my comments hurt a little. He was now actually concentrating on what I was saying and, while he was in this state, I tried to get it into his thick skull that I still regarded him as one of my best friends. The difference now was that, when we were in uniform, the laws of military discipline would be strictly observed until we were both at the same rank. There were not going to be any Christian names between us, because ranks and surnames were what the regulations demanded. I think that he got the message.

※ ※ ※

Betty now called in on most evenings that I did not go to the squadron. Apart from the warmth of her pleasant company, she also helped with the odd difficulties that the remainder of my college work produced. National Service had been announced and the first recruits to that scheme were almost on their way. Betty quickly realised that within a year or two my name would appear on the list. Although I would avoid serious warfare, I would undergo two years of compulsory military training. She pointed out that my physical fitness had declined slightly and I had to get back to it. She made a schedule of events for me for each evening, listed in order of priority, and once the college work was completed I was commanded to put on a pair of shorts and go running. I probably ran slightly less than a mile in one go at first, but it was enough. I looked forward to a final kiss and cuddle afterwards, before Betty left for the evening. While I was improving my leg muscles, Betty often went to see Donald. He was much improved since January and was now back at school and the squadron. He was still not very active and kept well clear of all the physical training. Donald's father was still in the Army, somewhere in the Mediterranean area as far as he knew.

Now that I had a pair of stripes on my arm Tony was less interested in the ATC and, because of Betty's interest in me, I did not see him quite so much. I tried hard to get him to go running with me and eventually I succeeded. After a few evenings he discovered that a good way to reduce the amount of human effort needed was to take a short-cut, but that landed him in a patch of marshy ground more than once. The final straw came when his mother made him wash his own kit. Tony was getting short of close friends but quite by chance I discovered that he paid an occasional visit to the local Sea Cadet unit. He had often told me he wanted to join the Navy to travel the world, and I guessed that he might leave the ATC soon.

❊ ❊ ❊

One particular day in May is still vividly stamped on my memory. While I was happily involved with the band at a Saturday afternoon concert for a local fête, Donald and Tony had gone fishing. Fishing was not something that attracted me as I could not see much fun in catching a miserable little fish and then throwing it back into the water. In my earlier days, while living on the Dorset coast, at least we sometimes used to catch a good sized fish that provided the basis of a excellent meal and it earned me some pocket money at the same time. Now I could not understand how Tony and Donald managed to sit still for hours on end and find it interesting at the same time.

The afternoon's melodies were still buzzing through my head as I marched down the road, partly thinking about the joys of afternoon tea when I got home. I was some distance from the front gate when a policeman passed me, pedalling with some urgency on his bicycle. That would not have seemed to be very unusual, except that he stopped and leant his bicycle against our garden fence. I froze in my tracks wondering what it was all about. My mother opened the door and they went inside. I stood there, trying to think what could be the matter. The music had gone from my head and tea was not now so important. Having convinced myself that I was not in trouble, I used my key to open the front door. My mother's eyes were watery as she ushered me upstairs to my bedroom. I could hear them both talking downstairs but it was not loud enough for me to make any sense of it all. My mother called me and I went down to face her and the policeman. They both wore expressions that indicated a real disaster. My mother was sitting on the settee, staring at the wallpaper, then slowly got up and went next door. The policeman told me that Donald had collapsed and had fallen into the water and drowned during his fishing expedition. Then he went next door. My face developed a tingling sensation and I felt faint. I conjured up visions of Donald in his scout uniform, and of him later in his ATC uniform, of him looking over the garden fence, and I remembered some of our scheming plots to avoid church. I was trying to imagine what it would be like without Donald. By now his mother and sister would have heard the news but his father was still somewhere abroad, helping with the aftermath of war. My mother came back in about half an hour and put the kettle on for a cup of tea. Then we embraced each other, and shed a few tears. My father arrived later with my sister. It was awful trying to say the right things amongst ourselves and the evening was remarkably quiet, punctuated by cups of tea, thoughts of next door and a few more tears.

Tony came to see me on Sunday morning. He had seen the disaster happen, but was still stunned and did not want to talk about it. Tony had led a sheltered life and, apart from the occasional good hiding, this must have been his first ever

138

shattering blow to his nervous system. It was only when he and I were alone almost a week later that he started to talk about some of the details. It was not a simple case of falling in and drowning. The facts were that Donald tried to wade out to the deeper water of the lake, soon to find that the easiest way back was to swim, but then his heart failed. When they got him back to dry land his rescuers did not have the right facilities to keep him alive long enough. Tony tried to help with the rescue and was probably still blaming himself for failing. He was so upset that I could hardly believe that it was the same Tony that was talking to me, and for many weeks afterwards he was neither eating nor sleeping properly.

Meanwhile, Donald's father had been sent for and the funeral arrangements had been made. Tony and I had not been invited to the funeral as it was to be a quiet family affair, but the squadron held a church parade several weeks later, which included a service of remembrance for Donald. I had never seen so many officers and cadets so upset as at that service.

18

A different kind of holiday

Now that I had thought seriously again about National Service, I saw it as a forthcoming threat to my social life and an unwanted interruption to my career. Although it would be another year before it caught up with me, I had already decided that the least of the available evils would be to try to get into the RAF for two years where life was reported to be easier, but there were no guarantees that this would happen. Betty wanted me to volunteer immediately for the Army, and we often argued the point without coming to any final agreement.

The college staff were busy trying to find me a job in the building industry. My first encounter with a prospective employer was at an interview in west London. I was disappointed to see the state of the front entrance of their office building with its display of gravestones, which reminded me of Donald and the Scouts. It was a masons' yard with a rather untidy old office that was in serious need of refurbishment, and it closely resembled the squadron headquarters. I had no inkling of how I should present myself, and the college had not given me any training on dealing with a prospective employer. I started off by being polite but the whole encounter was very formal and I was not at all pleased with the end result. The manager appeared unable to smile. It seemed that he had his heart set on taking on a boy to do the odd jobs, without any suggestion of how the job might progress in later years. I was just glad when it was all over and I went back on the train to college feeling quite dejected. By the time the college buildings were in view I had made up my mind that I was not going back to that dump, and I conveyed that message to a shocked headmaster in a very positive way.

My next interview was quite different. Someone at college could have taken note of my earlier comments. The office was an old-fashioned Kensington mansion built in the days before houses were numbered in an 'odds and evens' sequence and was therefore quite difficult to find. My imagination ran riot. I should not have been surprised to see a horse-drawn carriage appear at any moment. I was offered tea and jolly nice top quality biscuits while I waited and only my father's training at the table prevented me from scoffing the lot. I was introduced to an extremely happy gentleman who kept enough questions coming to keep me talking. Unlike the first interview, I felt so relaxed. When the inevitable enquiry came about what I did in my spare time, stories about cadets and Betty came tumbling out almost without effort. That was it. I was certain that the job was mine, and there could not possibly be any doubt about it. Waiting for his letter to tell me whether or not I had the job was going to be torture.

The dreaded examinations came. I decided that if I had not learnt sufficient in class during the three years at college, then no amount of swotting would improve matters at this late stage. Apart from going to bed just a little earlier and casting all college work aside in the hope of spending some extra time with Betty, there was nothing to be done except to labour away in the examination room. While working away at the last exam, my mind suddenly wandered and I thought of Betty doing exactly the same thing several miles away. It was the final exam for both of us, and love was pressing, so I skipped off college after lunch. She had invited me over for tea. I knew it would please her so I was determined to go in my Army Cadet uniform. It was probably quite legal as I had not formally severed my connection with the college cadets. When the front door opened we had an instant and urgent desire for a kiss and cuddle. Afterwards we sampled the comfort of the lounge, with the added joys of a well-prepared snack and soft music. We were tactfully left on our own to indulge in small talk and recollections of our first meeting. I got home awfully late, but it had been such a pleasant evening. I made as little noise as possible and went to bed. I had to go to college in the morning, although it was not important what time I arrived. There were two reasons for going, first to record my attendance and second to attend a leaving party during the afternoon to put the final touches to my full-time education.

That morning, two letters were delivered. Each held an offer of a job. The stone mason was prepared to pay me 35 shillings for working five and a half days a week in that horrible office. The Kensington builder only wanted me for five days a week for 30 shillings, and both allowed ten working days' holiday during the year in addition to bank holidays. I did not need very long to make up my mind. I opted for the latter. I was expected to continue my education at evening classes on three evenings a week and there was likely to be some homework as well. Reports on my progress at evening classes would be sent to my future boss at intervals. At least it was a move in the right direction. I later discovered that I had been offered a wage of two shillings a week more than another student who had better marks on his report, so perhaps something in all that training as a cadet had its effects.

The leaving party was a bit of a mess. The headmaster was advertising his beloved cadet force by having the entrance to the hall lined with cadets from the first year classes, each in their appropriate gear and carrying a rifle. He had provided food, music and a few decorations. There were lots of little groups of students exchanging details of their answers to the examination questions in the hope that they could predict the results. By 5 p.m. we had all had enough of his party, and we drifted off home.

Between leaving college and before starting work, I could just squeeze in a week in Dorset with my parents. The little town where I had spent some of my youth had hardly changed and it brought back pleasant memories. Some of the local residents were still there. In my favourite sweet shop on the opposite side of the road, the dear old lady still remembered the chocolate bars to which I was particularly partial. I was welcomed at the fish and chip shop, once owned by my cousin, and the landlord in the historic hotel remembered the conspiracy between us, that I could obtain rough cider by entering the cellar via the tradesmen's entrance. My uncle had since died, but my aged aunt was pleased to see us and expressed surprise that I was now old enough to go out to work and earn money. The memories were so vivid as I wandered off on my own up the steep cobbled street and over the cliffs. I remembered how I made a toboggan with my school friends when I stayed there one snowy winter, and had come down the hill into the town at an uncontrollable speed, with the pedestrians scattering out of our way to avoid a collision. One such journey ended in disaster when we ran off course and hit the sea wall. Not only did we urgently need most of the contents of a first aid kit, but we also got drenched by the waves smashing against the other side of the wall while we were attempting to recover our belongings. There was such pleasure in making our own fun.

Within two days of getting back home I was to be on my way to camp at Oakington. I needed all of those two days to gather together and sort out my kit, including one euphonium that had to be cleaned to perfection. My negotiations with my mother to determine exactly where in the dining room the ironing board was allowed to go, and for her valued permission to use the new electric iron, had just been concluded when I was aware of a tapping on the window. Betty was making signs that she wanted to come in. She took her time coming through the kitchen, having chatted with my mother on the way. She still looked as radiant as ever, and the big kiss that followed nearly caused a crease in the wrong place on my tunic. The feminine touch was much appreciated and the end of the day's work on my uniform coincided with my father getting back from the office and the official start of our evening meal.

Betty wanted to come to cadets with me that evening. It could only be one of those unexplained whims that the other sex comes out with from time to time, unless it was feminine intuition. I could not possibly take her into the squadron huts. It was for young men only. But I had to allow her to accompany me there and she agreed to meet me outside at the end of the evening. It was no use explaining the rules to her. I just pointed out how highly impractical it would be if all girlfriends, parents, sisters and brothers came to have a look or wait around, and it would not have left much space for training or parades. As my uniform was ready for camp and I would be with Betty, I had considered going in civvies, but I remembered other cadets being sent home for that infringement of the rules.

I did not think that my uniform felt any different for being pressed and polished but it was good for my ego and it was nice to have Betty there as a supporter. There were inquisitive looks from other cadets as we parted company at the gate and there were some passing remarks during the evening's training. The most difficult question to answer was how and where we met. It was all very well to say it was by chance on a tube train, but I dared not let anyone one know that I was in the khaki uniform of a cadet from college at the time. The reaction to that might have been quite unmanageable.

Before final parade I sensed that something was afoot especially when the duty NCO wanted me in a particular place among the three ranks. There were little whispers among the officers. It might have been my imagination, or it might be that the presence of Betty had had some effect. When the CO came on parade everything seemed normal until he started giving out details for going to camp. I was thinking of Betty again and had almost lost track of what he was saying, when I heard my name mentioned. I only half heard, but there was a reference to a sergeant. It was me! There were lots of corporals going to camp, but Adrian Clark was the only sergeant attending. Once again I was in the right place at the right time. As I saluted and turned about to take my place back in the ranks after the presentation I saw Betty outside, watching through the open door. That would surely mean another big kiss was waiting to land, and I would want an inquest to find out how she got the advance information.

On my way out of the hut I received lots of congratulations from the cadets, until Betty pushed her way through to tell me that some of her friends were waiting by the gate hoping for one smart cadet each. Along the road, next door to the Red Lion, was a fish and chip shop that was usually open until the public house closed. Those who had provisionally paired themselves off, and a few others who had suddenly become hungry when the idea was launched, almost filled the shop. It was a bit of a pre-camp jolly, with a leaning towards a celebration for my stripes. When the bell rang in the Red Lion and the drinkers wanted fish and chips, the slightly overworked fishmonger did not have much left for them.

I was late already and by the time I had seen Betty safely onto the bus I was having visions of a very worried set of parents. Walking home gave me time to think about how to manage the little problem of parents. I saw the bedroom light on, so my mother was on her way to bed. As I turned the key in the front door I heard my father move in the lounge, so I waved the three stripes at him. He probably guessed at the reason for my lateness. He muttered the words 'Well done!' and I hurried upstairs.

Now with those splendid three stripes and a band badge above them, I must have looked quite spectacular. I was off to Oakington for a week. The squadron plans for the journey to camp had been tried and tested many times. The same groups of people made the same mistakes every time. The cadets forgot to pack little items from their kit list and the officers made a mess of the travel arrangements, usually getting out of trouble by the skin of their teeth. The officers were having their fun by frequently reminding us that accommodation was in tents. I had already experienced the problems that developed in this kind of environment so I had an advantage. Some of the younger cadets had vivid imaginations and were uneasy about their fate, in just the same way as I had been.

Fifty-five miles from London by train, followed by half an hour in an uncomfortable canvas-covered truck through the lanes of Cambridgeshire, brought us within about 100 yards of a small field of tents. By now, the Royal Air Force was beginning to accept that their property would be over-run several times a year by cadets and they were taking the necessary precautions. They had set up a guardroom specially to cope with us. Most cadets were not too keen on those tents until they found out that the officers were having the most severe sense of humour failure. They had discovered that their tents were also on the same site, each identified by a metal frame supporting a canvas wash basin outside. The brick-built officers' mess was within sight but without any spare accommodation. That was the kind of justice of which I had previously only dreamt.

Once we had organised the cadets, at the density of six to a tent, and pointed them in the direction of the next meal, Adrian Clark and I were free to explore the area. Every cadet had standard service-issue bed with blankets, a pillow and sheets, one much-too-small locker and a duckboard on the ground. An electric cable supplied power to the two bulbs that dangled from the ridge pole of the tent, but we had no control over the light. That was firmly in the hands of the duty officer in the guardroom. At least it was more humane than some tented camps. Even the toilets had small heaters in them.

My first aim was to make sure that the officers suffered in the same way that I had at my first tented camp. I conferred with Adrian. Puncturing their wash basins would damage them permanently and, if we got caught, replacement could cost our parents a lot of money. That made puncturing a very risky business. Moving their things around would be detected too early and could jeopardise our other pleasures during the week. Our plan of campaign had to be more devious than that. We waited until the officers had left to sample the delights of dinner and drinks in their mess, then the duty officer would be alone and bored stiff, so I volunteered to spend an hour feeding him with the cadets' names and locations in the camp. Adrian detailed the more senior cadets to give him a hand, while the rest of the NCOs ran a game of football near enough to the guardroom to convince its one official inmate that all was well. That kept him out of the way while Adrian organised the removal of most of the tent pegs, which were then carefully replaced at a lesser depth in the ground. Adrian was a real outdoor type and this was right up his street.

We settled down for the night, much earlier than usual. No information was available on what time the lights would go out and organising ourselves in the darkness could be inconvenient. A first night at camp in an unfamiliar bed is never conducive to a good sleep. By one o'clock I had been through several short periods of dozing and I woke to find the other five in a similar state. The occupants of an adjacent tent were making one hell of a din and I wanted to do something about that, but the air outside my bed was cold. In the corner bed of my tent was one cadet who was always bright and merry, whatever the conditions, so I asked if he would like to go and see if he could do something about it. No further persuasion was necessary once I offered him my tunic, complete with its three stripes, to wear for the occasion. I was pleased to hear a sudden silence as he went into the tent and in a moment he was back. I had often taken much longer to achieve the same effect. Sleep was possible after that.

When I was next aware of time, it was nearly six o'clock and the temperature outside the bedclothes was unacceptably low. Four cadets were already out of bed in various states of undress.

'Oy, Sarge, the officers' tents are down,' said one.

I leapt out of bed to take a look, grabbing a few items of clothing as I went. The flat landscape had allowed the wind to do a superb job on the officers' tents. They were not all down. The majority were just leaning at precarious angles, while officers were wandering around discussing what had happened. I had never realised how silly these old men looked in their underclothes. No wonder their knees rarely saw daylight. I did not stay out there too long, but hurried to wash. When I found Adrian he was in the advanced stages of washing and already knew the result of the previous evening's effort.

At breakfast, the officers' tents were the main topic of conversation. During a quiet moment I caught up with the cadet whom I had sent to quieten the adjacent tent. I asked how he had achieved such an instant result. He reported that his entry into the tent, wearing my tunic with sergeant's stripes, gained initial silence, then it was only a case of threatening to throw in a couple of stink bombs if they made any more noise. He added that he regarded stink bombs as being almost as effective as a loaded pistol, but far less dangerous. He kept them with his kit, in a small tin packed in sawdust and sealed with sticky tape, and he often had great success with them at school. I would remember that for the next time a similar problem arose.

The first parade of the morning was very brief and formal. I noticed that certain officers did not seem to be 'on top of the world', but there were no comments made about the poor work in erecting tents. The Station Commander spoke to us about the role of the station and a session of foot drill followed. There never did seem to be a great deal of imagination applied to try to vary a camp programme. I had already been involved in the techniques of fighting demonstration fires, of lots of drill and parades, shooting, flying and being shown round the odd specialist technical section of an RAF station. After that, annual camps were all much the same. I scanned the programme for something really different, but it was not there. Training was scheduled to finish at around 5 p.m., with nothing planned for the evenings. I anticipated that Adrian and I were going to be lumbered with keeping the cadets occupied while the officers socialised in the mess.

Adrian decided that he would run some sporting activities if nothing else had developed by early evening. I was not very keen on that idea, but at 4.30 an order came from above to get the band together immediately after tea. A large room had been set up for a rehearsal in one of the camp buildings and we were joined by what seemed to be the remains of the RAF station band. Wednesday morning was detailed for the Station Commander's parade and because of leave and other duties, there were too few members of the station band to cope. Our fame had spread and the combined efforts of the RAF and ATC were to provide the music. At least I did not have to try to find the cadets something to do on that Sunday evening. When I met Adrian after band practice he was not at all happy. The guardroom NCO had not been authorised to issue any of the sports equipment that Adrian needed, but Adrian was a wonder at getting what he wanted. He eventually struck a deal with the NCO in the guardroom to release the equipment, having persuaded him that he could choose between seeing cadets fully involved in sports, or fully involved in mischief. At that point, the choice was fairly easy.

By the time Monday evening came, we were on good terms with NCOs of the other squadrons in camp. We agreed that we would take it in turns to provide the evening events, and tonight it was the turn of Adrian and myself to investigate Cambridge. The rules had been changed to permit the use of civilian clothes in off-duty periods, so I retrieved my college clothes from my suitcase and found a plain tie to go with them. I knew that my parents were many miles away but if there had been any scrap of information filtering back that I did not wear a clean shirt and tie for the evening, it could have caused another stain on the family's honour.

Cambridge was old and historical. It boasted a cinema but we had both seen the film before. From the outside, the local cafés looked gloomy and very expensive. It was a warm evening, with a few hours of daylight left, but offered no amusements that were attractive to us. In desperation for something of interest, we sat by the river for some time watching people come and go. After a prolonged period of silence, Adrian mentioned that lots of young people were going in and out of the public house across the road and he wanted to give it a try. I sensed danger. I had, almost without realising what the full effects might be, got drunk once before. I did not like it at all. We had to go back to camp that night and getting past the guardroom could be hazardous if we reeked of alcohol. Eventually Adrian convinced me that it would be all right. He said that just one pint would be nice and it was unlikely to be noticed.

Inside, the place was crowded with young people and a pianist was banging out popular tunes from the far corner of the bar. I had to stop myself singing the naughty words, but we joined in and enjoyed it. I enjoyed that pint and we both had another one. It was only when I glanced at the clock that I realised how close we were to the departure time of the truck back to camp and we knew that if we missed it, a taxi could cost us a fortune.

We found the truck without difficulty, but there were far fewer cadets than there had been on the journey from camp. The driver did a head-count and our observations were right. We decided to wait for another ten minutes. Ten minutes later, I wished that we had not waited, as the remainder of the cadets had now arrived, in varying states of intoxication. The floor of the truck was a long way above the road, and it took assault course tactics to get over the tailgate. The driver and I did the lifting, or was it pushing, to get the cadets inside, while Adrian laid the more helpless ones face downwards near the tailgate. He found a spot for us both, near the cab, where it was less draughty and on the upwind side of the cadets. I had never seen this objectionable side of humanity before, in such proximity.

Arriving back at camp, I felt the handbrake engage very firmly as we pulled up at the guardroom, then the driver was out of his cab and round the back of the truck in an instant. There was a revolting mess on the floor and he was not going to clean it up. He was looking to the offending cadets or a gang of volunteer cadets to deal with it. Adrian indicated to me that we should go over the tailgate first to help the driver to unload the sober cadets. The guardroom NCO was taking the names of the cadets, but he had some difficulties with the drunks. They were carrying no identification documents so each body was presented to the NCO, someone shouted out a name, then the body was hauled in the direction of his tent.

The next morning, at parade, there was a truck on display with a driver and a collection of officers. Adrian and I, having been identified by the driver, were brought out to the front of the parade. We were asked to identify the cadets who had been on the truck but we pointed out that as they had all been wearing their civilian clothes, we had no way of identifying the squadron to which they belonged. As far as we knew none of our squadron was there, and we did not recognise the others in the dark in Cambridge, as we had been otherwise engaged, helping the driver. Adrian explained all that, wearing a worried look and showing great concern, and I backed him up. It let us both off the hook nicely since we believed that the investigations and subsequent cleaning of the truck were quite rightly the concern of another squadron.

The Station Commander's parade on Wednesday morning was to start after breakfast at 7.30 a.m. Tuesday evening was detailed for a short rehearsal and bull-night combined, with time for a quick visit to the NAAFI then off to bed. Most cadets were up at the crack of dawn and the band got itself in position with only minutes to spare. The parade marched on to the music of J P Sousa, played a selection of popular tunes during the inspection, with the traditional Royal Air Force March Past at the end. Just before lunch time we had news that the Station Commander had been extremely impressed with our performance. It may have been rumour, or another practical joke in the making, but during our midday meal details were circulating about flying on Wednesday evening. The source of the information was dubious so, before the afternoon training session started, I located my CO and asked him. Although he was curious how I had found out he did confirm it, but only for the band in recognition for their efforts on the Station Commander's parade. It was proposed that we would be needed at about 9 p.m., and he would give us more details later. I was not to tell the other cadets just yet. After tea the band was briefed with all of the details. The aircraft was to be a York and, for technical reasons, a test flight was necessary. The band cadets were needed to fill the seats and they would enjoy the unusual experience of night flying.

By 9.30 we had marched to the hangar, amusing ourselves on the way by counting rabbits that were taking their exercise before going below ground for the night. By now it was dark and the temperature was falling rapidly, aided by an increase in wind speed. During the heat of the day my uniform had been very uncomfortable but now, with another layer of clothing underneath, it was just about right. Once aboard, it seemed that we were stuck there for the night. I did not expect luxury, but my body was a good firm fit in the seat. Having sat down we were advised of our return time of about 4 a.m. I was adjacent to the gangway and being interested in maps was able to guess at our position by the shapes of lakes and rivers, and I correctly named some of them. About an hour into the flight, I was grabbed by one of the crew and directed to a seat with a radar display in front of it. Earphones went over my head and I noticed a map in front of me, very dimly lit from a light at one side. Instructions came from somewhere in the aircraft that I was to locate our position and then talk the pilot down to an aerodrome on the map. I fiddled with the knobs on the front of the radar screen and discovered that I could select a scale of height and distance from a beacon. I read off these details to the pilot and I hoped he would make sense of them. Very soon after that, a firm jolt indicated that the aircraft had touched down. I had only outline knowledge of what I had been doing, gleaned from a diagram in a textbook, so when we eventually came to a stop on the tarmac I presumed that either I had done the right thing by logic, or the pilot knew exactly where he was going and I was being assessed. Later on I convinced myself that it was the latter. We took off again and made several more landings, each time with a different cadet in front of the radar screen. It was a long way past four o'clock when the noise of the engines ceased at Oakington. I warned the cadets not to make too much noise getting into bed. We just threw off our uniforms, climbed into our cold beds and quickly fell asleep.

I woke to the sound of aggressive voices outside the tent. It was now a good deal warmer underneath the bedclothes than it had been an hour or so earlier and when I opened my eyes to the daylight I saw a tall body silhouetted against the blue sky. The outline revealed itself as an officer with one ring round his arm. I was tired and not very interested, but he was trying to order me out of bed and on parade. He said that it was late but I considered it to be early. I protested that the band had been working all night and had not long returned. I tried to refer him to my CO and got the answer that he was also asleep. I sat up in bed to confront the officer. A quick calculation was necessary. I made it very plain that we had been flying at the Station Commander's invitation and this was our first period of sleep in the last 23 hours. The mention of the Station Commander must have taken him aback slightly. He went away and I went back to sleep.

Around midday, I was woken again. My one open eye located a cadet's face near to mine. I did not recognise him as one of ours.

'If you climb out of bed, sergeant, there will be food in the mess in half an hour.'

'Thanks. I'll try and make it.'

Well, at least he either understood the position, or had been given his orders by someone else who knew what had happened. I decided to engage him further in conversation but he was now using the same technique on the rest of the cadets in the tent. Mental arithmetic made me realise that I had not eaten for nearly 20 hours and for me that was serious. I washed my essential parts and put a uniform over the top then, struggling against tiredness, made my way to the mess. Once inside, I found that there was a table earmarked for the band. Our CO turned up a few minutes later and, without criticising him, carefully explained that it had been the orderly officer who tried to get me out of bed for parade, only an hour after I had fallen into bed. I thanked him for arranging the flight, stopping myself in the nick of time from commenting on how difficult it seemed to be for officers to communicate these little details to each other. We all did a lot of eating at that table. I felt the old body clock falling out of step with my other components, so I persuaded my CO to let us loose in the NAAFI club for the afternoon. He agreed that we should be able to get back to normal safely in there.

After tea, I was outside the tent when I heard the duty officer shouting for a flight-sergeant. I thought that I knew who he meant as he was looking in my direction. At his next attempt, it was plainly obvious that he was after me. I decided to ignore him and moved out of his sight. Moments later, I was standing to attention having saluted first. He looked quite upset.

'When I call for a flight-sergeant, that is exactly what I want,' he stormed.

'Yes, sir.'

'Well, why did you ignore me?'

'I'm not a flight-sergeant, sir.'

'What is that on your arm, then?'

'That is a band badge with three stripes below it, sir, which indicates that I am a band-sergeant.'

He understood his mistake and looked embarrassed.

'Well, get me a flight-sergeant, then.'

'Yes, sir.'

I saluted, but he did not return the compliment. That was perhaps worth reporting to my CO when the opportunity arose. I sent a cadet to go looking for a flight-sergeant, then I decided that I had had quite enough, so I changed into my civvies and went off to look for Adrian with the intention of going out for the evening. He was very receptive to the idea but visiting Cambridge by truck was not going to be our first choice.

The duty NCO had changed since I last called in at the guardroom. This one moved around like a newly-born lamb and had the most active blue eyes. He might have been the camp athlete. We explained that we wanted to visit a quiet spot locally, within walking distance, preferably with food and unspecified drink, and not haunted by officers. Was two miles too far? He knew of a little village pub with a quiet room at the back. It served fish and chips and lots of other sundries. If we rattled the servery flap a beer might appear. It sounded good. We were impressed, agreed and accepted his recommendation. Village pubs fascinated me. Each had me guessing which door led to the bar. When we entered, we were surveyed by the locals and a game of cribbage came to a temporary halt. The barman removed his pipe to get a better view of us without his customary cloud of smoke getting in the way. I felt that I had invaded their precious privacy. Someone in the corner muttered 'from the camp'. One door just had 'Back Room' etched on its surface. We went through to another silent reception. We must have been in the right room in the right pub because the flap was there. Adrian rattled it as directed, and it opened. The barman now had his pipe back in his mouth. Adrian asked if they had fish and chips. There was not much choice of fish, but it sounded cheap and very acceptable.

'Anything to wash it down with?' asked the barman.

Adrian knew what I drank and he ordered. The flap dropped back into position. In a moment of great confidence, we introduced ourselves. Initially, they all seemed suspicious of us but were soon friendly enough. Then the food and beer arrived. Everything we said to each other was, we were sure, silently noted. I thought it strange that our money was not required until we were on the point of leaving. It was most unlike the public house local to our squadron, that we had occasionally dared to enter. The same NCO was on duty when we got back. No names were recorded and my lovely bed soon welcomed its occupant, ready for another day at camp.

After training on Friday, I spent most of the evening with the cadets in an effort to get things ready for handing back to the camp staff, and much of the early part of the night trying to prevent damage to cadets and property. It was nearly two o'clock in the morning before sleep was possible. The following day would see us back at home, with a further inquest on the week's activities. At least I now knew what information to offer so that it would be acceptable to my parents.

19
New neighbours

One Saturday morning I woke to see the effects of the rain on the garden and an overcast sky with no possible chance of the sun breaking through, so I decided that the conditions were just right to go for a run. I had not been out for a run for some time and there were fewer and fewer opportunities to do so. When I stepped outside the sky was sprinkling the area with fine drizzle. It was not raining enough to make the going uncomfortable, but it was the temperature that mattered today. I just felt more active, so I took the hilly route over the golf course. The birds had gathered to harvest worms as they came to the surface. I stopped and watched birds and golfers while I got my breath back. I ran much further than I normally did and I felt satisfied with my morning's performance. Arriving home, I used the alleyway at the back of the house and entered by the kitchen door to avoid both the risk of dirtying the carpet and my mother's wrath.

Later that morning I expected to find my mother preparing a meal as I came downstairs after an extended soak in the bath. The house was unusually quiet and at first I thought that she must be in the garden. A slight noise from the lounge very soon provided the clue. My mother was standing far enough back from the window so as not to be too obvious as she looked out across the road to where a large furniture van was being unloaded. I joined her. We had seen the departure of Mr and Mrs Clark from number 5 only last weekend. Now here were the new residents arriving, presumably from east London if the address on the side of the van was any clue. The removal men were unloading some large and old-fashioned items of furniture and a good quantity of heavy boxes. Mr and Mrs 'New Neighbour' did not look too elegant, but it might have been the way they were dressed for the occasion. There was a very industrious boy who looked about sixteen years old and a little girl who was assisting with some of the smaller items, occasionally getting a shove from her parents to move out of the way. At least they looked well organised. By now my mother had a pressing need to get lunch prepared and my help was needed. When my father had arrived from the office and we had all eaten, we were itching to get back to the lounge window. There was a lot of work going on inside the house and the van had gone. A cup of tea was the answer to all social problems, and my mother wanted to go across the road and invite them over. My father did not agree because they did not look as if they were 'our type'.

On Sunday morning, after Tony and I had been to cadets, eaten lunch and met up outside my front gate, there was a shout from number 5. The boy whom I thought was aged sixteen came running across the road.

'Hello, mate, the name's Ronnie!' he called, in the most genuine Cockney accent that I had heard for some months.

'We've just moved in. Come from Poplar, we 'ave. What's it like 'ere?'

'Not bad at all. My name is Mike, this is Tony.'

'What yer wearing those uniforms for. Are you in the Air Force or somefink?'

'No. In the cadets until we get called up.'

'Can I join?'

'How old are you?'

'Seventeen.'

The front door of number five opened and another male voice, also with a Cockney accent, commanded him to go inside.

'Meet yer tomorrow night.'

The front door slammed shut behind him. Tony and I looked at each other. My father was probably right and perhaps they were not 'our type', but at least he had made the effort to be sociable, which was more than we had done. Tony agreed that the best place to meet was in his house until the social differences were sorted out. That afternoon the sun showed up for the first time during the weekend, so Tony and I went for a walk over the golf course, taking roughly the same route as I had run on the Saturday morning, but passing the old gun site then round the boundary of the RAF station. On the way we chatted about Ronnie and concluded that if he wanted to join as a cadet that would be fine, but we agreed that we were also committed to having him as a friend.

On Monday evening Tony called for me. We went over to number 5 to collect Ronnie, planning to finish in Tony's back room for the evening. Ronnie was having none of that. First, we had to meet his mum, dad and sister. They explained that the family had been living happily in Poplar until a bomb hit the house. In the disaster Ronnie had lost his younger brother, his puppy and a lot of prized possessions. They had been moved around several times by the council until there had been an offer of a permanent house across the road. During a remarkably short lapse in the conversation, Ronnie looked at me in a straight eye-to-eye contact.

'Come on, let's have a look at your place.'

I was not quite prepared for that. Tony nodded his agreement, so I took them into our lounge. My mother, father and little sister quickly detected the unusual visitor, and I launched the round of introductions. Ronnie spoke up again.

'This is all bleedin' posh, ain't it. Where I come from, the visitors come in the back door.'

Tony giggled. There was clearly an urgent need to reprogramme Ronnie in the ways of living in modern suburbia, including the tradition that the back door was normally used only as a link between the kitchen and the garden. Ronnie told us that he had been accustomed to looking out of the scullery door into a small yard, wedged between a terrace of houses, in the same way as my grandmother had. I made the point that our house was not particularly 'posh'. It was new when my parents moved in thirteen years earlier, and it was modern. Ronnie was confused to find the toilet upstairs rather than in a corner of a back yard. We had a front garden and a back garden, whereas Ronnie was used to the front door opening straight onto the footpath with no grass within sight. He was trying to come to terms with a serious culture shock, moving to live in what he described as the depths of the countryside, miles away from the nearest factory and with a language that sounded like the Home Service on the wireless.

My mother thoughtfully made tea and emptied the larder of her home-made cakes. Ronnie was trying hard to conform to our general eating habits and was being as polite as he knew how. Our evening eventually came to an end. Tony and Ronnie left to go their respective ways and then I came face to face with my father who objected quite strongly to Ronnie's language and the general state of his clothes. We argued quite seriously. I felt rather sorry for Ronnie, as it was no fault of his that he had been bombed out of a house and his upbringing was not up to our standards. My father became more subdued when I reminded him that his own parents lived in an ancient old terrace of houses with his many brothers and sisters crammed into two bedrooms. However, my father held the trump card as the house was his property. I went to bed without any firm idea of what to do when Ronnie called for me again.

When Ronnie called for his second visit he wanted Tony and me to go out with him during the weekend, and we all met on Saturday morning as agreed. Ronnie insisted on taking us to Poplar. As soon as we came out of the underground we could see that the area was splattered with depressing terraced houses and mounds of rubble. The shopfronts needed glass and the road was in urgent need of repair. People were laughing and joking but they had obviously suffered a lot of hardship during the air raids. Ronnie soon brought us to a bridge over a polluted river, from which he indicated that he had once lived in a house somewhere amid the mess some 200 yards in front of us. In the very early hours of one morning he had been blown out of bed and was rescued from the river. The site had now been covered by that big pile of rubbish. With tears in his eyes, he just added that his brother never made it. After several minutes of intense thought, he took us towards the fish shop which was the traditional meeting place of the local gang. They were mostly in their teens, but a number of youngsters were also hanging around. They seemed to be happy, despite their colourful adjectives and worn-out clothing, and even happier to see Ronnie again. In sharp contrast to what would have happened in our 'posh' suburbia, Tony and I were instantly accepted into the gang. It worried me at first that I might get attacked by them, but they seemed very kind-hearted and I was soon put at my ease. Between eating chips we must have met a good selection of the Poplar youth, most with nicknames and an outstanding vocabulary of Cockney jargon. Several hours later, after feasting and having a jolly time, we decided that we ought to be going home.

Ronnie wanted us to join him and his father in the market on Sunday morning, but we declined. For us, Sunday was reserved for going to the squadron for training. He did not miss telling us that his family had a stall in Petticoat Lane, and Sunday was the highlight of his weekly activities and the day when he earned the bulk of his pocket money. My father wanted to know all that had happened as soon as I got home but I managed to leave out the bits of which he may not have approved. I did make a good story based on the fate of Ronnie's previous home. Ronnie still did not gain my father's complete approval, but I felt that the objections to him were abating slightly.

Tony and I soon accepted Ronnie as a jolly good friend. He was a great character in all senses of the word. He had left school and now went out very early in the morning to help his father in the family business of market trading. He never came with us to join the cadets despite his initial enthusiasm, and it was not until many weeks later that we discovered the truth of the matter. I had crawled out of bed one Saturday morning with the intention of going flying with the cadets, thankfully assisted by an alarm clock and with my mother's permission to use the kitchen for making tea and breakfast at that remarkably early hour. I quickly checked in the mirror to make sure that my uniform was correct, then I pulled the front door closed behind me as quietly as I could and turned to face the chill of the morning air and the glimmer of daylight. I saw Ronnie on the footpath, handcuffed to a soldier who was forcing him into an army lorry, while another soldier very firmly locked the tailgate behind him. Then the lorry drove off. I knocked at number 5 before I got home that evening and discovered that he had failed to report for National Service and had been arrested. Occasional enquiries at number 5 during the next few months did not bring any positive news so I guessed that they were all embarrassed by the affair. My father adopted an attitude of 'I told you so' whenever the matter was mentioned. I conveyed the news to Tony, and although we occasionally spoke about Ronnie, there was not really much to say.

It was Christmas Eve. The matter that was uppermost in my mind was the joy of a few days off work. I had bought the few presents that I could afford and had posted greetings cards to the remainder of my friends and relations. Early that evening there was a very loud knocking at the front door, somewhat similar to the racket that heralded the arrival of Tony, but the rhythm of the knock was not quite right for it to be him. My mother was busy preparing food so I opened the door to find an extremely smart soldier on the door step. The only area that was not khaki, highly-polished black or gleaming brass was the well-shaven smiling face of Ronnie. I invited him in. He made it no further than the doormat before he asked if I was still in the cadets, and what rank I held. He came to attention when the word 'sergeant' came out and he explained that according to the rules he had to stand to attention while in the presence of NCOs and officers. He found a corner of the hall that was not occupied and carefully placed his kitbag there. He explained that he had knocked on the door at number 5 but there was no one at home, so he had called in to see me. My mother opened the kitchen door, having heard unusual noises, but quickly shut it again. Here was another of those unique opportunities that occur in military life. As a cadet sergeant I had the chance to inspect a real soldier. I was not going to miss this for all the tea in China. The uniform, the webbing kit, those boots, the haircut were all absolutely perfect, and how could I offer him tea after he had been brainwashed to eat only with those of the same rank? I had to guarantee him that the rules of the Army would not apply within our house today, but he was still uneasy when I told him to take off his cap and kit, and sit in a comfortable chair.

My mother supplied tea and quickly retired to the kitchen to continue her chores. Ronnie explained that, in his several changes of residence, some of the official letters, including his call-up papers, had been mislaid or destroyed. The Army had assumed that he was formally 'absent without leave' and had decided to arrest him. His greatest shock had been to find a soldier standing over him as he awoke from sleep one morning. Unfortunately he had used his east London phraseology to tell him to buzz off and come back when he was ready. The soldier insisted on staying put while he got out of bed and dressed himself, then he had a pair of handcuffs fitted to his wrists before he was marched out of the house to where I saw him on the footpath on that Saturday some months ago. Ronnie very quickly discovered that the Army do not accept pleasant explanations, and it was several hours later that he found himself under the strict control of a nasty corporal at a basic training camp. He had narrowly avoided being condemned to a cell in the guardroom pending a formal charge. It was no wonder that he was being so careful when I opened the door to him.

Having survived his first encounter with the Army, after a few weeks he decided that he liked it. He told tales of how different it was to be away from home, of self-reliance, a wonderful set of mates who all helped each other out of trouble, of everything being organised, and of being away from smoky London. I had a momentary vision of Betty telling me of her brothers' tales of army life. He had his second army shock when he discovered the high level of smartness and absolute discipline that was required of him before he was allowed out of the barracks. His beloved encounters with the opposite sex, beer, the market stall and general freedom were all out of reach for a while. He was due to come home on weekend leave a good time ago, but he failed to reach the required standard and was ordered to repeat some of his basic training. His mates had helped him out and it was only because of them that he was released now.

My sister had slipped very quietly into the room and sat beside Ronnie, listening to the story as it was unfolding. In one of the gaps in the conversation she commented that Ronnie would be much better at cleaning the brass door knocker than my mother was. A few moments later my father came in and asked lots of questions of Ronnie. The problem was that his parents were not aware that he would be allowed home at Christmas, and he could only assume that they had gone away and locked the house up. The family had lots of friends and relations around London and they could have been invited anywhere. So there was Ronnie sitting in our lounge, not knowing what to do until he was due back with the Army on 3 January. I think that my father had changed his opinion of Ronnie. The scruffy market trader's mate that he first saw was now transformed into a very smart soldier. My father said that he had only two options. He could report to the police station and let them sort it out, or he could make himself comfortable on the settee in the lounge until the matter resolved itself. Ronnie stood up and thanked my father. Pam was sent off to bed and Ronnie was read the rules of the house before we were all fed again. We listened to more stories from Ronnie. My father seemed even more interested, and thought that if I went in the Army, then it would do me much more good than being in the Royal Air Force. I was not too sure that I agreed.

The house did not get going very early on Christmas morning, and I got up when I heard conversation on the ground floor. I found my mother and Ronnie in the kitchen. It was very rare to find someone in the kitchen when my mother was working, but they had come to an arrangement in which they took turns to prepare meals. I told Ronnie that he did not have to be in uniform and I would much prefer to see him in some casual clothes, but Ronnie only had two sets of uniform and one set of kit with him. All of his civilian clothes were very securely locked up across the road. However, he assured me that one set of uniform would be worn and the other set would be cleaned on alternate days. He had really begun to love the Army.

Our friends and relations came and went during the day. Presents and greetings were exchanged and the liquid refreshments flowed freely. That army waiter-cum-doorman was the best visitor that we had had for years. Our friends and relations wanted to find out how we had got hold of a soldier to help at Christmas. My father was delighted with him and it made mother's chores so much easier. Pam and my mother stayed up late to entertain Donald's parents and little sister. My father had his friends in until his excessive intake of wine and spirits got the better of him. Ronnie and myself were last to bed, mainly because we were talking military matters until the early hours, but we also had to wait for our visitors to vacate the lounge so that Ronnie had somewhere to sleep.

I don't quite know what the Army did to Ronnie, but when I woke to a gentle noise in my bedroom, Ronnie was there with a cup of tea. Everybody else had had one too. A good quantity of daylight was trying to force its way in between the curtains. It was much later than usual. I looked at all that khaki with Ronnie inside it, waiting for me to leap out of bed. The day before had been a most pleasant Christmas Day. Today was going to be much better because Betty and her parents had invited us for lunch, and her father had volunteered to collect us. I told Ronnie that we were going out. I explained very carefully who Betty was and the basis of our relationship, but I did not want him to feel that he was intruding and he was most welcome as a friend. My mother had made coffee and then proceeded to adorn herself for the occasion. Pam put on a nice dress after endless visits to the mirror to look at her reflection. My father and I just found informal suits. Ronnie was not going to ask any questions. Perhaps the Army had taught him to be discreet.

Pam was only nine years old and urgently wanting to have her first ride in the big Daimler, as she had not been in a car before as far as she could remember. It was now parked outside and Pam ran to meet Betty. Pam was full of excitement and made the introductions in the congested area of the hall. Then Pam conducted everybody outside and allocated us seats in the car. My guess was that she had learnt something about entertaining at school. Then Pam made the introductions to Betty's mother when we arrived. Now having got into the way of doing these things, and having instantly acquired some more confidence, she promptly got Private Ronnie Williams talking to a Ministry official with the rank of Captain. Ronnie went a little on the white side, using the word 'sir' twice in every phrase until my father spotted the problem and smoothed it over successfully. But Ronnie was not at all happy. He whispered to me afterwards that he had never spoken socially to an officer before, and it might almost have been a military offence to do so. Amongst the jokes that followed his disclosure, he was just told to do a bit of name-dropping when he got back from leave. Betty understood his predicament and took him off upstairs to show him a nice comfortable spare bed if he needed it at any time. Knowing Betty, she probably got him to try the bed for comfort while he was there. Ronnie returned from the bedroom in time for lunch, carefully holding Betty's hand and wearing a big smile that he was trying to erase before too many people got the wrong impression.

The standards of food at Betty's house were always excellent and our lunch that day was no exception. My mother and father looked well pleased as they headed for the lounge, probably to talk over the problems of their respective children and other niceties with Betty's parents. Pam and Betty went off together to compare all the pretty things of life, leaving Ronnie and myself. I took Ronnie into the garden where we would be out of earshot of the rest of the party and where I could have a few serious words with him. I found a gate at the back, leading to a sports ground, and I guided him in that direction.

'Ronnie, were you hoping to have a further quiet period with Betty this afternoon, or get chatting to her?'

'Only if you don't mind.'

He was very calm in delivering that last remark.

'Then may I explain something to you?'

'If you wish.'

'You do realise, I hope, that we are invited guests here and I very much appreciate Betty and her parents. I have no wish to change that arrangement, but in Betty's view, you are a very special guest.'

'So what?'

'Well, it is very important that you behave yourself. You were invited to view a possible place to sleep on some future occasion should the need arise, but I gather from your smile and the slight rearrangement of your dress that you may have embarked on something more than a simple chat. Is that true?'

Ronnie's face was getting much redder. He must be feeling the heat by now. He was not going to say a word.

'Ronnie, your face gives the game away. Any contact with Betty must be quite honourable and correct. The Captain is not daft, and is quite likely to detect any deviation from the straight and narrow.'

Ronnie knew that he was in trouble. He had difficulty in coming out with his next few words.

'I'm ever so sorry. What shall I do now?'

'Well, if you have made any improper moves towards Betty, you had better go and talk to her in confidence, and apologise or put the matter right in some way. It's up to you.'

'Oh. Er, yes. OK.'

'And when you think you're getting into trouble, all these social niceties have to be put aside. You call me by my rank, and you call the Captain sir.'

He got the message.

'Yes, sergeant.'

We walked on a bit further. Ronnie was getting really worried. I reminded him that he had been well looked after during the Christmas holiday and he ought to be grateful to everybody present for that. Ronnie decided that he would thank people individually as he parted company with them later in the evening. I then assured him that he was welcome to stay with us until the end of his leave.

Just before tea, I noticed Ronnie having a quiet conversation with Betty. They parted with almost strained smiles and a clasping of hands. We had tea. It was time to return home. Ronnie was doing what he was told. When he got out of the Daimler, he took his final opportunity to thank Betty's father. They were both by the front of the car for some time. I looked out to see Ronnie standing to attention, and Betty's father was doing some serious talking. I did not suppose that he liked standing out there in full view of the neighbours. Betty ran out to the car and it was driven off in more haste than usual. Ronnie went across the road to his house and again failed to get a reply.

Our door knocker was used lightly, and Ronnie was let in. He took me on one side.

'Sergeant, I've just had a bollocking. The Captain did notice what went on with Betty, and I got told not to meet her unless I get invited and I have your permission.'

'What else, Ronnie?'

'He inspected my documents and made a few notes, and I had a lecture on bringing the Army into disrepute. While I am here, could you please accept my thanks for the hospitality. If there is anything I can do for you, then please could you let me know?'

I thought for a moment.

'In my wardrobe there are uniforms that ought to look as smart as yours. I do not have to go to work tomorrow morning, but I need to call on a college friend to sort out a problem with his homework. I shall be back later in the day, so you might find some time to improve them.'

'Yes, sergeant.'

That may not have been the end of the matter, but I ushered him into the lounge and we spent the evening together.

✳ ✳ ✳

My final day of the Christmas holiday from work had been planned in advance. My college friends had invited me to go and see them to compare notes. There was quite a crowd of us in the morning and there was no point in going home at midday, so three of us settled in a little café for a snack. When I left them,

I just went for a walk. It should, perhaps, have been a run but I was not kitted out for that kind of thing and, in any case, walking was more conducive to thinking. I had to solve a few little problems. Both Betty and my father now wanted me in the Army. They had said on a few occasions that the RAF was too soft. Ronnie was the salesman for the Army, and he had finally convinced both of them. I had to discover the facts before it was too late. It was very certain that I would be in one of the services during the next year. The real problem was that there was no one whom I trusted to give me an unbiased opinion. I just had to look out for someone with a lot of experience. I could not decide until then, assuming that I would have a choice.

Ronnie had gone to see his friends in Poplar and when I got home, there were lights on at number 5. Ronnie's kit bag had gone and my uniform had been brought up to Army recruit standards. I went across the road to see if Ronnie had returned and was surprised to see Tony there as well. He was also getting an earful of how good the Army was. Ronnie was still wearing his uniform. I mentioned that one of the reasons he told me that he wanted to get indoors was that he wished to wear his civilian clothes. Unfortunately for him, Mr and Mrs Williams had decided otherwise. It was at this point that I began to wonder if Ronnie really liked the Army as much as he said he did. Perhaps he saw a uniform as a means of attracting the opposite sex.

Tony was beginning to be interested in the Army in the same way that he was interested in everything else for the first day or so. He came in to see me for a few hours in between periods of having nothing else to do. We talked of many things, and during a lapse in the conversation he suddenly asked,

'Did you hear about the chickens?'

'No. What chickens?'

I thought that it might have been the prelude to an awful joke.

'Well, Ronnie saw a chicken on his basic training.'

'So?'

'Well, he never realised that they were real, live birds that ran around. He just thought that they were made from something or other, and then hung up in the butcher's shop. Apparently, he had never seen one complete with feathers on before, running around making clucking noises.'

'If you lived in the depths of Poplar, would you expect to see fields and animals?'

'No. I suppose not.'

'Well, have you seen coal being dug up?'

'Of course not.'

'There you are then. If you are not around at the time, then how do you expect to find these things out?'

Tony looked confused.

'I'll give you a tip, Tony. Don't mention it to Ronnie at the wrong time. You might just end up with a damaged nose.'

'Oh. OK.'

Tony quickly changed the subject to joining the Army.

Apart from my first serious session with alcoholic drinks at the New Year, I saw very little of Ronnie before he left to return to camp during the late afternoon of 2 January. He came to the door, very correctly dressed and loaded up with his kit, and said goodbye to us all individually. He must have appreciated our hospitality more than we realised.

20

I get documented

My mother had been reading the local paper. She almost aimed it at me as I came through the front door. I had already had a difficult day at work, with much more aggravation than usual, and I did not really want to be bothered with anything until I had eaten. My mother was more excited than I had seen her for some time but, at that moment, I was more interested in a nice, juicy piece of beef arranged with its vegetables on a hot plate. My mother wanted me to have a look at the newspaper. When the meal had been eaten and the tablecloth had been taken away, she folded the paper to display a large official announcement by the Ministry of Labour and National Service. Between the explanatory and formal jargon was a list showing the initial letter of the surnames of those who were required to register for National Service on a specific date. I was within the category specified, and I saw it as the first positive threat of being in the armed services. Instead of being a cadet and making four visits a week, I would be a full-time serviceman. My mother was immediately convinced that she would not be seeing me at all for two years but when my father saw it later in the evening he said it would do me a world of good, was highly delighted and had no sympathy for me at all. I made a note of the date in my diary because there were dire threats of severe penalties or imprisonment for not registering. On my next occasion at the squadron, I made a point of talking to the bandmaster to see if he thought I could be posted to a band. After all I was now fairly experienced as a musician. It would be so much more preferable than finding myself posted into the Army or to a trade that I did not like. He liked the idea and said that he would find out what he could, and write to let me know the result. I did not anticipate that I would get off lightly, nor avoid the initial weeks of 'square-bashing', but it was worth a try.

My employer was compelled to allow me time off work to go and register, but he had hoped that I would only be away for half a day, until I demonstrated that the timing of the appointment plus travelling time would not allow that to happen. He asked about my interest in military matters. We had discussed my involvement with the cadets at my interview for the job, and he must have made at least a mental note at the time, but he was now much more interested. His opening questions revolved around what I had gained from the cadet organisation in experience or training. Then he tried to relate my answers to what it did for the company. My status as a sergeant really did make him look up, and he interpreted that as meaning I was becoming a leader of men. I told him about the demands made upon me to keep fit, which I achieved by going for a run as often as I could, and my responsibility to keep up appearances. He lounged back in his managerial chair and said that I was one of the few juniors in the company who was always well dressed, and he had noted that I walked in a decidedly military manner. I reflected on my first impressions of Ronnie, and then my impression of him during his leave. When I thought about it, I realised that it was not only the uniform that created the effect. Clearly my employer would be keen to support me in any cadet activity. He told me that if there was any training which encroached slightly upon the company's hours of work, I just had to go and talk to him and he would see if there was anything he could do about it. That indeed was a mark of confidence in me.

❊ ❊ ❊

This was one of those days when I just had to make a good impression. The CO had advised us to put on our uniforms when we went to register. It was not compulsory but highly recommended and it might even be to our advantage. My uniform was up to Ronnie Williams' standard already. I had a band badge, so I decided that my white belt and gaiters, not normally worn for routine parades, would be in order. It was known that a little bit of bullshit went a long way. The straggling queue at the Labour Exchange could be seen from some way off and it seemed to be moving at a snail's pace. As I approached I could see many uniformed cadets waiting their turn, most of them dressed in khaki but quite a number displaying authorised and colourful additions, so I guessed that my smart white webbing was not out of place.

Having tacked myself on to the end of the queue, I had the chance to speak with many other of the young men who were also waiting. Some had not yet found jobs and some were struggling to get settled into one. Some seemed to want to join the Army and start shooting some Germans in retaliation for their attacks on us during the war. Some who had not been cadets were viewing their fate with some horror. Even the thought of having to be away from the comfort of home and parents was terrifying. At least I had experienced camp, with the rough and tumble of military training, lots of discipline and without relying on my parents for all my little needs. One young man was clad in a set of clothes that made it appear that he was in the rag and bone business. He was viewing my uniform in some detail. He asked questions of me that made me think that he had been hiding himself away from the real world for several years. I asked what his parents thought about it all. He admitted that he did not have any parents but lived with an aged auntie who was reluctant to let him out of the house alone. I explained that, provided he was reasonably fit, then there was not much chance of avoiding doing his National Service for two years. It was written in an Act of Parliament, and there was nothing that his auntie could do about it. I suggested that if he wanted some experience in the ways of a military organisation before he landed up in the Army, then he should join a cadet unit.

The desk was manned by an elderly, beady-eyed civil servant dressed in an approved pin-stripe office suit, complete with bow tie and ancient monocle, whose pen could easily have increased its velocity if only he had some enthusiasm for the job. The young man in front of me was trying to ask questions about what would happen to him now, but he was not getting any useful responses. He left with a look of despair, muttering something about a silly old grandad. When I arrived at the desk, the old chap adjusted his monocle and peered at me, trying to read the flashes on my uniform. His lips worked as if he was trying to say something intelligent but nothing came for a while.

'I see that you are in the ATC. I shall record your details, as I must, but I am afraid that I cannot guarantee that you will serve in the Royal Air Force as there are very few places left. Do you want me to make a note that you are interested in the Army or the Navy as an alternative?'

That may have been the extent of his authorised vocabulary. Army or Navy? Either alternative was quite out of the question even if Betty or Ronnie would try to persuade me otherwise.

'No, sir!' I said, as firmly as I could. He looked up, perhaps to gauge the expression on my face, or perhaps the 'sir' confused him.

'Oh dear, I will write down what you say, but the officer will have to decide once all your tests are over. Name?'

'It's on this envelope.'

'Oh, yes. Address?'

'That's on the envelope, too.'

'Date of birth?'

He got that wrong twice. The rapid change from receiving details by means of vibrations through the air to working out how to put it on a form must have upset the operation of his brain for a moment. He tore up the form and started again twice. No wonder there had been a paper shortage. And this did explain why the long queue was moving so slowly. Eventually I was given a card in standard government buff colour. I now had a number as well. What a waste of time it had been, hanging about for over an hour to get a card with a number on it. Perhaps old grandad's purpose in life was to consume ink and paper and other people's time. Anyway, that was it. I had my details engraved in His Majesty's records and escape was now impossible. I was sure that I was destined for the Army.

Now I had not a lot of things to do and lots of time to spare, so I walked to the shops. I just wanted to buy a few odds and ends and since I had the rest of the day away from work, it would save me a journey on Saturday. I needed something to eat and a cup of tea. There was a café near at hand so I went inside, sat at a table and ordered. I suppose that I must have been staring vacantly out of the window, deep in thought about my imminent change of career. I heard the chair at the side of me scrape on the wooden floor. I expected a cup of tea to have arrived but the table was still bare.

'Hello.' The voice belonged to the orphan chap who spoke to me in the National Service queue.

'I saw you in the High Street, and wondered if I could have a word with you.'

'Of course you can.'

The tea and sandwich arrived.

'Anything else, sir?'

I looked at the lad sitting beside me.

'Tea?' I enquired.

'Yes please.'

The waitress went off to the kitchen.

'Now, what did you want to talk to me about?'

'I want to join your cadets. I must have training of some kind before the Army get hold of me. It would be better for me if I started off with a little bit of knowledge.'

I dug a small piece of paper out of my pocket and wrote the squadron address on it. Underneath I wrote '7 p.m. tonight'.

'Meet me there, don't be late and don't bring auntie.'

His cup of tea arrived.

'What about my mates. Can they come too?'

'Yes. How many mates?'

'Are four OK?'

'Yes. Now what do you expect us to do for you?'

'I want a uniform like yours, and I want to learn to do drill.'

'It will take you a few weeks to get a uniform and the first thing we teach you is drill.'

His hair had not been brushed and it could almost have been an advertisement for a hedge on a windy day. I took my cap off to show him what well-groomed hair looked like.

'And each of you will need a haircut like mine.'

My hair had been kept short since my attendance at the Army Cadet camp when other NCOs stripped it all off at my unofficial promotion ceremony. I was not bald but I was the squadron's visual aid for a service haircut.

'By the way,' I enquired, 'I don't know your name.'

'Jim.'

'We use surnames in the cadets.'

'Sorry, Jim Hughes.'

'And you don't need to know my name. I have three stripes so you just call me sergeant.'

He drank the remainder of the tea.

'Yes.'

'No. You mean, "Yes, sergeant".'

'Sorry, sergeant. I'll see you tonight at seven.'

I arrived home at a very respectable tea time, removed my belt and gaiters, cleaned my trousers of the blanco which was always a legacy after wearing white gaiters, and I was off to parade. I was one of the early arrivals. Orphan Jim and his mates were not far behind, all now with precious little hair, expertly dealt with by auntie, and with clothes that had now had most of the dirt brushed off them but still looked old and tatty. I took them to see the adjutant and warrant officer in turn, for them to sort out the preliminaries.

Only moments after first parade I saw Tony arrive in his civilian clothes, with a big shopping bag full of uniform. He had collected Donald's uniform which had been outstanding for some time after his death and, as he wanted to leave the ATC, he brought his own uniform back at the same time. He went off in the direction of the stores and then came into the band room to see me.

'I saw you in the recruiting queue today,' he said.

'Then I suppose that you were playing truant again.'

'Oh no. Not that. I was signing up for the Navy.'

'But you're too young for naval service.'

'That's what they said. They took my details and told me to join the Sea Cadets for six months and then come back, so that's what I'm going to do.'

I saw the funny side of that. He could not even swim and I was sure that he would be the worst misfit the Navy had seen for years. I wondered what would happen if he had a cold or did not like the job that he was given.

'That's a jolly good idea, Tony. You've got all the right qualities to make an excellent sailor.'

My encouraging comments might just help him on his way, I thought.

✳ ✳ ✳

By the next Sunday morning the warrant officer had managed to get Jimmy Hughes and his four mates issued with their uniforms. They were wearing them for the first time and loving every minute of it. They were to be left to my tender mercies for their first session of drill so I arranged them in a straight line on the parade ground. As with all new cadets, the concentration needed to stand still was a new experience and they were finding it difficult to avoid taking admiring looks at each other. This was one of those days when having three stripes on my arm was so rewarding.

'Stand still. Look to your front. Arms at your side. Don't move anything. No talking. Don't look at me, I'm not beautiful.'

I walked slowly along the line of scared recruits and placed myself in front of the end cadet.

'Name?' I demanded.

'Hughes, sergeant.'

Then I moved down the line one pace to the next cadet.

'Name?'

'Hughes, sergeant.'

Then I moved on to the next cadet.

'I'm Hughes as well, sergeant.'

'I did not ask *you* your name because I know it already. I can recognise a family of similar, saucy faces. Only speak when you're spoken to.'

'Sorry, sergeant.'

I walked away at that point. I had guessed correctly that they were brothers. No wonder their auntie had problems! By the end of the morning they were quite good. They begged me to come back in the afternoon for more drill, and I persuaded the CO and the school caretaker to agree. In the afternoon they were even better. They loved those uniforms, uncomfortable or not. They praised auntie for their haircuts. Then I found out that they worked at home, helping auntie make toys. Despite delicate enquiries over the next month, no one ever reported seeing them out of uniform. They certainly attended every night that the front door of the squadron was unlocked.

In the weeks that followed I imagined the file of my personal records increasing in size as it landed in 'in' trays and 'out' trays alternately at the Ministry of Labour and National Service. I wanted to be in the RAF. I could perhaps handle the Army, as I had already been dangerously close in the cadets at college and I had seen the Army's effect on Ronnie Williams, but the thought of the Navy horrified me. I regarded encouraging Tony as the best contribution that I could make to supporting the Navy. I did not like salt water, nor the ships that wallowed around in it, although my fishing from the Dorset coast was an exception because it made money. After what seemed an eternity, there was a result from my CO's request for me to join the RAF band. I should soon have a letter with a date for an audition. My boss was a native of Wales, with an outstanding singing voice, so pleading with him for another day off work for an audition would not be too difficult.

I really had been busy again and I did not appreciate how close the Easter weekend was until I heard an item on the wireless about Maundy Thursday. Now there were some more statutory holidays to look forward to. Both Ronnie Williams and Tony had knocked at the door within ten minutes of each other. Ronnie was in his immaculate Army uniform and Tony was in his Sea Cadet uniform. There were several things that intrigued me. I asked Ronnie why he was still in uniform, when all the other National Service soldiers that I knew were travelling home in their civilian clothes after their square-bashing was over. I soon had the answer. Ronnie admitted that he had not yet passed his basic training after many attempts, and secondly he was hoping that I would approve a visit to Betty who was a known admirer of anybody in khaki. I would 'have to see' as my father used to say.

We were both intrigued by Tony and where he was going today. He told us that he was off on a sailing course and was leaving within the hour, but Tony was a showman and had seen Ronnie at home. If he was going sailing then he must have learnt to swim, so I asked about that.

'Easy,' he said. 'What they did with me was to throw me in the swimming pool. They said that if I sank they would fish me out and start again, but I stayed on the surface so they left me there until I got the idea of moving forward. Then every hour they repeated the plan.'

'So where else have you been swimming, Tony?'

'Nowhere else. I passed.'

I was rather dubious that it had been as simple as Tony made it out to be. I was certain that they would have had more trouble with him than that. I was not going to say a word but there was a distinct possibility that the sea would not be quite as pleasant as the swimming pool at this time of the year. I would be interested in his view of the Sea Cadets in a week's time.

Having seen Tony on his way to his seafaring activities, I now had the problem of Ronnie and Betty on my hands. I needed to go and see Betty and find out whether she wanted to see Ronnie or not. The only way was for Ronnie and me to go and see her together, and if she or her father did not approve or if they were away, then we would both have to come back again. Ronnie was not going to take his uniform off, in fact he might not be allowed to. So that I could compete on equal terms, I would have to wear my ACF uniform, with its one stripe, which I had stored in my bedroom. While Ronnie waited downstairs I got myself dressed. I had one stripe more than he did and Ronnie was very conscious of that.

Before we left I quizzed Ronnie about his motives for seeing Betty again. I reminded him of his mistakes on the last visit and I pointed out the ranks that he must acknowledge. When we reached Betty's house I rang the door bell and her mother came to the door.

'Good morning, gentlemen. The Captain wanted to see you both as soon as possible. He is in his study upstairs. Please go up but knock at the door first.'

My suspicions were aroused. It sounded as if Ronnie had made approaches to her already and that he was expected. I think that Ronnie was also a little worried about that reception. I knocked on the study door.

'Come in.'

We both made a very careful entry. We both aligned ourselves with his desk, at the correct distance from it, and saluted. He looked up and surveyed the scene. Then he looked down at his desk, and then looked at us again. Officers are good at setting the nerves of their troops on edge.

'You obviously need to talk to me about some point or other.'

I spoke first.

'Yes, sir. For some time, I have enjoyed your daughter's company and I appreciate your hospitality. However, when we came after Christmas, you gave me a positive order that if this soldier wished to see your daughter he had to have an invitation first and he needed my permission. It so happens that Private Williams spoke to me this morning, with a request to see your daughter. I was not able to make contact in any other way than coming personally, sir.'

He glared straight at Ronnie.

'Wait there.'

'Yes, sir.'

He left the room and we heard him go downstairs. Ronnie and I did not dare to move. Then we heard the stairs creaking as he made his way up again. He entered the room and sat at his desk then looked at us for an almost unbearable time. Then he addressed me.

'Corporal. If I ignore your status as a cadet, you are by rank the senior and I shall regard you as such in this affair. I also accept that it was you whom Betty chose in a chance meeting some time ago and you have acted quite properly since then. I think that is very good of you.'

That was a delightful credit.

'Thank you, sir.'

Then, after another nerve-racking delay, he looked at Ronnie.

'Private Williams. You were invited to this house at Christmas and you failed to behave yourself. In view of your background it may be that you have not been educated to the standard that I find acceptable, but it is also possible that you now understand what is socially required of you and the regulations associated with being a soldier. My daughter has agreed to meet you provided that a number of conditions are met. These are that the corporal must be in attendance at all times, and he is to be responsible to me for your actions. Apart from going to the toilet alone you are not to take off or adjust any part of your uniform, particularly while you are in her presence. You are also to part company with my daughter within five minutes of being ordered do so. In the event of your failure to comply with these requirements, I shall hand you over to the Military Police and report the matter to your Commanding Officer, who may take whatever action he thinks fit. Do you understand.'

'Yes, sir.'

'You may leave. My daughter is waiting for you.'

'Thank you, sir.'

We saluted and left. Betty was waiting for us in the lounge. She gave me the customary big kiss first, then looked me over. Then she took Ronnie for a cuddle.

'Did you get a big bollocking from Daddy, then?'

'Yes, I'm sorry, Betty.'

'Well, don't you dare get your prick out of your trousers again.'

Ronnie went a brighter red than I had ever seen. A tear was beginning to trickle. Betty wiped it off. In the hope of relieving the tension, I changed the subject, suggesting that we all go out somewhere. There was a show in the park not more than a mile away and Betty accepted the invitation. While Betty was getting ready I warned Ronnie that, as I was responsible for him, he was to stay with me at all times until he got back to my house and any attempt on his part to misbehave would be reported. Ronnie was the perfect gentleman that afternoon, and it was all very pleasant.

When Ronnie and I returned home I made a point of telling him what a lot of trouble he had caused for both Betty and myself. He said he was scared that his CO might find out what had happened, because that would definitely have meant a spell in the glasshouse. Ronnie went off to see his friends in East London for the next few days and neither Betty or I saw him again during that holiday period.

21
More of the Army

Three days before my audition for the RAF band was due I was sent an appointment date for a medical in London. I went off to Holborn on the tube thinking that it would be all over in a short time, just like the ATC medical or the quick once-over before I went into hospital. I walked in the door before 9.30 a.m. in the hope that I would be dealt with without too much delay, but there were already many young bodies that had been waiting since some early hour. I was issued with a pair of shorts and a locker key in exchange for my clothes, then had a number written on my forehead in greasy crayon to help them with easy recognition. I found myself in the company of a crowd of teenage ruffians while trying to communicate with yet another civil service duffer. Admittedly, having the greasy crayon treatment was actually a bit of a laugh in itself. No sooner had the medical clerk labelled a forehead and moved on to the next candidate than the inscription was adapted to read something else. I suppose that most of us could not have cared less about our numbers but it did bring an element of humour and delay into the proceedings. Someone very bright and obviously destined for the Intelligence Corps discovered that the elastic in the shorts was a loose strip inside a fold of the fabric. He made a slight modification that allowed the elastic to break upon command and caused quite a commotion. Naturally, this encouraged others to follow suit. The medical team, labouring on with their inspection of human beings, were not in the least amused as they tried hard to battle on with their task in the face of enormous adversity.

Most of our time was spent waiting around in one queue after another. Everything was taking place in one big room with a few movable partitions to provide the odd discreet corner, but otherwise there was no privacy whatsoever for the victims. By 10 a.m. there were male bodies of all shapes and sizes, some looking terribly sorry for themselves and shedding the odd tear, some looking as if this was a prelude to a holiday on a sunny beach. Others were extremely conscious of their bodies, wanting to cover as much of it from view as possible and giving the impression that they were still attached to their mothers' apron strings. Many did not seem to take matters very seriously. They employed tactics such as missing the bottle instead of peeing into it, and feigning deafness but failing to continue the pretence when the doctor, using a very quiet voice, told them to join the next queue. There were also the near-professional dodgers who wore dark glasses and complained about the light when they were asked to remove them, or had deliberately eaten food which they knew was aggressive to their stomachs. The bodies behind them in the queue had a wonderful view of all these pranks and were able to develop their own variations for disruption. The doctors must have been well experienced in these tricks, probably having seen them all before, so they retaliated by handling each disruptive victim more like an animal than a human being. Few of us were extended the courtesy of being asked to sit or stand in a particular way so that the doctor could conveniently do an examination, but were silently shoved into position and held there until it was all over. Several bodies were given severe tongue-lashings when they were sent round a second time because of their earlier practical jokes.

After the physical tests I was sent to the upper floors of the building to embark on an intelligence test. Did I heave a sigh of relief! The tests comprised simple mathematics, English and general intelligence consisting of matching up irregular shapes, all so simple that I could not imagine how people could possibly fail. All the candidates in the room with me seemed to be those who had stated a preference for the RAF or Royal Navy. When I returned to the lockers at the ground floor level, I discovered that the pranksters of the day had been continuing their japes. It seemed that, working as a gang, they had exchanged numbered keys among themselves and were now furiously complaining to the staff that their clothes were missing. The locker area was sealed off while the staff discovered that there were more bodies than sets of clothes. I did not have any difficulties myself but while I stood on the underground station platform I could see members of the gang, some still wearing only their issued shorts, redistributing their belongings among themselves. By exchanging locker keys and organising an amount of chaos, they had succeeded in releasing each others' clothing from the lockers and taken them to the station in advance of the main part of the gang. They all disappeared into a train moments before the police arrived and were last seen dressing themselves in a relatively empty carriage, many having gained a pair of official issue shorts in the process.

The airman on duty at the gate of the RAF camp at Uxbridge directed me to the headquarters of the RAF band. There was no ceremony about it. I was received not as a prospective National Service conscript but more as a bandsman looking for a job. They had not received my paperwork but they knew that I was coming and were very pleased to see me. For my first test I was asked to play a piece of music alone, then this was followed by an oral test on theory. Neither of these tasks caused me any difficulty. It seemed to satisfy the band-sergeant so, after a free and substantial lunch, I was invited to join the band for their rehearsal in the afternoon. That was a wonderful experience, very far removed from both the squadron band and the nuts and bolts of service life. In the squadron the conductor would stop the band because someone had played a wrong note, but here I was among professionals and a halt in proceedings was to correct a point of interpretation of the composer's directions. This was indeed real music-making. If only I could get into this band during my National Service, it would make the pain of initial training so much easier to bear. The rehearsal was over much too soon. I could have enjoyed myself here for hours. The band was dispersing for tea and at that stage I thought that it was all over and done with for the day. I did not expect to have an interview with the band-sergeant just then. However, he wanted to know all about my past history at school, college studies and cadets and I felt totally at ease. Only at the end of the interview did he hint that he would send for my documents and I could expect to be a member of the band after a period of square-bashing.

I went away from Uxbridge in state of absolute delight, assuming that I was now to be free of the Army or Navy. My not being in line for the Army might upset Betty, so I should have to be very careful how I broke the news to her. I had landed a position for my National Service that might upset Tony as well. On the way home I thought about my good luck. Perhaps it would be better if I said nothing at all until I got my call-up papers or some more definite information came my way.

Three weeks went by and nothing came in the post. I remembered the old chap at the Labour Exchange and reassured myself that civil servants just don't work that fast. I remembered the saying that no news is good news. Then another month passed. I asked several other cadets and it seemed that there was no definite lapse of time between medical and conscription. I did not want to start any formal enquiries, just in case it made matters worse, nor did I want to get caught up in a muddle of ministry paperwork and suffer the same fate as Ronnie Williams in the early hours of one morning. I waited until my CO was in a good mood and then I asked him. His reply was non-committal, and he suggested that I did nothing. I protested that I wanted to know where I stood but I was not able to extract any more information from him.

One Saturday evening, I made my customary visit to see Betty. I told her carefully edited parts of the story, how I was concerned with the possible delay in my being called up, but studiously omitting the bit about my encounter with the RAF band. She listened politely and suggested that if I really wanted to know more, she could ask her father to make some delicate enquiries. I was not too sure about that idea either. Betty's father came into the room and I was invited by Betty to tell the story all over again. He had friends in influential positions and he would ask, if that was what I wanted. I thanked him for his interest in the matter, but pointed out, with as much tact as I could muster, that I would prefer not to go into the Army, but I did want to know where I stood without wishing to precipitate my entry into the services.

It was another week before I took delivery of an OHMS envelope. I put it in my pocket and went upstairs, my heart pounding and an uncontrollable sweat developing. I was not even sure that I wanted to open the envelope, but it was laying on the bed and, whatever it said, I guessed my fate was sealed. When I did pluck up courage to open it, it was an anti-climax. The envelope held a note from Betty's father to say that my records could not be traced although they might yet appear out of the woodwork without warning. However, if I did have a desire to do my National Service as a matter of some urgency, or to join the Army as a career he would see what he could do, then I might be called up to join the next available intake. Because of Betty's interest in the matter, he would make sure that I joined one of the Guards regiments, adding that I ought to be a proud member of the armed forces and there was nowhere better than the Guards. That was definitely not what I wanted. It just needed someone to discover that I had been an Air Cadet, then my two years might be spent bashing away on the designated strip of pavement outside Buckingham Palace as a tourist attraction. I was determined to consider my next move much more carefully and not do anything else until I had weighed up all of the possibilities.

It worried me during the whole of that week. I could not possibly join the Guards. I had to force myself not to think of all my present friends and colleagues in the cadets taking turns to make fun while I was on duty in a public place; even worse, my father might bring his friends to see that elegant guardsman and announce in a loud voice that it was his son. My present place of work was also too close for comfort. To be seen bashing away on the King's paving stones would be an unbearable nightmare, however honourable it may seem to others. Perhaps I ought to take my courage in both hands and find out if the RAF band wanted me. That would be the lesser of the two evils but it would mean waiting for all those Ministry in-trays and out-trays to be emptied first. If only I had not opened my big mouth.

A few days later the postman came with another OHMS letter that set my nervous system into panic again, until I opened it and found that it was from the headmaster at college. They were having a weekend exercise for the senior cadets and I was invited to join them for three days. I did not really class myself as a senior cadet in the college cadets, nor was I madly enthusiastic about wallowing around in an unknown wood. They had not given me any more than that one miserable little stripe but, on reflection, age might have had something to do with it. When I went to see the boss at the office, from the safe side of his door I could hear that lovely tenor singing voice of his in full flow. It might one of his good days, providing an ideal opportunity to ask about a Friday off, and perhaps the chance to nip off early on Thursday as well. This was pay day and the office tended to be a much happier place. He listened to my request carefully and instantly approved.

Then another Saturday came round and I had money jingling in my pocket. The sun was out and I liked wandering around London. It would make a nice change. My father would be at work and I arranged to meet him outside his office so that I could scrounge another lunch out of him. I wanted to do some shopping first and where else but Oxford Street? I went into a clothing shop just to look around but on impulse I bought two of their most violently coloured ties. I could not wear them before lunch as my father might not approve. As I turned the corner into Regent Street I saw a face that I thought I knew. He had been at college with me. His name, Andrew, instantly came to mind but I could not think of his surname. Our eyes met. The conversation ran quite normally. He asked what I was doing to earn money and how many women I was spending it on. He started off doing his National Service in the Army, having volunteered almost as soon as it was announced in order to get it over and done with. He was on leave at present, on the look-out for the opposite sex. In London, the good ones were snapped up quickly and a lot of the rest were prostitutes, so he was not holding out much hope. He had hated the first six months of the Army. It was nothing but being bullied, cleaning everything in sight and walking around like robots. When he decided to sign on for a phenomenal number of years, their attitude rapidly changed and it was very much nicer. I saw a bus coming. As time was pressing I bade him a very rapid farewell and hopped on to the platform of the bus as it was passing. Luckily my father was a few minutes late, although he was usually very prompt with his timekeeping. We settled for a large restaurant near Trafalgar Square. I had a pleasant meal and straight afterwards I headed for the toilet with the intention of wearing my new loud tie. My father would have gone mad if I had flashed it under his nose anywhere else but at the pay desk. That was one location where my father was guaranteed not to do anything out of the ordinary. However, it took him the whole length of the journey home, sitting opposite me on the tube, to calm himself and accept that they were only colours after all.

On the Thursday morning before the weekend exercise it was a bit of a struggle going to work in my formal office suit, carrying my entire uniform in a suitcase. The boss wanted to see my uniform and so did the other chaps in the office. The girls giggled, like girls always did. I had to meet the rest of the cadets at Paddington station late in the afternoon and I needed somewhere to change. There was only one thing for it: I had to use the office canteen area then make a quick escape on the tube. I already had an arrangement with the canteen manageress that she would look after my suitcase until Monday. I expected to get away from the office without being seen but that was not to be. I was spotted before I got through the canteen door, and a good number of the office staff mocked their military office junior.

Under the big clock on Paddington station was a good place to meet. It was on platform 1, away from the congestion within this great monument to Brunel. There were five other cadets on this training weekend. I was, according to the stripes on my uniform, the most junior NCO there. There were none of the jollies on the train that I had experienced on the way to my first camp. This one was crowded mainly with business folk on their way home. To misbehave on this journey would be quite out of order. An hour and a half later we were in Oxford, and during the next 45 minutes we were conveyed by an army lorry, bouncing along the country lanes to a tiny army outpost in the middle of nowhere. The lorry was parked outside an office at the side of a guardroom and we all climbed out. The sun was just beginning to set over a most picturesque stretch of countryside. It was one of those scenes that looked so peaceful that it made you want to live there for the rest of your life, provided of course that the Army did not spoil it. At a small desk in the office was seated an officer who seemed to know most of the details. Documents were shuffled to and fro, then our names were confirmed and duly noted. The telephone rang and conversations about us were in progress.

Soon we were instructed to form a straight line outside the office. To an experienced cadet that meant a very straight line, out of the way of soldiers, standing at ease and not talking. I heard the sound of many pairs of boots as their inmates approached. They halted. Someone in authority was issuing instructions and they were at my end of the straight line. One soldier broke off from the group and halted in front of me, menacingly close. His face was twisted into a grimace and I could just see his teeth. I stared, mesmerised. There were two stripes on his arm. The heels of my size 8s came together powerfully. He looked me up and down in the now fading light.

'You're mine until Sunday,' he snorted. 'Come with me. March, with your arms swinging up to your shoulders, towards that hut with the lights on. This weekend you will only do what you're told. Nothin' else.'

I halted at the door.

'Get inside. Fourth door on the right. Put your kit on the table.'

I did not like his growling or his arrogance.

'Right. Lets have a look at your kit.'

He spread it all out on the table and checked it over. It had been assembled at college and brought to Paddington for me to collect, so I hardly knew what I had. A sleeping bag and a ground sheet were there with the major necessities for camping. There was no food, but a vast collection of odds and ends. The hut was divided up into small rooms and I could now hear similar activities going on elsewhere in the hut. I had never heard of professional corporals smiling before, but this one was beginning to. He took me to the other end of the hut. There were two lines of beds, mostly occupied by soldiers in a sitting position, each swearing about his luck, while they were cleaning their kit. They all looked about my own age. I was shown a bed, just like the one at my first camp, and I was told to get myself organised for the morning. The soldier in the next bed put his trousers down for a moment and surveyed my arm for badges.

'Been a bleedin' 'orrible little cadet, 'ave yer?'

'Yes'. It was probably better than saying 'No'.

'What wiv?'

'The cadets at college.'

'Bloody 'ell. 'E's got a uniform and goes 'ome to mummy every night to get 'er to clean it?'

'No, I have to clean it and I don't let mummy touch it because she's not very good with military things.'

'Then you'd better get down to the shop and buy some boot polish, and a duster, and get back 'ere quick.'

'Yes, sir.'

'I'm not a bleedin' sir either. Only officers are sirs in this dump. I'm yer mate.'

I had seen a hut marked with the word 'Shop' near the guardroom. It was unlikely that there would be another shop open at that hour. I turned round to go to the shop when, from behind, I heard, 'March there, you little prat.'

I thought that I was marching. Obviously I was required to expend more effort. I wondered if he really was 'my mate'. I spent my last few coins on boot polish and got back to the billet and started using it. I had seen all this before, from cleaning everything in sight to marching like a robot when I was not inside my billet; from trying to get bullets on to a distant target to eating up food that the NCOs rejected, and then starting the cycle all over again. What I found different was the petty rules made by the NCOs and the resulting humiliation than ensued, while trying to keep on the right side of the regulations, assuming that you could find out what the regulations intended. I was sure that we were planted in this billet with soldiers of about two weeks experience, so as to relieve their boredom, rather like giving a baby a new rattle. Unlike those on cadet camps, their beds had to be slept in. An NCO was around to see to that and these soldiers were tired out at the end of each day in any case.

Friday morning was not nice. After I had been fed with suspect food I marched, I stood to attention and I cleaned things. This corporal watched my every move; after lunch it was not much better. I had to do it all again but with much greater efficiency and speed, with a gun to look after and kit on my back. After an hour it all came to a halt. I was given a dead rabbit and was soon being taught how to prepare it and cook it. During the war I had watched my mother clean out a rabbit but this was my first messy attempt at the job. Then I was taken across the field to see what plants could be eaten. We walked through woods and across streams, then came to a small area where the undergrowth was quite thick. The corporal pushed me back against a large tree and held my lower jaw with a strong grip. The back of my kit was touching the trunk and my head was forced up so I was looking at the sky. There was someone else around me too – a soldier who succeeded in tying my kit, with me inside it, to the tree with a webbing strap. They both glared at me for some minutes. I saw a twinkle in the corporal's eye as if he was enjoying it. No one said anything for several moments while they viewed their victim. I was trying to stop myself showing signs of panic.

They walked away and all I could hear was very distant sounds. Then they came back. They both glared at me again.

'Why are you still here?' he demanded.

'Because yesterday you told me that I had to do what you said and nothing else.'

'Very good, you're learning fast. Now you are here to survive the night. The first thing you do is to get yourself free. Then you've got to find yourself something to eat. Then you've got to make yourself comfortable for the night. Inspection in full kit at eight in the morning.'

I was approaching a state of panic, but I told myself that if I succumbed it would just get worse. I wriggled, with my kit jammed between the tree and me, but nothing was going to give or come loose. I felt around for the end of the webbing strap but could not find it. I stopped and tried to think. Another soldier came past and I tried to enlist his help.

'No, mate. The enemy have got you. I had to sort it out when I joined. You'll find that it's difficult sleeping when you're standing up tied to a tree so you really have a problem. Breakfast is difficult too.'

Then I had a brilliant idea. The panic had cleared from my mind. All I had to do was undo my webbing belt, leaving the rest of the kit tied to the tree. It was so simple that I cursed myself for not thinking of it before. Surely, I was not this stupid?

Food was next. Rabbits were no good. I remembered trying to catch them at Woodbridge, so I abandoned that idea. Another cadet on the same exercise came wandering past and we joined forces. He was much younger than I was, with one stripe on his arm and still attending college. Food was elusive so we sat down to think about it. There was no meat walking around waiting to be killed, even if we had something suitable with which to kill it. I thought of home and going for a run. Those birds on the golf course always found a meal. They ate worms. That was meat. We discussed it. We went looking for a soft patch of ground and found a stream. On the banks of the stream there might be worms. There might even be fish there. The birds were sitting and watching us. We watched the birds. No fish were being caught but the birds were finding worms, so we raided their source of supply. We wanted water as well and we had a small container in our kit, still clinging to the tree. At least we found an old box and we soon had a seething mass of muddy worms to take back. We got back to the tree to find a notice pinned to it declaring that we had lost points by not looking after our kit, and the ground sheet had been removed. That was a blow. The other cadet went back for water. We had an awful lot of mud, a good quantity of worms and no recipe book to refer to. We washed them, put them in a billy can and left them boiling for some time. We had seen a cottage with a small garden which had a good selection of vegetables growing in it. Some of those went missing, without the owner's knowledge, and were added to the pot of worms. I had to discount the image of worms wriggling in their wild state. It was not an excellent meal by any stretch of the imagination, but it would keep the hunger away until the morning.

Next came bed. We decided to sleep together for warmth. The sleeping bags had not been confiscated so we set about collecting a good quantity of twigs and similar vegetation. We found bits of military debris lying around and we took them and tried using them as a windshield. We used our webbing kit to protect us from the damp rising from the ground. Despite our precautions to keep the wind out we were able to see a good distance around us, with the aid of the moonlight. At around 11 p.m. we heard the sound of a car engine and saw some headlights. We peered out through the gaps in our defences to see a car stop very close by. I expected to see someone on the lookout for us, but the headlights of the car were extinguished and the interior light came on. There were two people in the car and we could just see them moving around. Later there was a distinct and regular rocking motion. It was all very quiet except for the natural sounds of the countryside and occasional feminine giggles from the car. It must have been there for an hour, during which time its engine was running intermittently, presumably to keep the occupants warm. Someone got out and walked round the car, wanting to relieve himself against a tree. We decided to make some whistling noises and sang out 'I see you' in high-pitched voices, but not for long enough to give our position away. Our lone piddler made a hasty dash for the car door and it was driven off much faster than it arrived.

It was all a rather uncomfortable night and we did not get any continuous sleep. We were both awake as soon as the birds started singing and the first glimmer of daylight showed. That gave us at least two hours to get ourselves organised before the threatened eight o'clock inspection. The worst job was cleaning the mud off everything and the hard brush in our kit was soon clogged with dirt. We made repeated visits to the river to fetch more water and we made a valiant attempt to clean the essentials in the hope that this would be acceptable. We agreed to miss out breakfast in the hope that we might have the opportunity to eat later in the morning. Eight o'clock came and went. There was no sign of anybody arriving to do an inspection. By ten o'clock nothing had changed, except that now the mud had dried and it was becoming easier to remove. We were not going to wait any longer and decided to make our way back. I remembered the direction of the sun at the end of the previous day and was able to calculate our route back. By a further bit of good luck we found the timber buildings of the camp. We also found the same officer near the guardroom and explained our reasons for returning. The remaining four cadets had not been seen. It was just past midday and eating was our high priority now. We found a cook who was prepared to serve food and that problem was then solved.

Saturday afternoon was a debriefing session. I did not have to be told what my mistakes were. I suppose the first one was volunteering. The second was not looking after my kit, but this was compensated by the fact that I got myself out of trouble, had survived without mishap and now knew who the driver of the car was. I had some more intensive and advanced survival training afterwards, then I listened in on the debriefing of the remaining four cadets when they eventually returned.

There was nowhere that I was authorised to go during the evening, except to commute between my bed and the WC, but interesting conversations developed. I learnt a lot about sex and much less about fags. I was in among soldiers who did not like the Army, and most were already counting the days to the end of their service. There were no gentlemen among them. All were rough, with miserable faces, looking as if they had been kicked out of a run-down block of flats. I should rather have run away that night, if I had only known which way to run. But I didn't, so the alternative was bed in the company of those whom I did not trust. While I lay there, in the hope of getting some sleep, I persuaded myself that I was not in serious danger. Anything that was stolen from me would be the property of the Army and someone else would have to deal with that problem. My personal possessions only amounted to a few coins and a handkerchief.

More physical activities came on Sunday. I had to go up in the trees, between them and down again on lengths of rope, just to prove that man originated from the same source as apes. I was not the fastest but at least I made it after lots of effort, and I was not last either. 'My mate' told me that the rest of the lads thought I did pretty well, and I might even make a decent soldier if I tried a bit harder. I could not judge whether or not that was pure bullshit, but it might have had a slight ring of truth. However, trying harder was not at the top of my priorities. After tea on Sunday I had to march and run alternately round the parade ground, cheered on by all of the inmates of the billet, until I saw the lorry that was to take us back to Oxford for the train home. That lorry was quite a pleasant sight in the circumstances, particularly as it had now an officer in the front seat together with one of the offensive soldiers. It was the same one that I now knew to be the phantom car driver in the woods on Friday night.

'Excuse me, corporal. When I saw your car out on the training area on Friday night, I noticed that one of your rear lights was not working.'

The officer glared at the corporal. The corporal looked very embarrassed indeed. I did not stay long enough to hear any of the conversation that followed, but it must have been quite interesting. The one problem still remaining was that my only suit was still with the canteen manageress at the office, and the only outfit that I could wear to get there on Monday was my uniform. Sadly I also forgot that the manageress did not arrive until about ten o'clock, so this office junior had the awkward misfortune of having to wear his uniform at the office. Someone with a wicked sense of humour kept my suitcase locked away, refusing to release it until the end of the day. Lots more giggles from the girls but a lot of credit from the boss. The same practical joker could have pinned a note on the office door that I was to be addressed as Corporal in future.

Photo 1 *A cadet of the Air Defence Cadet Corps (the forerunner of the Air Training Corps) 1939–1941.*

Photo 2 *A cadet of the Air Training Corps (from 1941 onwards). Note the rearrangement of the identification badges and the simpler form of belt buckle (compared to the Air Defence Cadet (Photo 1).*

Photo 3 *Cadets often wore a white or blue webbing belt to indicate that they were part of a ceremonial party.*

Photo 4 *Some units dictated that their bandsmen wore additional items to embellish their uniforms, and band badges were issued upon the authorisation of Commanding Officers. Sometimes they added plumes in their headgear, but in those days the rules concerning additional items were largely ignored.*

Photo 5 *The Army Cadet Force followed the rules for the Army, but their status was obvious from their variety of badges.*

Photo 6 *The Combined Cadet Force was introduced, usually in public and grammar schools starting at around 1949, and its training was incorporated in the school curriculum. Uniforms for the Army and RAF sections were similar except for the colour of the cloth.*

22

Manston

It was in 1948 that we first realised that getting to an annual camp was going to be different. Our point of assembly was no longer the railway station, in front of an audience of curious onlookers. This year we had to report to our squadron headquarters and travel by coach. It was not going to be a quick journey, but at least it removed the problem of getting from a railway station to the camp, and the inconvenience of making the change between stations in London. It was a little less comfortable because we could not now wander off to the toilet or stretch our legs while travelling, but after all the fuel shortages there was a degree of novelty about going by road. The main towns on our route were made aware of our presence by our wolf whistles aimed at the local females, who quite often responded by waving back to us. Young men in uniform were still being regarded as heroes for saving the country from German occupation. Our only hope of closer encounters with young ladies *en route* was to persuade our officers and the driver that there was an urgent need for a visit to the toilet, always assuming that it would be in the centre of a town.

Having arrived at Manston without any disasters, we were delivered to the doorstep of our accommodation. It was outside the main fence of the RAF station, in a very clean and newly-painted hut which was not of the nissen variety. It had a single room at each end, for two of the senior cadets, and the luxury of indoor washing facilities so we could achieve the requisite cleanliness without going outside. During my previous periods of living on an RAF station, I had seen beds which collapsed under the load imposed on it by a bouncing cadet because the springs had been replaced by string. After dumping my kit on the bed, my first priority was to investigate. The bed did need some alteration to get it back to the makers' specification and this was best carried out from underneath. By laying on my back on the polished floor, I could exert quite a force on the springs, sufficient to get them back into place. I ignored the background hubbub of cadets organising themselves until I suddenly became aware that there was too little noise. It was usually a positive indication that either mischief was afoot or there was a sudden good reason for everyone present to give the impression of complete innocence. I was aware of a hushed giggle and a whisper. When I saw two feet close to the bed I became a little concerned. Those feet were not wearing boots but officer's shoes, and the cloth from which the associated trousers were made was not of the same quality as those issued to cadets. I wondered if the owner of this footwear knew of my presence, and if so, I had to consider if the time was right to emerge just now or stay where I was. Then I heard my name mentioned, though I did not recognise the voice. I was being looked for.

I wriggled out from under the bed and looked around to see a small group of my fellow cadets in one corner of the room. My CO was much nearer. He was the wearer of the shoes. I dusted myself down as best I could and found a cap to wear. The CO had a notebook in his hand. He told me that he had met the station accounting officer in the mess who had asked if I had arrived, and wanted me to report to his office before 3 p.m. I could not imagine why I was needed as accounting was way above my head.

I was advised to stand in front of the only mirror in the billet to make sure that I was dressed correctly for the occasion and I commandeered a very helpful corporal to inspect the final result. I had been given precise instructions on how to get into the station headquarters without entering through the front door, and a very brief clue as to where the accounts office was located. Once outside our hut, I found that the whole place was buzzing with activity; airmen and vehicles were busily going about their duties. This venture into the accounts office was taking on some importance. I was sure that the station commander had strict rules of discipline for his men, as all of the NCOs and the airmen were marching everywhere, so I thought it best to follow suit. The RAF must have called together all of its officers that day and released them, one by one, to proceed along the road that I wanted to use. There was no way of avoiding them so my right arm had the saluting technique down to a fine art during the next ten minutes or so. The back entrance of the headquarters was fairly busy and was the only door by which the non-commissioned staff were authorised to enter. This led to a long corridor. I recognised the name on one of the doors. I had an interfering old auntie, on my father's side of the family, with the same surname. She was a miserable old woman who always wanted more attention than the rest of the family were prepared to offer her, and she was not at all popular. The plot was now becoming clear. My father had planned this as a surprise for either my uncle or me.

I knocked on the office door. Nothing happened. I was surveyed by the headquarters staff who were going about their duties. I knocked again, with no better result. I felt better when a sergeant understood my plight. He explained that the flight-lieutenant often disappeared for half an hour or so, and it would be better if I waited. Waiting always made me nervous, rather like volunteering for pain outside the dentist's surgery. I wondered what he wanted me for. Two officers came along and I saluted yet again. I wondered what he looked like, because I could not remember him from the family gatherings, if indeed I had seen him at all. I felt out of place and certainly of lesser importance than anyone else that was moving. It would not be right to wander around or read the notices. They were of no interest to me and might be confidential, and the sound of my boots on the floor would almost certainly persuade someone to investigate exactly what I was doing there. I did not have a reasonable explanation ready for any questions of that nature. Despite my three stripes, I also had a badge to indicate that I was a cadet and was still an insignificant member of the services. Standing to attention was the only acceptable option if anybody in uniform was in the corridor. I did pluck up enough courage to relax for just a moment to look at my watch and glance around, until the sound of more footsteps and voices and doors squeaking on their hinges alerted me to the possibility of being caught off guard. Another two officers came along the corridor. I saluted. One of them returned my salute, stopped and fumbled with the key to the door. He went inside for a moment and then came out. I was invited in and offered a seat in a rather heavily upholstered chair. It did not feel right to be in the presence of an officer and to enjoy this level of comfort.

He was a little man and spoke in an unfriendly voice. I noticed that he had the same mannerisms as my father, with similar facial features. He took a cigar out of its packet and lit the thing. I was offered one as well but refused it. The air was soon heavy with the cigar smoke that hung around the office like a dark rain cloud. He looked as if all humour had been banished from his life over the years, and the cigar did not seem to help matters. The depth of the chair left me below the smoke level and almost below desk level as well. I would have felt much happier standing up. There had not been any hint of a pleasant welcome. He enlightened me, in a rather formal manner, about the family relationships. My father had written to him to say that I was to stay at Manston for a week. We chatted about the rest of the family for ten minutes or so until possibly he became fed up with it. The conversation took an interesting turn when I was asked what our training programme included during the week. I was not aware of its details, but I tried to make an intelligent guess based on my knowledge of earlier camps. He offered to make facilities available for any particular training event that the cadets might like. On the spur of the moment, I could not think of anything in particular that we needed. Trying not to appear totally stupid I remembered that there was a funfair of some doubtful repute at Margate and the cadets might appreciate an evening visit there. He muttered about finding out if there might be a chance of some free transport, but certainly no more. The airmen usually went on the bus and were often late getting back. Then I remembered that the band had brought some credit on itself at a previous camp and had got some extra flying out of that. Could the band do something to earn itself a visit? I tactfully indicated that my CO was the organiser of the training, and while I was prepared to suggest ideas, it was he who would make the final decision. I left knowing that matters might be discussed further over a meal in the officers' mess and it might be possible for me to manoeuvre things to our benefit. The only problem was whether I would be able to make contact with him again. Picking my words carefully, I asked how I could formally get to see him again if I needed to. The surprising answer was that I knocked on the door and walked in. Surely that could not be right? Perhaps I should have to consider the situation as it arose.

I was delighted to get away from the tense atmosphere of the station headquarters and the stink of his cigar smoke. I was now free to undertake more solo marching, with a good measure of thinking and saluting thrown in, before I got to the billet. I realised that I was the senior cadet NCO on the camp, so the level of the discipline was going to have to be of a high order. The rest of the squadron were still in the billet. Either they had politely waited for me so that we could go to our evening meal as one very smart squadron, or they were hoping to find out more about my visit to Station Headquarters before they decided to go anywhere. I had other matters on my mind. The first was that the cadets had to march everywhere and I was responsible for making that happen. Standing in front of the squadron and assembling them into three ranks to march them to an evening meal did not seem to be very demanding, but I was aware that airmen were looking on from a safe distance. They were perhaps expecting to see a mammoth flouting of the station standing orders or a failure of military discipline that would bring the station warrant officer out of his office. The alternative was to ensure a continued happy relationship between the station staff, my CO and my father by making sure things were precisely correct. I felt very alone standing in front of those three ranks. It was far different from an enclosed parade area where a moderate level of raising the voice was normal. I really had to shout and my musical instincts fortunately led me to use the direction of the wind to carry my voice. I spent as long as I could telling the cadets about the level of discipline required from them and which must continue for the whole week. If they wanted to do anything that they had not been specifically ordered to do, then they were required to let me know, even if it was only going to the NAAFI or for a walk round in their spare time. My second concern was to ensure that we all identified officers promptly, and that they had their rank respected by a salute. I still felt rather uneasy but we arrived for food without incident.

During the eating process I found out that I had become a very respected member of the squadron now that it was known that I had contact with an influential officer of the RAF. If I could pull off something a bit dramatic it would help my ego a little. I discussed it with the other NCOs for a time until the catering staff made it clear that they wanted us out of the dining hall so that they could clear up. It would have been impossible to hang around outside the dining hall for fear of attracting the interest of the station security staff, and then there was the problem of getting all the cadets back to the billet in one squadron and in their three ranks. A meeting at the back of the billet seemed to be a much better idea.

We chose an area away from the rays of the setting sun and on a convenient bank of grass. It was difficult to come up with any ideas without knowing what the RAF station had to offer and, if our alternatives were to be considered, they had to be better than the existing programme that we had yet to see. My instant idea of the funfair at Margate was popular and if the RAF could save us the cost of the bus fare it would be worth a try. Otherwise, we were all short of good practical ideas.

There was nothing for it but to wait until the morning. It was just possible that a visit to the NAAFI could be fitted in before it was time for 'lights out'. The cadets needed a nudge to remind them to remove their caps before they went in, and before any problems set in. The place was alive with soft music and dancing couples. Some cadets had already arrived and most of them were looking on from the perimeter of the hall without taking any part in proceedings, but were probably trying to work out the routine for embarking on all this social activity. Generally, the girls were all in their best civilian attire and the men were in uniform. Two of the cadets were knowledgeable about dancing before they came to camp, but service footwear was not quite right for this activity. That restricted us somewhat to a chat and a bite to eat.

When I found what I thought was a quiet unoccupied and dimly-lit corner, I discovered empty beer glasses on the table. Further investigation led me to the bar. I had not yet spent any pocket money and here was my golden opportunity. By now there were seven cadets in the party who had succeeded in collecting nine young girls. Buying soft drinks for that lot would land me in desperate trouble for the rest of the week. A plump little girl, complete with flickering eyelashes and a big smile, was looking hard at my stripes. By golly, she was a fast worker. Her arm was round my waist almost before I realised it, while she fired questions to find out if I was a real sergeant. I confirmed that I was 'real', but a cadet and not in the RAF. I thought it best to point out straight away that we were all at camp for just one week. I still wanted a drink, and this new attachment clinging to me also wanted one. I knew what the rules said about under-age drinking of alcohol, but by now she had ordered, the beer was already poured into a glass and money was changing hands. It was much cheaper than I expected, but I had to devise a plan to persuade her to open up her handbag again for my next drink. I dropped a hint that we all might be free on another evening during the week, but we did not know any more details yet.

Our successful chatting was being viewed from a distance by other cadets. Some of the very small fourteen-year olds ventured to the bar and they got served too! That opened up the floodgates, and the rest of them followed suit. Without any further prompting, my partner got a ten-shilling note out. I watched her long dress swirling as she strutted off to the bar. She looked so beautiful. I watched her return to the table, holding a small glass of something that was not beer. I sipped it carefully while she watched, and I suspected that she might have been waiting for some kind of result. It was extremely strong and not very sweet. The chatting continued and I had not noticed the time until, quite tactfully, a cadet reminded me that we should now be on our way back to the billet. I took my leave of the young lady and hurried back. I piled into bed and remembered nothing more until the combination of sunlight and voices woke me.

The scramble to get washed and dressed and get the cadets off to breakfast and back again was sheer routine, and they were all behaving themselves. The CO was waiting outside the billet for our return. I halted the squad and saluted.

'Good morning, sir.'

'Good morning, sergeant. Dismiss the cadets. Get them to tidy the billet, and then come to see me.'

'Yes, sir.'

I set the cadets about their duties, not fully convinced that all was well, but the CO wanted me first and he was waiting for me a bit further away from the billet.

'Sergeant, did you talk to your uncle yesterday, and what was the result?'

'We first talked about family matters, sir, but then the subject of our camp training programme arose and he volunteered to help if we needed anything in particular.'

'Then what did you suggest that the cadets might like?'

'All I could think of at that moment was a visit of some kind, perhaps to Margate in the evening, sir, if that did not interfere with your training programme.'

'Well, I thought that was a reasonable idea until, at breakfast this morning, I met an officer whose daughter got herself slightly the worse for drink, and arrived home in the early hours apparently in the company of a sergeant whose description fits you quite accurately.'

I felt my face go cold. I seemed to be so deep in the shit that I had visions of my stripes coming off.

'I'm sorry, sir, but we only had two drinks and I left her in the bar and was back in the billet before 10.30. She could have bought some more drinks after I left, and I definitely did not take her home.'

'Then there is the problem of you consuming alcohol while under age.'

'Yes, sir.'

'Now there is also some damage to bedding because one corporal, who was also drinking, got back to bed but could not hold his water, so he wet the mattress. That mattress cannot be used again and will cost money to replace.'

'Yes, sir.'

'And you were the senior cadet present.'

Now it occurred to me that uncle might be talking to my father before I got back home from camp. I was absolutely stumped as to how I was going to get out of this one.

'I'm ever so sorry, sir. Is there anything I can do to make amends?'

'Sergeant, the first thing you will do is get those cadets on parade and into church, and get into church yourself without conjuring up another story about belonging to some unique religion which is not likely to exist in this part of the world. Then after church you will get hold of that drunken corporal and see if he has any bright ideas. I suggest you get these cadets praying a bit harder than usual in church because there are lots of sins to answer for today.'

'Yes, sir.'

I dared not even move, or ask if that was all.

'Get those cadets on parade.'

'Yes, sir.'

I never did like church, except for attending family weddings. Joining the cadets was one of the ways I had found to avoid it, but it did not always work out like that. During the service I was more concerned with the problems of the previous night than listening to sermons and singing hymns. I had earmarked the interval between getting back to the billet and leaving for lunch to talk to Corporal Maynard to get his version of the events. He had no clear recollection of what had happened to him. He remembered having a few drinks, then the next he knew, he woke up in a wet bed, awash with the stench of urine. I decided to abandon further investigation into Maynard's activities since it was unlikely that I would get any more useful information from either him or any other cadet. I tried to think about each point that the CO had mentioned. Under-age drinking, getting an officer's daughter drunk and being the senior NCO present when Maynard had got himself into trouble and damaged his bedding.

After lunch I ran the CO to ground in a small office in an adjacent hut. I had picked up some useful tips from my father from time to time, one of which was that people were often in a good mood just after eating a pleasant meal. Another, particularly applicable in an office, was always to wear an immaculately pressed white shirt to lend an air of authority. I could not manage a shirt but at least I could pay full attention to my dress. I approached him with all due compliments. He lounged back in his chair, possibly relaxed by an intake of wine with his lunch. At least he looked as if he was in a good mood. I explained that the bar staff on Saturday evening were readily serving anybody who came near the bar, and that included all of the cadets. I stuck to my earlier story that if the officer's daughter got herself drunk and arrived home in the early hours, then it must have been in

193

the company of someone who was not a cadet. I suggested that she could have taken note of my appearance from our initial meeting, during which there had actually been very little time for drinking. The only crimes for which I could be blamed was drinking while under age myself, although I had not bought the drinks, and perhaps being unaware that Maynard had not returned to bed, or possibly that he might have returned and then gone out again. I was certain that all the beds were occupied on my last round of the billet. He stared at me for a good few minutes while I stood to attention, making sure not to engage my line of sight with his by staring at a mark on the wall at my eye level.

'Sergeant, you are to go back to the billet and explain to the cadets that the NAAFI and all other places that provide alcohol are now out of bounds to them. You are to speak to Corporal Maynard and tell him to remove the stripes from his uniform so that he now assumes the rank of cadet.'

He paused. I was waiting to hear my fate. There was a tense silence, during which I hoped that I would not have to explain to my father why I had become a corporal. I wanted to say something, but it was still his move and his next words would be crucial to me.

'You will tell Corporal Maynard that as soon as he has removed his stripes, he is to report to me immediately.'

'Yes, sir. Am I to be demoted too, sir?'

'Not immediately. I will decide during the week.'

That was a close shave. I instantly felt relief but I tried not to show any reaction to his decision. I was still not moving, still staring intently at that mark on the wall.

'Thank you, sir. I am sorry that I was involved in these problems. Is there anything else that you need me for, sir?'

'No.'

He was unusually abrupt in that last word. I decided to remove Corporal Maynard from the rest of the cadets to tell him his fate, having first armed myself with a pair of scissors for the job.

I was certainly in a difficult spot. Apart from the threat to my stripes, if my father found out what had happened he would beat the living daylights out of me when I got home, and the channels of communication were very efficient between the ATC and my father. I sent a cadet to call Maynard out of the billet. The cadet returned alone, with the excuse that Maynard did not feel well and was staying in the billet for a sleep. I told the cadet that I had just given him an order. He was to obey that order and bring Corporal Maynard to me. Fortunately, Maynard appeared after a few moments. He made a weary effort to present himself to me.

'Corporal Maynard, the CO and I have been discussing what occurred last night, mainly your intake of alcohol and the resulting damage to the mattress.

Because of your behaviour, the CO has decided to demote you to the rank of cadet and he requires you in his office to return those stripes now.'

Maynard looked shattered and a small tear rolled down his cheek. He did not speak.

'Maynard, here are the scissors. Get going.'

'Yes, sergeant.'

He turned round and went inside the billet. A few moments later I saw him go into the CO's office. He was in there for some time, then he eventually came marching out in a very formal manner and went into the billet. He just sat on his bed and cried, with his head hung down so that the others would not see too much. There were odd remnants of cotton thread, that once kept his stripes in place, still hanging from his uniform.

The training programme, now in typewritten form, detailed a visit to aircraft that were parked around the airfield. Maynard did not take part in this visit, as he did not wish to be seen until he had composed himself and, presumably, contemplated his next move. When we arrived for our next meal Maynard was already eating and was most of the way through a second helping of a large portion of suet pudding, with a mug of tea awaiting his attention near at hand. He had tidied himself up quite noticeably and now there were no signs of tears or tiredness. He looked up occasionally while the rest of us chatted during our meal but he did not speak. He waited until we were all ready to leave before falling into position amongst the three ranks to march back. In the billet, his friends gathered round him and engaged him in hushed conversation.

Unless we were very seriously involved in religion, no entertainment whatsoever was on offer that evening. Two footballs appeared from somewhere so the cadets enjoyed a rough kick-about, but score-keeping was hampered since everyone seemed very uncertain about the rules. I was rather pleased to see that after some delay Maynard and his colleagues joined in. Later that evening I sat down with Maynard and we talked about the previous evening's events in some detail. It was generally agreed that the officer's daughter had achieved her drunken state without any assistance from the cadets, and I was probably the only one that she remembered meeting while she was sober, and could describe with any accuracy. As I thought about it, I remembered that I did not actually go up to the bar to get beer. It was more a case of anyone who went within striking distance of the bar being presented by a glass of something, for which payment was demanded. Perhaps Maynard had acquired a drink in the same way, and then became ill enough to lose control of his normal functions.

After the usual activities and breakfast on Monday morning I was waylaid by the CO, who was waiting outside the billet. He ushered me into his office in great haste.

'Sergeant, what do you know about this officer's daughter getting drunk again last night in the NAAFI and the cadets being served with beer again?'

I was pleased to hear that. The plot was thickening. Someone on the camp was out to cause trouble.

'Absolutely nothing, sir.'

'You are in charge of the cadets. Where were they?'

'We all played football outside the billet after our evening meal, then we went inside the billet, sir.'

'Can you account for every cadet?'

'Yes, sir. The NAAFI was barred to us and there was nowhere else to go.'

'Tell me again, sergeant. How many cadets disappeared from your game of football?'

'None, sir.'

'And how many cadets left the billet after football?'

'None, sir. I counted them at intervals.'

He was silent for a few moments, and I was looking at that mark on the wall again.

'Let me think about this.'

'Yes, sir.'

He had a few more moments of silence.

'Sergeant, get the cadets on parade. I shall be out in a few minutes.'

I had just the germ of an idea that the CO believed me. This could solve a lot of problems. I wondered what he would do next.

The cadets were assembled in three ranks. The CO just said that this morning's visit was to the air traffic control tower and that I was totally in charge for the entire morning. That was a very unusual statement from him and I issued a severe warning to the cadets that if anything untoward happened it would have consequences that would make them wish that they were not in the ATC. The visit was very interesting and the control tower staff seemed very happy to meet us. I took the opportunity during the last three-quarters of an hour to run through some drill instruction before lunch. Drill always encouraged the appetite before a meal and it would be useful, if my intuition was right, for us to be on our best form during the afternoon.

I led the squadron on its usual parade after lunch. Our CO was missing from his office but he soon arrived, accompanied by my uncle and another officer whom I did not know. They wanted to inspect the cadets and the state of the billet, then they had a short discussion about the results while we waited. It seemed that we were waiting for the announcement of something rather important. Our CO started by saying that there had been a lot of wrong information circulating about the events in the NAAFI on Saturday evening. He and another officer had investigated the matter and decided that the problem was not of our making, but there were still more serious matters yet to be resolved. As a result, we would be allowed to use the NAAFI for the rest of the week provided that we did not drink alcohol. Also, there was an offer from the station commander to provide a coach to take us to Margate and back on two evenings. In addition, there would be an opportunity for the band to play to the public on the open day of the Battle of Britain weekend. Then he issued a stern warning that these concessions would only be honoured if there were no lapses of discipline and we came up to the standards normally expected from airmen during their basic training. This was rather a tough challenge to us, but a party of airmen would be detailed immediately after evening meal today and again in the morning to give instructions.

That afternoon there were several main topics of conversation. One was the challenge of meeting the RAF standards of discipline, another was the joys of the funfair at Margate, and yet another was the Battle of Britain weekend. We returned from our evening meal, the younger cadets already as peaceful as lambs and the more senior cadets taking the view that at the end of the week at least we would still be alive, having been fed, watered and given time to sleep. Then our beloved parents would welcome each of us back in one piece. In the billet morale had risen and cadets were already looking at items that could be improved or tidied up. However, this soon came to an abrupt halt when one tall, gloomy-faced RAF corporal entered the billet, stamping his boots on the concrete floor, and shouted, 'Every cadet by his bed.' I had, fortunately, met this kind of individual at the Army Cadet camp, and I had a quick vision of McKenna and his father. It was not a question of being polite to him. He effectively froze the whole billet, like statues in a museum. Even the flies were not flying any more and the light evening breeze seemed to stop moving the outside door. As far as I could see, each cadet was standing to attention at the end of his bed, looking at the cadet opposite. The corporal slowly walked up and down the centre aisle of the billet, then between beds to inspect each cadet and locker in turn. Not a word was spoken but when he got to my bed he spent a lot of time looking at me and the contents of my locker in much greater detail. I observed this by watching the reflection in the window opposite. He was interrupted by the sound of marching feet some distance away. A group of airmen came to a halt outside the billet and the corporal went outside and spoke to them. Before long these airmen were inside the billet, each one allocated to four beds. The corporal spoke in an unmistakably military voice.

'These airmen are here for your benefit and to get this billet and you in an acceptable state for tomorrow morning's inspection. Do what they tell you. Carry on.'

He marched out as formally as he had come in.

His last words had been 'Carry on', but I assumed that this was an order to the airmen. I was going to stay at attention until I received a definite instruction and the cadets acted likewise. Being the only cadet with three stripes, I felt rather vulnerable. One airman came in my direction.

'Fall out, sergeant. You don't have to stand to attention in front of me, but you have to set an example to the cadets. I used to be an ATC cadet before I joined up.'

He must have been about the same age as myself but there were marked differences. He had arrived the day before from his basic training camp in the Midlands. He spoke with a West Country accent as far as I could detect. He looked so fit, with sparkling blue eyes, and spoke in a way that left no doubt at all about what he meant. I heaved a little sigh of relief that we had something in common. I looked at the airman. He was nothing like the majority of airmen that I had seen elsewhere on the station. His uniform was immaculate. Not a thing was out of place or untidy and it was clear that basic training had had its effect on him. I asked if the cadets could relax from their position of attention too.

'No, not until we have both looked at them.'

On the other side of the billet Maynard looked as if he was becoming impatient, so we went to his bed first. I looked at the rest of the billet to see other cadets enduring the same kind of treatment. Soon there were several little groups of four cadets, each with an airman who started off by showing them how the contents of a locker must be displayed, then revealed the intricacies of folding items of bedding and how to lay out the remaining essential accoutrements. More memories of McKenna flashed into my mind. For the remainder of the time available that evening the airmen applied themselves to the removal of dust and dirt, after which they departed, now supervised by the corporal. We noticed that they marched away, with perfect precision, in the direction of the NAAFI. There must have been some drinking time left. We worked away for another hour, knowing that our Margate visit depended on it.

The following morning I was awoken by lots of shouting. As I pushed away the bedclothes to let in the light I saw airmen. Their purpose was to pick up where they had left off the previous evening and our training programme had been altered for the morning to accommodate it. Although it was very early, the airmen were already washed and dressed. There was no chance of maintaining the horizontal position any longer. I recalled the violent exits from bed at Woodbridge and the treatment of the cadets from college who failed to move before daylight. I decided to get out of bed voluntarily. At least I could watch the fate of those who were slower. I was disappointed. The orders of the airmen were not going to be questioned. We ceased our chores just long enough to go for breakfast and come back again. Then the morning's hard labour started in earnest, with yet another review of the state of the billet. It was a further hour before the airmen were satisfied. Our uniforms did not need too much attention, as they were always on display. Then one of the airmen wanted a word with us.

'This week, all you cadets are in the Royal Air Force. Most of you will soon be joining up for several years whether you like it or not, so you had better get used to the idea. You have all done a great job tidying up and the results are sure to please the corporal, so the Margate trip is on for this evening.'

Looks of concern changed to beaming smiles.

'Those of you who own clean and pressed civilian clothes will wear them after tea. Those without clean civilian clothes will wear their uniforms with full webbing. There is plenty of webbing in the stores and every cadet will march there now to get some in case it is needed. You still have two hours before lunch, so get things right. It's up to you.'

Getting webbing kit and making it fit properly was something I had experienced before. We helped the younger cadets who found it strange but they soon accepted that if the RAF did things this way, then they ought to comply.

That was very a hard morning's work indeed, but we were rewarded with two visits to Margate and another camp later in the year. Most of us remembered the words of the airman who threatened us with being in the RAF for a couple of years in the not too distant future.

We had vacated the airmen's mess after lunch and the cadets were now full of food and enthusiasm again. They were in their three ranks ready to move off when the RAF corporal arrived.

'Sergeant, your billet looks much smarter than it did. I want to finish off the job properly, so within the next thirty minutes you will have all your cadets on parade in full webbing and outside your billet ready for a period of drill.'

'Yes, corporal.'

That sounded pretty dull to me but, during the few moments of getting organised, I found that the younger cadets seemed quite thrilled by the idea. Whether that would still be the case by the next mealtime was in some doubt, in my mind. The packs were empty as they came out of the stores, but one enthusiast found that blankets fitted inside nicely. What else could I do but offer support to a keen cadet and get everyone else to do likewise? The drill session, commanded by the corporal, was surprisingly successful. He had at his command the full range of sarcastic comments of the experienced serviceman, and many of his criticisms during the training had a humourous slant to them. In the middle of the afternoon he declared an interval, during which he explained the use of webbing equipment and its many additions and variations. Then it was back to more drill until our evening meal.

I was becoming increasingly interested in the sheer enthusiasm of these younger cadets during their first week at an annual camp. Perhaps that is what someone had thought about me when I was a young cadet, and perhaps this is why I landed up with three stripes. As we were preparing to go for food again, we were interrupted by a group of five young cadets who did not want to go to Margate. I asked them about their civilian clothing and had a look at it. It was in a satisfactory condition and I explained about the funfair with its mechanical attractions, and possibly its female ones, but it was of no avail. One cadet came out with a plausible explanation.

'I don't like women. My mother is a woman.'

Quite an observant cadet, I thought.

'She is always fussing about and she spends lots of money and then goes to my dad for more. And look at that girl in the NAAFI that got us into trouble. No, I'm not getting involved with any women.'

I tried a bit of persuasion, but he was not having any of it. My next aim was to make sure that they had a definite plan for the evening so that there was no chance of mischief. They did have a plan. They wanted me to talk to the corporal and ask him if they could do some more drill. So why the sudden urge to do drill I enquired.

'Well, I'm not very good at reading or writing, and I don't get good marks in anything at school, so I want to join the Army or something. They pay good money for men to march around all day. That's what I'm going to do.'

'Then I will find the corporal to see if he is willing to organise it.'

'Thanks, sarge. And will you try to get a rifle to use with the webbing?'

'I'll ask.'

'Thanks.'

He had clearly given the matter some thought and involved some of his mates. At the evening meal, I would have to find the corporal to see what he said. The corporal was absolutely delighted that a cadet had actually asked.

'Tell them to be outside the guardroom in an hour from now. I'll see what I can do.'

I relayed the message to the cadets, at a time when the rest of them were dressed in their respectable civilian clothes and listening for the arrival of the transport.

The five cadets decided that they were not going anywhere without lots of webbing kit on their backs. It seemed to have provided them with a new kind of thrill. They inspected each other, decided who was in charge according to length of service and took off in the direction of the guardroom, more in the style of guardsmen rather than cadets.

Several pairs of eyes tried to peer into the guardroom from our coach as we went by, but there was nothing to be seen. Our trip to Margate was a great success, if only judged by the quantity of female addresses logged during the evening. The delay in getting the cadets aboard for the return journey was caused mainly by the time it took them to unhitch themselves from members of the opposite sex. Our return to camp offered a huge surprise. Five cadets, who by now had each also acquired a rifle to put on his shoulder, formed a guard at the side of the hut door. I asked whether they had enjoyed the training. They had met with a problem to begin with, since they thought that I said that they were to meet inside the guardroom. The airman on duty had seen them in all arrive in their webbing and assumed that they were there for a spell of jankers. To stay on the right side of the regulations he had put each cadet in a cell until the matter got sorted out. They had loved every minute of being put in a cell and being marched around. They even marched to the local village and gave a display of rifle drill outside the inn until the light began to fail.

News gets around quickly and for the rest of the week the ATC could do no wrong. On our second visit to Margate these five cadets finished up paying half price at the fair. The innkeeper had telephoned our CO before we left for home inviting the five cadets back, although that might have been very difficult to arrange. The invitation to the band to play at the Battle of Britain celebrations was to be confirmed as soon as the cadets could commit themselves to the date.

Just to add a finale to the camp, Maynard got his stripes back. The sewing produced a few technical problems, but there were lots of cadets around with a bit of domestic knowhow.

23
Lots of bodies

There was a knock at the door one Saturday morning. It was not any of the usual knocks that I instantly recognised but a very delicate knock. I opened the door to see a very well dressed middle-aged lady standing there. She smiled courteously and quickly explained that she had recently moved into the house next door with her family and wanted to introduce herself. She had not met many people as yet and, being so close, we were at the top of her visiting list. I called for my mother, who was around the house somewhere doing the cleaning. My mother came downstairs, a little conscious that she was still wearing her apron, but they met and introduced themselves in the comfort of the lounge, and chatted for a good while. Her husband had gone to organise things for the household. She had two sons and was proud of them. Stephen was sixteen and had just started to attend a college some distance away. Paul had had his fourteenth birthday the week before, had lots of ambition and was still at school. My mother was not very good at explaining things but I gathered that she and Pam had gone off to see my auntie for several odd days while I had been at Manston, so they had failed to greet the new arrivals next door. It was all very nice for the two ladies to exchange their respective family notes and they were certainly enjoying it, but Pam and I were feeling left out of the conversation. During a short pause I took the chance to ask about Stephen and Paul. There was not much immediate response but it prompted an invitation for us all to go next door during the evening to meet them socially and to partake of unspecified refreshments.

My first impression was of an extremely tidy and well kept house, with everything in its correct place. It was quite a contrast to the state of the property when Donald's family lived there. Her husband was a salesman in a local company and used the lounge frequently for meeting his business friends. My parents were invited into their lounge, leaving Pam and myself with the two boys in the dining room. Paul and Pam were getting on very well together, with a gramophone close at hand and a pack of cards. Those two were engrossed and were likely to be so for some time. While all that was going on, Stephen and I swapped notes on our college work, though mine was of a more specialist nature now. Stephen spoke of the college that he used to attend, and then his new college. He told me that, having selected this new college, he had discovered a recent rule by which a cadet force had been established and attendance was compulsory. I suddenly became interested and realised that some of the comments that I had heard about a Combined Cadet Force were coming true. Stephen was not very happy at all with the idea of having to wear an army uniform to college at least once a week and sometimes, during important occasions, on all five days of the college week. He had never worn a uniform before and he had some serious doubts about whether he would like to be a cadet. He suddenly found out that there was no way of escape when he had been told to go and collect his uniform on his second day of attendance, and was given a date on which he was required to wear it. He looked again carefully at the college prospectus from which both he and his father had made the selection, but there was no mention of any cadet force. His uniform was being kept out of sight in his bedroom cupboard. He had convinced himself that he was going to dread the training at weekends. He was also worried about a threat from his rather saucy younger brother that he would take any opportunity to make fun of him when the opportunity arose, and that would be quite embarrassing.

I had not mentioned the cadets until then, but I said that I had similar doubts when I was enticed to join and I had had a few problems, then I offered to help him if it would make things easier. I suggested that part of his problem might go away if he directed Paul towards one of the cadet organisations. As a gentle introduction to his new uniform, I volunteered to meet him during the following afternoon, on condition that he tried it on. We could then sort out any snags and put them right before his first parade at college on the following Friday. It surprised Stephen to discover that I was already a cadet. Just then a good selection of food arrived at the table. Paul had heard bits of our conversation and we had to go over it all again, picking our words carefully, so that Paul was sold the idea in a fairly painless way. Stephen could see no other way to get his uniform sorted out, and he told Paul that he might feel that he was being left out of the deal. I did not tell Stephen, but I had already thought of that. The spare ACF uniform that I had acquired a long time earlier might fit him. We agreed that Paul would have to join something, and even Paul was beginning to like the idea. Later on that evening, I wondered if the college that I attended some two years earlier had in any way contributed to the development of this new cadet force. There were certainly a few chance remarks circulating at the time and there seemed to be some similarities.

On the Sunday morning I had been to the squadron for band practice and I was still wearing the accoutrements that went with my basic uniform. Paul knocked on the door in the afternoon, with a rather sad and unwilling Stephen trailing behind him, carrying a large bag of uniform. Paul was a bit startled when he first caught sight of me, and Stephen instantly became much happier. We emptied the contents of the bag onto my bed and I invited Stephen to get himself dressed. For him, it was not really a question of what to wear, but in what order it had to be put on. It was easy going, as far as the trousers and battle-dress blouse. He was starting to complain about the boots and gaiters, and he had to practice to get the beret exactly right. My guidance for adjusting and fitting his webbing accessories caused a few problems, but eventually the day was won. I pointed out to Stephen that the whole process had taken over an hour, so for his first formal encounter with the cadets on Friday he had better plan to get up that much earlier.

Paul had been watching all this with great interest, and I asked him what he thought about it.

'Smashing. It looks jolly smart. I wish that I had a uniform like that.'

That was the remark that I had been waiting for.

'Well, Paul, as it happens, I think that I have got one that is about your size.'

Paul's face was a picture. Stephen, while showing some signs of physical discomfort, was delighted that Paul had dropped himself into this one. I dug out the college ACF uniform from my cupboard and held it up for him to see it.

'Can I wear it now?'

'Yes, but the rules say that you both call me "sergeant" at all times when we are in uniform.'

Paul's face was now a really happy delightful picture and I tried to predict how long that would last.

'Er, yes, sergeant.'

Paul was a fairly intelligent lad. He had taken note of what his brother had done and managed to achieve the same effect in about the same time as Stephen. I decided that a few rules ought to be explained at this stage. I pointed out the major differences between the Army and the ATC uniforms, and the regulations about saluting. They both commented about how harsh the material was to their skin, and how heavy it all was, at which point I reminded them that they would eventually get lumbered for two years of National Service. They could put some training in now, or it might be much more difficult when they did get called up. They saw the point. Paul was now absolutely thrilled and desperately wanted to be a cadet.

'What do you want to join?' I asked.

Paul surveyed the uniforms for a moment.

'I want to be an ATC cadet like you, and in the band with that white belt and white gaiters. I always wanted to play a musical instrument. If I have to be an airman or a soldier for two years, I might as well start now.'

Stephen looked really pleased. My plan was beginning to work. Paul was unlikely to poke fun at his big brother and, if he did, Stephen now realised that he could do likewise. Paul's luck was in. It had not been long since the ATC had lowered the age limit for joining to fourteen. Paul looked at himself in my tall mirror.

'Can I wear this uniform today, and let you have it back tomorrow?'

'You have overlooked something, young man.'

'What, then?'

'I'll say it again. You have overlooked something, young man.'

There was a nudge and a wink from Stephen.

'Sorry, sergeant. Can I wear this uniform today, and let you have it back tomorrow?' then a pause, 'Er, sergeant.'

'Well, it is not your uniform, and you are not really entitled to wear it until you get enrolled and issued with an ATC uniform from the stores, but I'll break the rules only on certain conditions, and only until tomorrow morning.'

'What's that?' then another pause, 'Er, sergeant.'

'Condition one is that you join the ATC before the end of next week. Condition two is that your brother also wears his uniform today, and condition three is that you both go to school or college tomorrow in your usual clothes. Condition four is that you both put on your uniforms tomorrow evening to let me have a look to see if they are correct. How about that?'

They looked at each other. By their facial expressions, they were exchanging messages of approval.

'Yes, sergeant.'

We shook hands. Stephen thanked me most sincerely for my assistance and said that he felt much happier about things now, and Paul thanked me for the enjoyable afternoon and hoped that the ATC would accept him. They left a few moments later to break the news to their parents. For me, there was just one thing outstanding from the afternoon's events. In the process of changing, Stephen had left his money behind, so it presented me with a wonderful opportunity to go next door and return it. I wanted an excuse to see the reaction there. The whole family were pleased with the results, and they were loving every minute of it.

My next aim was to get home from the office a little later that usual on Monday evening. It would create some tension until I arrived, and it would give them time to sort themselves out before I had a look at how they had dressed themselves. I actually got home much later than I had intended. I had been asked to stay on at the office to help with an urgent task and I did not get home until eight o'clock. My father had kept them entertained for a while and he had taken it into his head to do an inspection himself. I did it again and came to the same conclusions. We were both impressed. Theirs were better than my initial attempts when I first joined.

Two things were certain in my cadet life. First, whenever I went off to an ATC camp, Tony always managed to find a good reason not to go. Whenever he suspected that there might be an initiation procedure or similar, then he probably had a good reason for avoiding such things but initiations usually only happened once. They put the fear of God into you at the time but you knew where you stood afterwards. The second certainty that I had come to accept was a visit from Tony, usually just after I arrived home, to catch up on the latest news.

Tony had been a member of the Sea Cadets for most of the year. There were no initiations there, except that he failed to foresee that he would be thrown into the water when they discovered that he could not swim, but that fact was kept very quiet both before and after the event. Now Tony had decided to leave the Sea Cadets, and I had the feeling that he thought he was now qualified to join the Navy. It had always been one of his declared ambitions in life and he had tended to keep me in the dark about the progress of his application to join. On this occasion, as he banged out his usual rhythm on the door knocker he was waving a bunch of papers at me to prove that he was off to sea almost immediately. I did not tell him that he would not come into contact with the sea for some weeks, and that he was more likely to come into contact with cleaning materials and parade grounds first. Tony was good at volunteering for anything that sounded thrilling, but he often found out about the details the hard way and sometimes when it was too late. I was sure that the Navy was in this category, although he would, in any case, have to undertake his National Service somewhere. One evening my mother called to me from the lounge, which sent me running in to see Tony with a girl round his arm. Was she the reason for his having made himself scarce recently?

On a Friday morning not long after this, I was startled by the belabouring of the door knocker. A glance at my clock showed me that it was just seven o'clock. I was still in bed but was awake and thinking of food. My father had left early for work and mother was in the kitchen preparing breakfast for the rest of the household. She left the caller to be dealt with by me, knowing that this was a very efficient way of getting me out of bed. When I opened the door I found there were two visitors. Tony was there, with a suitcase, to say his last goodbyes to us. I could not understand why he was going on a Friday, until I saw his girl wandering along the footpath too. I hazarded a guess that they had arranged some joint weekend accommodation, and he planned to put himself into the hands of the Navy on Monday morning. I wished him the best of luck in his new career and could not help myself thinking that it would soon sort him out. The other visitor at the door was Stephen. He waited very patiently on one side, until I had disposed of Tony. I knew that it was his day for parade at college.

'Do I look all right, sergeant?'

He stood there, not quite at attention, but near enough for this occasion. The CCF would not miss that detail. For a first solo attempt at wearing a uniform, it was not bad at all.

'In the circumstances it's passable, and there are bound to be lots of worried cadets looking far worse than you.'

'Thank you, sergeant.'

'And if there are problems today, then we'll make it Saturday morning in your house this time. Go and buy some blanco, some boot polish and brass cleaner, and make it nine o'clock and no later.'

'Yes, sergeant. Thanks a lot.'

On Saturday morning, Stephen had spread all his purchases out in his bedroom. Paul watched while Stephen cleaned. Paul kept on talking incessantly on ATC matters. He had been to the squadron on Thursday and had been given a form to fill in, and had since developed even more enthusiasm. By midday Stephen had done a good job and his dad wanted to view the final result. He was sent up to his bedroom to dress himself, and came back looking very smart. Stephen viewed himself in the mirror. His dad, Paul and I searched for any imperfections, but there was almost nothing to criticise.

'Now, Stephen, you look jolly smart, but I want you to think about what the rules say. First, the written rules require you to salute when you meet officers, and to be correctly dressed when in uniform. And you've got to act in an honourable way. Then there is a rule about standing at attention when you speak to those senior to you.'

He tried harder to stand to attention.

'Yes, sergeant.'

'We also have rules which require you to look after the King's uniform. That means maintaining it at the standard that you have now, or better. In my squadron there is an unwritten rule for ATC cadets which requires that once you have put on your uniform, you are expected to wear it for the rest of the day. For CCF cadets, it may be different.'

'But, I'm going out with my girlfriend after lunch.'

'Then I expect she will think that you look very smart but if the CCF have got different rules, then you will have to comply with those.'

'Do I have to, sergeant?'

'Yes.' His dad said that before I did.

'But, but, oh, sod it. All right then, you win.'

Stephen was not pleased. His father had asked some questions at college and the answer he received from them still left some room for doubt, but he could not escape the demands of the CCF, college or his father very easily.

He was well and truly stuck with the CCF for a couple of years. He asked me to stay for lunch, which I gratefully accepted, and his girlfriend called to collect him just as the washing up was finished. He suddenly became top of the popularity list when he opened the door to her, but Stephen was blushing quite seriously as he walked down the road.

The plans for the Battle of Britain display at Manston were in place. All except one cadet in the band had paid for the weekend. My boss clearly understood another of my carefully worded requests for a Friday off work, and those who were at school either had an arrangement with their masters or would play truant. Paul, who was the most recent cadet to have a uniform and having heard about the event, had engineered himself a place as well. He was not a good musician yet, but had promised to be helpful if there was anything that he could do. I had discussed the matter with my CO and we had agreed that there was often a need for someone in the wings, even if it was just to fetch or retrieve a piece of music. There was a spare bed at Manston and a vacant seat on the coach, so Paul was rather pleased to be accepted. I strongly suspected that his real reason for wanting to attend was quite different. At the time of getting his uniform, he made a very polite and firm request to the stores officer for some white webbing as he wanted to join the band, so it may have been the urge to show off.

The band had been working hard in the evenings, practising for the event, and I had the music sorted. In the bottom of the box of music I put a few spare items of uniform which, by tradition or incompetence, often went missing at a difficult moment. The CO was concerned about any recurrence of cadets drinking in the NAAFI and its later effects. The cadets who were in the band were generally much older than the average cadet who came to the last Manston camp. He had decreed that cadets were not to take any civilian clothes with them. He even found a supply of khaki army shirts to go under our tunics, and he personally inspected our bags for any sign of non-uniform wear that could possibly go over our outer clothing to disguise the fact that we were cadets. He had written to several of the places that supplied alcohol to make sure that boys dressed in cadet uniforms were not served, and he took the precaution of briefing us about the problem some days in advance.

Paul came knocking on the door almost an hour earlier than was necessary, looking as smart as his brother did. After a final check of band instruments and other kit, we were on our way by midday. The young damsels in the many shopping areas on the way were just as thrilled to see us as we were to see them. The windows of the coach could be lowered and there were occasional contacts with female hands when the coach was going slowly enough. Then there were the rugby songs that could not be sung on a railway train for fear of giving offence, but were ideal in the coach while travelling in rural areas. I think that Paul was at first quite shocked by all this but he soon learnt the words. Manston came into view and I recognised the timber billets from the previous visit. It was already bringing back fond memories. The kitchen had ceased serving food to the airmen, but we were expected and there was sufficient set aside for a lot of hungry cadets, four warrant officers and the CO. There was an almost empty building next door and that was the venue for yet another rehearsal. It took up most of the evening, so the NAAFI and the associated drinking problem did not have any chance to raise its head.

The great day had arrived. We went to breakfast and we were recognised by several airmen, from our previous visit. They sat down with us in the airmen's mess and we explained about our duties for the weekend. I don't know how it all started, but the conversation got round to the NAAFI and its problem with our cadets getting drunk at the bar. It had not only happened during our particular week at camp, but had being going on for months. I listened to the conversation from a safe distance, making good use of one advantage that I had. My ears had plagued me for years, resulting in my being completely deaf at one stage in my life, and that was when I learnt to lip read. The problem had since been cured, but thanks to my secret skill I was able to understand parts of the conversation, including the few odd words that were drowned by background noise. The airmen knew all about cadets and their lady friends, and the ones who were getting into trouble were said to be those who were there for an overnight stay.

My flight-lieutenant uncle was sure to be around, so I decided to leave a message that I might not be returning to the billet until mid-morning and went to station headquarters in search of him. I knocked on his office door and was invited in by an apathetic murmur. As soon as I had completed the routine of making my military presence known, he became of a better disposition. He invited me to sit in that luxury armchair again. I had felt rather uncomfortable in that last time, so I declined with what little tact I could muster, adding that I was pushed for time. I stood to attention and reported what I had heard, adding that if the cadets went near the NAAFI that night they might be set up to take the blame for something and the problem would continue. He thanked me for the information and I left.

In the event I had not been missed. In the billet the cadets were carrying out lots of odd jobs, in preparation for our afternoon performance. We had a wonderful selection of music available and the band looked impressive. There was the usual selection of food at lunch time. A raised platform had been built as a bandstand overlooking the main arena and runway. Paul had made himself useful doing odd jobs, then later on voluntarily became a very effective publicity man among a crowd of people whose interest was in music rather than flying. Our rehearsals had paid off and the music was going well. Then we started one of the preludes by Chopin that were usually played on a piano, but had been adapted for brass band. This one needed very careful concentration. It had started very well, when suddenly there was an almighty bang from somewhere behind us, not too far away. I noticed a look of horror on the CO's face as he continued conducting. At the earliest opportunity we turned round to see a mighty column of black smoke. Then we heard the bells of the emergency services, between the public announcements that the show would continue, while the rescue operation took place around a crashed Mosquito. It was a very sad interruption to an otherwise wonderful day.

On the way back for tea we tried to approach the crash site to have a better look but to no avail, so we devoured our evening meal without further delay. We were not looking forward to an evening without entertainment but then things changed in a most unexpected way. Our CO had arrived in the billet. He told us that in the accident the crew were believed to have been killed and some spectators had been taken to hospital but there was no positive information about their condition. Now there were two things of importance. The first was that the warrant officers had a number of sacks with them, and the police needed some help in searching the area to recover any personal property or aircraft parts. The second was that he needed two smart cadets for a special job that he would explain later. He chose Malcolm Gibbs and Corporal Richard Maynard, and then added me to the group as an afterthought. We were to wait behind until he was ready.

We waited. Four men and five cadets came into the billet and our CO and my uncle followed. They locked the outside door behind them. My uncle spoke first.

'Thank you all for coming. I accept that you don't know what this is all about, but we have information that there are some illegal dealings going on in the NAAFI and we have a chance tonight to sort the matter out. What I want the cadets to do is to occupy two tables as far away from the bar as possible and preferably partly out of sight of it. The rest of you know where you are to be. I want the cadets to go to the bar, not all at once, buy beer and take it back to your table. If, after that, you get offered more drinks, then accept them too. You will find that when you get back to your table, one of these four gentlemen will remove the drink that you have bought and replace it by a drink that looks like beer. It will be a cordial that is OK for you to drink, so treat it like any normal drink, preferably just within sight of the bar. Then leave the rest to us.'

We waited around for a considerable time and asked lots of questions while we waited, but our suspicions were that what was being sold as beer over the bar was not beer at all. Something potent was also being added to the beer sold to the cadets to upset their stomachs. This had drawn attention to the cadets who therefore took the blame for much more serious matters involving the young girls.

It was almost dark when we got to the NAAFI. Our purchases were being carefully exchanged by the four detectives who intended to have them analysed later on. It all went according to plan, and we were supplied with a vast quantity of soft drinks.

Much later in the evening, we met up with the cadets who had been searching for debris. They brought back the news that at least seven other people were known to have been killed in the accident, in addition to the crew, and several cars and two other Mosquitoes were also involved. Those cadets who had a telephone at home were advised to ring their parents to let them know that they were safe.

Most of us got back to bed later than usual that evening, and consequently were not up early enough to get to breakfast. The warrant officer knew of a local café that was open on Sundays. It was prepared to cook a big breakfast, so the official place of eating was abandoned in favour of 'Dirty Dick's'. When we returned, the band was wanted immediately to accompany hymns in the station church. I took a slightly different view of proceedings in church after our visit. Above all, we got a mention for the quality of our music and for helping the police with the aftermath of the accident. However, nothing was said about our visit to the NAAFI, so perhaps that would appear in a forthcoming report in the local press.

Our transport was waiting for us soon after lunch but before the handbrake was released the station commander stepped aboard and thanked us for the music and for helping the police in more that one job. He said he was sorry that we did not have much time to ourselves, but he would write to our CO about that.

24
The aftermath

All was very quiet for a week or so after the Battle of Britain weekend at Manston. I was rather glad about that, as it allowed me to divert my activities towards my homework and it gave me further opportunities to see Betty. I was able to enjoy a few late nights with some extended sessions of loving cuddles, and the consequent dubious pleasure of missing the last bus with a two-mile walk home.

Fridays were pleasant and I always looked forward to a change in routine more than anything else. It so happened that one Friday, on the last stage of my journey home from work, I met Stephen at the bus stop. He looked fairly miserable and seemed unwilling to continue any of the topics of conversation that I started. It was not until we got off the bus that he felt that he was able to pour out the day's troubles. The problem had started at home when he could not find his beret, so he took a chance and went off to college without wearing one, hoping that he could find a replacement when he got there. Unfortunately for him, the sergeant-major could not avoid noticing it as soon as he got off the train and he made him pay for another one, adding on an exorbitant price for the badge. In the afternoon he discovered that the sergeant-major continued to be seriously upset about the missing beret, berating the fact that incidents like this were not supposed to happen in the organised environment of a private college. Stephen was not the only defaulter. Several other cadets were lectured on the requirements of the King's Regulations and the misuse and loss of government equipment. There was an effective reminder service in operation which usually ensured that there was no recurrence of the problem. Every day for the following two weeks all the defaulters were required to get to college thirty minutes earlier than usual, in uniform, and to provide an armed sentry at the gate. Stephen did not mind wearing his uniform, but it was the earlier start that would upset his regular morning routine. The sergeant-major had told them that if there were any similar problems, the punishments would get more serious until they showed some effect. I made soothing noises about his predicament, but inwardly hoped that he would understand that this military experience was just as important as his college work. I learnt afterwards that Paul thought it was terribly amusing and his mother had to intervene in what was becoming a serious conflict between them.

I parted company with him at the front gate, to find that there were two letters on the table waiting for me. Both had my name and address written rather haphazardly on them, with postage stamps that had been aimed at the corner of the envelope instead of being carefully attached. One was from Tony, headed with his military address. It was more a muddle of words rather than a series of logical sentences. Once I deciphered it, I discovered that it gave his account of what the Navy was like. I was right about the drill and cleaning, because I knew that it was true of the introduction to any military organisation. He had not seen a ship yet, but there were some nice pictures of them around. He had yet to get to grips with naval terminology, judging by the crossings out and the replacement words in another handwriting in his letter. It seemed that 'heads', 'galley', 'bulkhead' and 'aft' were not yet properly installed in his vocabulary. The last page was a sorry tale of no women and the fervent wish to be home again. I had no sympathy whatever. He volunteered, it was his avowed ambition and he had declared his allegiance to King and Country. It was also his compulsory contribution in accordance with the National Service Act.

The contents of the second envelope on the table was more of an invitation than a letter. It was from Private Ronnie Williams. He had started making plans for a party on 26 December, though it was yet several months away. It would be at a club in Poplar. He proposed to invite all of his friends for a special occasion and Betty and I were included. There was a hint that the invitation list included an awful lot of people. I had no clue what the special occasion might be, so I went across the road to number 5 to enquire from his parents. They had had a similar invitation in the post and were not sure either, so the mystery remained.

It was a night that I ought to have gone to the squadron. I deliberated for a while and finally decided. It was a bit late but I got there. There was a notice on the board with a couple of letters and newspaper cuttings giving an account of the accident at Manston. Other than the crew members of the three aircraft involved, twelve civilians had been killed. Among the letters was one from the station commander thanking us again most sincerely for the services of the band and enclosing a cheque for our funds. He also thanked us for helping with the problems in the NAAFI. After his internal investigation, he confirmed that there was to be no criticism of the cadet services and that he had taken 'appropriate action' with his staff. The actual wording left us to guess the details, but the words that followed illustrated his confidence in the ATC, and our squadron in particular. The letter ended with an open invitation for us to go to Manston again. Next to it was a letter from the police, thanking us for our work in searching the area after the accident, and enclosing a further cheque.

In due course, Ronnie's formal invitation arrived. It was a bit too grand to be a mere sampling of the local intoxicants of the Poplar area. At the bottom of the invitation card, where one would normally put 'RSVP', was written:

Dress
Uniform for members of HM Forces and Cadets
Other male guests – lounge suit
Ladies – optional

Then there was another handwritten note:

'I shall be ever so upset if you miss this one, and it's your only chance.'

There was a small wad of invitations in the envelope and a loose piece of paper torn from a notebook, asking me to distribute them as I thought fit, and amongst as many of his friends as I knew. I thought it must be something important as I could not imagine Ronnie having everything so formal, with the request for uniform and a note almost demanding our attendance. But neither could it be a dance with refreshments. When I read the invitation for the third and fourth time, I could not understand the stipulation of a lounge suit, as that was quite out of keeping with Ronnie's style of dress. It certainly had a positive military touch about it. But he was only a soldier, and that in itself was not usually a cause for celebration. It could have been a simple party if it was not for the great emphasis on formality.

I went across the road to number 5 again and asked his mother about Ronnie's friends. She was not sure but, after a search of his bedroom, eventually produced a list from some notes that he had left behind when on leave. Tony and Betty both appeared on the list, with some other local names and addresses that I did not recognise. I was now more confused than ever. Was this list only of friends, or did it include names which were known to him and not necessarily his close friends? His mother was even less sure now. We agreed that invitations should certainly go to Tony and our respective lady friends. His mother decided to write back to him to clarify the matter, but after two weeks there had not been a reply.

✳ ✳ ✳

It was not a very active Christmas. We were invited to our most recent neighbours next door for lunch, and they came back to us in the evening to try to make some headway into the food that was left over. Tony turned up later in the afternoon, full of life and jollity and looking much fitter than he had ever been. We were instantly briefed on the history and fate of Admiral Nelson. Stephen, Tony and I spent most of the time comparing our military notes and experiences, with Paul taking a lot of interest and perhaps wishing that he was much older. Tony seemed to have acquired a degree of maturity in his conversation and I could only presume that the effect of joining the Navy was beginning to produce results. There was no clue that he disliked it, but neither was there any comment about how good it was. On the other hand, Stephen could not stop talking about college. He thought that it was great and he was getting on well in his studies. He now liked the cadet unit so much that he thought that being in the CCF was the best thing that had ever happened to him. We all quietly enjoyed ourselves until we almost fell asleep and by midnight all except my father were in bed.

One of the remarkable curiosities of the calendar, as it is applied in Britain, is that Boxing Day traditionally never falls on a Sunday. On this intermediate day of 26 December I woke up with nothing on my mind except the thrill of Ronnie's forthcoming party, and nothing on my body except a pair of shorts. It was frosty outside and I decided that, while the rest of the area was still recovering from Christmas Day, this morning I was going to be a man. I added a vest and a pair of plimsolls to my attire then went straight from the bedroom for a run round the local roads. When I got back my father told me that I was mad. I knew that already, so in an effort to emphasise the point, I did another lap. When I returned for the second time, I found my father muttering away about the problems of the younger generation while watching my mother clearing out the grate and trying to light the fire with wood and coal. My father did not really approve of all this activity, and we argued until he admitted that such things had always been well beyond his level of fitness. By then, breakfast had been delivered to the table so, just to annoy my father a little more, I got stuck into the eggs and bacon, still dressed in next to nothing. Breakfast was excellent and especially welcome after all that physical effort. The rays of the sun had percolated through the obstructions to form shadows on the wall and I felt like getting up to mischief. I whipped my vest off.

'Look, Father.'

My father reluctantly looked round.

'Look. There's another hair on my chest this morning. I'm a man now. That's five hairs to date.'

My father did not say a word. It might have been that he was fast becoming convinced that I was getting worse. I went upstairs and had a long look at that big bare body, with its the fifth hair, in the mirror. I wondered when the letter would drop through the door telling me to report for National Service. The body in the mirror was physically ready for them now, even though my brain might not like the idea. I had another dose of self-admiration, then scrounged a second cup of tea from the kitchen.

Betty arrived in time for mid-morning refreshment. I grabbed her with those uncovered arms and fixed her in place against my five-haired chest to give her a big, he-man kiss. She liked that. We had time for lots of confidential chatting before some further remains of the Christmas fare were eaten. Tony, our most recent square-basher, delayed his arrival until after lunch. Before I dressed myself properly, I went for another run round the block. We left home for the station to make our way to Poplar. Beyond the City of London limits the area was still rather unfamiliar to me, but by following Ronnie's precise directions and keeping Tony well away from them, we arrived at the right place. The large hall had its boundary walls against a public house on one side and a very dubious looking general shop on the other side. Across the road, tucked in a corner next to a terrace of houses, was something halfway between a market stall and a garden shed advertising eels, pie and mash all alleged to be instantly fit for human consumption. I was not sure that I liked eels and I decided I should have to steer Tony away from this source of food.

Once through the heavy oak doors, I was impressed by the inside of the hall, adorned as it was by ancient joinery, marine pictures and oriental inscriptions. It had a distinguished atmosphere, with a high roof in the style of a church. The gas lamps had been retained to light the place, and a chandelier hung from a timber beam at the centre of the roof structure. There were a few early arrivals and some people were busying themselves with the task of catering, but there was no sign at all of Ronnie. Most guests wore military uniforms of some kind, and stood around the edge of the hall in little groups, talking amongst themselves. Non-alcoholic drinks were on offer by the apparent organiser of the catering. At about five o'clock, the doors were pushed open and more bodies arrived. Someone stood on a chair and announced that drinks were now available, and once the show was over there would be food as well. Chairs were distributed round the outside of the hall, and the gas lamps were dimmed.

Music, complete with loud scratching noises, came from an old pre-war gramophone which needed to be wound up at intervals by a very active elderly lady who looked as if she was enjoying the task. Then the dancing girls arrived and the entertainment was first rate. I dared not look at Betty too openly as the almost bare females leapt and danced around the floor in time with the music. One by one they added frilly adornments to themselves, throwing us kisses from a distance and gradually getting dangerously near as the dancing progressed. It ended with a barrage of real wet kisses before the theme suddenly changed from dancing to an impressive juggling act. When the jugglers eventually dispersed, we saw a young dark-skinned boy sitting cross-legged on the floor with several snakes round his body and with his partner playing an oriental pipe. This was a rare sight for us and these two held us spellbound for a long time. Their smiles drove away any doubts that I ever had about associations with coloured people from abroad. Then the girls returned and persuaded us to move into an adjoining part of the hall where Ronnie was standing on a platform.

As soon as he had the attention of the assembled company, he started by thanking us all for coming. He wanted this to be a military occasion, and it was for that reason that we had been asked to come in uniform. Up until that time, he told us, he had helped his father in the market, but he did not want to do that for the rest of his life, despite the fact that he had made lots of friends there. He was now involved with the Army and was doing his National Service. It had been interesting so far, but he had been thinking about the day that it would end and had been considering his long-term plans and the many alternatives open to him. He liked the Army so he had decided to make a career of it and, while he had been making these deliberations, it so happened that he had met Pat. He told us that Pat had volunteered for the Army, having seen some problems developing at home and urgently wanting to get away from it all. She was hoping to get lots of practical experience with not much housework. Pat joined Ronnie on the stage, and they announced their engagement. They had told their parents on Christmas Day, and today had been earmarked for the celebrations. Then Ronnie announced that the food and drink were ready, and we were invited to do something about it. The elderly lady had since moved from the gramophone and was now seated at a piano, tinkling away at some popular tunes. Ronnie and Pat circulated amongst their guests, in the way that good hosts do, and made a point of introducing people as far as possible.

Tony was on the other side of the hall, where he had discovered several bodies dressed in naval uniform. They were very intent on a serious conversation. Meanwhile, Betty and I were each dealing with a large sausage and a few other delightful morsels of food, when Ronnie and Pat headed in our direction. Betty and Pat went off to have their own conversation about feminine matters, so I was invited by Ronnie to accompany him on his rounds. In each group of people that we met, most had a story to tell about the war. It was a mix of their personal disasters, funny stories and renewed encounters with their friends. I was not a great lover of beer in anything other than moderate quantities and, having been presented with half a pint, I wanted what was in my glass to last a long time to avoid a refill. I quickly worked out that asking people for details of their wartime experiences kept me clear of top-ups.

I was offered a cigarette but politely declined. Many years previously I had seen an uncle puffing away continuously at cigarettes, punctuated by intervals of excessive coughing, and I could see no point in getting into that state of health. However, I was fascinated for a time with the rising smoke and the way it curled around in the currents of air. While I was admiring the patterns, Ronnie had moved on and I came back to reality to find myself surrounded by a group of people who at first I took to be soldiers, but after some self introductions it was clear that I was among a party of Royal Marines. They were very inquisitive about my status as a cadet at the age of eighteen. I tried to explain why I had not been called up for National Service and I was persuaded to prove the point by producing the necessary documents. These were in my pocket and were inspected thoroughly, but they did not appear to be convinced that all was well. I decided to make my excuses and found Ronnie again. Ronnie's father was close at hand and he and I started talking about the much safer subjects of market trading and Ronnie's engagement to Pat. From some distance across the hall, I detected that the group of marines still seemed to be bothered about the matter of my call-up and at intervals they looked in my direction. I concluded that they were probably talking about me. I felt at risk and rather uncomfortable, and I was trying to make up my mind between going across the hall to meet them again, in the hope that it might relieve the visual tension, or ignoring them in the hope that the problem would go away. Once, as I glanced involuntarily in their direction, I saw one of them beckoning me with a single finger. Well, that was the decision made for me.

As I approached, the one who had called me broke away from the rest of the group and headed towards a side door and into a small room.

'Did you want me?' I asked rather innocently.

'Yes, young man.'

I had my back to the wall, and I was looking straight ahead, with a view of not much more than the top of his tunic, two collar badges and a rather bright gas lamp in the background.

'We are concerned that you said that you had registered a good time ago, yet you have not been called up.'

'Yes, that's right.'

The group of marines gathered round.

'This gentleman here was particularly interested.'

He pointed out one of the group who looked much older than the rest of them. He was dressed very well for the occasion. The others cleared a space for him. This was going to be a time for being polite and correct.

'I am an officer in the same regiment as Williams.'

I interrupted his conversation for a moment to salute.

'Thank you, sergeant. Why do you think that you have not been called up yet?'

I had to be careful about this answer.

'Probably because they have not got round to it yet. There are no complications to my knowledge.'

'Then may I have a look at your papers please?'

I took them out of my tunic pocket for the second time that evening and presented them to him. There was not really much to look at. They were inspected with great care as if a forgery was suspected. Eventually, he looked for the marine who had called me over.

'It looks all right to me. Quite genuine and correct.'

That was a relief. It was most unlikely, but I had the horrible memory of Ronnie having been arrested in his first encounter with the Army and hoping that I was not going the same way.

'Thank you for your time, sergeant. I hope that you and your lady enjoy the rest of the evening.'

They all went out into the main hall except the marine who initially beckoned me and was now barring the way between me and the door. There was a pause while he looked as if he was trying to pick out the right words.

'I'm sorry about the enquiry, but we were tipped off that there might have been several absent-without-leave servicemen about. Our role is to investigate absentees, and by chance I had an invitation from Ronnie. I had the misfortune to live near him when his home was demolished by a bomb. In my house I was the only survivor, so I joined up at once as the only way to carry on living away from all the resulting problems.'

'Thanks for letting me know. I'm very sorry to hear about your family.'

I thought that had concluded the matter, but he wanted to tell me more. He had been a cadet too. He had joined the Army Cadets, but he did not really like it. Now that he was in the Royal Marines, it was all very different. His parting words as I left that room were that he would like to meet me again, and in the Royal Marines if possible. We exchanged addresses before I left him to go in search of Betty.

I found her among a jolly group of Ronnie's friends, all with full glasses of beer. Betty felt that she ought to be on her way home soon, and I agreed with her. Tony was found with an unmanageably drunken female hanging on to him and, although conversation was difficult, it was his intention to stay there for the night. Betty and I thanked Ronnie for his hospitality and left to go home.

Public transport, even during the late evening, was still running quite frequently and would be for several hours yet, so there was no particular point in hurrying. It was my first encounter with the Commercial Road by night and I was concerned about our safety, having heard awful stories of criminal activity in that part of London. The gliding of the trolleybus over the cobbled road was remarkably smooth and reassuring. By contrast, the public houses looked dangerous but they were all on the other side of the glass window, and it was nowhere near closing time yet. I considered the underground train to be home territory and I felt even more relaxed. Betty snuggled up to me and I was thinking how comfortable it all was, but a stray thought cut through the pleasant things of life and brought back those comments about the Royal Marines. When I had a moment, I needed to find out more about that. I accompanied Betty home safely and handed her over to her grateful parents. Her father kindly got his car out to take me on the last stage of my journey. I walked from his car to my bedroom without turning on the light or making a noise, so my parents were not disturbed. They must both have been fairly deeply asleep if they were not aware of one pair of boots proceeding along the footpath towards the front door.

In the morning, my mother was very relieved to find me among the bedclothes, without any signs of damage. She admitted that I was old enough to look after myself, but that had not stopped her worrying about Betty and me. The time was almost nine o'clock and the drowsiness was quickly passing. I felt fit again, and I decided that I was going to take another run round the block before breakfast. My mother looked me up and down, once again in my bare running necessities, and consequently announced that food would be on the table in about half an hour. That meant that she did not want me to do more than a half-hour stint of serious running. I turned the lock on the front door and found that an icy blast of air was pressing hard from the other side. My mother shouted at me to shut the front door quickly, before the draught extinguished the flame in the oven. The unusual urgency in her voice prompted me to do just that and I went outside to brave the weather. Now I was faced with only one option, which was to run and keep warm in accordance with my first decision. It was a fight now, as I was running against the wind. I slowed down slightly outside number 19 to see if there was any sign of Tony, but not a light showed. I always found that running occupied my body, leaving my mind free for some basic thinking. My thoughts returned to that marine at the party who had hinted that I join the Royal Marines. I had learned that marines had to be fit, so perhaps this occasional urge to run around in the cold might do me some good. I wondered what else the marines did for the benefit of the country. Perhaps I ought to find out, just in case it became an acceptable alternative to the RAF or Army.

On the way home I made a careful survey of the Williams property at number 5. A second careful look led me to detect a slight movement of the upstairs curtains. I was seriously considering knocking at the door when I heard Paul's voice. He had heard me shutting my front door and had admired my eagerness as I went up the road earlier, and he now wanted me to accompany him on a second lap. I really was looking forward to food just then, but Paul was a cadet and I could not possibly refuse his request. It eventually made the demolition of a fried breakfast even more satisfying, and my father was at last getting used to the idea that he was going to see much more of his athletic son at times of communal family breakfasts.

After lunch, I wondered where Tony had got to. I knocked at number 19 and a bleary-eyed Tony answered the door. Some kind, reasonably sober person had dumped him on his front door step during the early hours, and his parents had dragged him inside and laid him out on the carpet. The family had not long been awake and Tony was beginning to realise what kind of a state he was in. He said that he was due to return to his ship on the following day, and there was a uniform to be cleaned before then. The cleaning job was being assessed as I knocked on the door. I queried his reference to a ship, as I had really had the impression that he had been committed to basic training at a shore establishment until then. He corrected me quickly and pointed out that nearly every place of work in the Navy is called a ship, whether it floats or not. When I left him he was in the final stages of brushing his trousers and not in need of any further help.

I had another sudden urge for more fitness and I went in search of Paul. His father answered the door and my simple request got Paul away from reading a book. He was not very keen to go running again but his father had heard my invitation and had decided to convert it into an order. Paul gave up after one lap round the block. I wanted to keep going but after the second lap the effort defeated me as well. It had to wait for another day. I was due at the office the next day and was not really looking forward to it, even though it was only a few days until another minor celebration at the New Year.

25

New experiences

Nothing dramatic happened in the early months of 1949, not even a letter from Tony or Ronnie. I was back in the routine of going to work to earn money, leaving home in the cold and dark hours of the morning and getting home from evening classes on at least two evenings a week long after the sun had shown its last rays of light. Even my enthusiastic runs round the block were slotted into an odd hour on Saturday or Sunday. Going to the squadron was a very welcome relief to the weekly routine and I put in as much effort as I could spare in this direction. It came like a breath of fresh air when another very experienced warrant officer joined the squadron. He had been in the RAF but they had severed his connections with the service when he was no longer required. However, they had sold him the idea of helping a cadet unit. We all felt that the RAF was much nearer to us now. Our drill and discipline had always been of a fairly high standard but he added something extra, and we noticed the difference and were proud of it. There had been a noticeable reduction in the number of cadets wishing to join, mainly due to the feeling that the world was becoming more peaceful and the male love for joining a military organisation was declining. The presence of our new officer had arrested this trend slightly, and the squadron was a happy place.

A message appeared on the squadron notice board, signed by the new warrant officer, requiring all NCOs to attend on a particular Sunday morning. I thought it prudent to make that extra little bit of effort, and it was clear that many others had felt the same. We were directed into a classroom where the chairs and most of the tables had been folded and stacked on one side. The senior NCO had quite correctly assumed that he was expected to assemble us in three ranks, ready for the warrant officer's arrival. That was quite unusual in a classroom because it had always been assumed that timber floor could not survive the impact of so many boots hitting it at the same time. The explanation was soon forthcoming as the warrant officer made it very clear that as NCOs our discipline was expected to be outstanding and only the best would do. For this reason, he had insisted that this class was going to stand while he was talking. He told us about some new orders concerning uniforms. The squadron now had sufficient supplies of berets to replace the forage caps, and there had been a recent delivery of greatcoats to the stores. Both of these items had previously been issued for special occasions only, but were now to be issued to NCOs before becoming general issue to the rest of the cadets. For us, this would take effect within the next few hours. Then, when the changeover was complete, there would be drill, if only to show the cadets how perfect he expected them to be. He also wanted to seek our opinion on boots. Successive commanding officers had identified that there had been a reasonable local source of studded boots over the years, and had ordered that they were worn. The regulations also allowed shoes to be worn, subject to them complying with an authorised pattern. Did we like what we had on our feet or would we prefer a change? The last matter concerned an initiative test for NCOs only. It might take up to four days and could require some time off school or work. No other details were going to be available, except that we all had to take part but not necessarily at the same time. The choice of date was ours and the application forms were on the one remaining unfolded table at the back of the classroom. He left us standing in the classroom and took the flight-sergeant outside.

Our audience of cadets was in place when the NCOs marched on to the parade ground, resplendent with the new items of uniform. This certainly concentrated my mind on what I was doing, as any little imperfection would surely be criticised by the cadets. We felt very satisfied with the results after half an hour. When the warrant officer got us back into the classroom again, he first congratulated us on our drill, and told us that it was his intention that all the cadets would be to the same standard by the end of the month. Then he brought up the subject of the wearing of boots. Only one NCO had not decided. The rest of us wanted to continue as the squadron had done since 1941. Our view was that shoes would not provide sufficient ankle support, would be a soft option and we would not be able to hear our heels hitting the ground at every step, from which we concluded that our drill standards would eventually suffer. He decreed that the one undecided NCO would also comply. We had discussed the matter briefly among ourselves while the new supplies of berets and greatcoats were being issued, and the change from boots to shoes was not at all popular. We still wanted to feel more like the real old-fashioned style of serviceman. That ended his morning's work and we were free to go.

Within the next few weeks, all the NCOs had decided on dates for their initiative test, and written permissions from our parents were being submitted. I decided that I would get my father's permission, mainly because he liked volunteering me for things like that. I had managed to scrounge a week off work on the days following the Easter weekend. It would fall within the period that college was closed, and it gave me a weekend to recover if I needed it.

Two weeks before the event I was required at the squadron on a Saturday afternoon for the details to be sorted out. Corporal Barry Jenkins was waiting outside the gate when I arrived. It seemed that he would be my partner for the week, both or us having selected the same dates. We waited for a ten minutes or so for the warrant officer to arrive. This was the first time that I had ever seen him out of uniform, complete with umbrella, trilby hat and briefcase. I looked at Barry and he looked back at me as we saw him coming along the road, and the same thought must have struck us. Were we supposed to be in our civilian clothes today? We had both assumed that anything to do with the cadets required a uniform. It did not seem right otherwise.

'Sir. Were we supposed to be in uniform today?'

'Yes, sergeant. I'm only here to open the gate. You are here to plan your initiative test and get yourself and the corporal organised.'

'Good. We've done it right then.'

He unlocked and we went inside. There was no atmosphere about the place with only the three of us there. It was gloomy and it looked like our garden shed, but without the spiders and the tools and the general mess.

'There you are, then. All the information you need, except your destination, is in the envelope.'

'Thank you, sir.'

'I'm off to make three cups of tea so I'll leave you to it for a while.'

There was a good bundle of paper inside the sealed foolscap envelope. I was surprised to find a map of Great Britain rather than a detailed local map, with separate pages of typed information. On one page was a list of kit needed, one page suggested useful odds and ends to take, one page bore a list of emergency food supplies, and one had a list of things that we must not do. We sat down and read them together. The 'must not do' list was important. It was mainly sensible things aimed at keeping us out of trouble, for example not calling the emergency services unless a real emergency arose. The list of food supplies was quite interesting and nearly impossible under the food rationing regulations that were in place at the time, until we found out that it would be made available for us during the afternoon, together with items on the 'useful odds and ends' list.

The tea came. The warrant officer said that it was free, and one of those perks for such occasions. He said the stores were now open and the kit was there ready for us to take home until the Easter Monday. That did not ring true. We thought that we were off on Tuesday.

'That's right, you report here on Monday. By the time you two get going it will be Tuesday,' he explained. 'Come into the stores when you're ready.'

Having disposed of the tea, we were both eager to get to the stores. Apart from anything else, we saw the chance of being exceptionally inquisitive. Our food and our extra kit were already spread out on two tables. Most of it was packed and of the non-perishable variety. We checked it against the list that we had been given and found that he had left a few things out. There was no 'housewife' set and a bakelite cup was missing. He said that he has purposely left these out to confirm that we had checked. While the warrant officer excused himself to go to the shop for cigarettes, we had a look round the stores and found some badges of interest. The day would eventually come when we might need these, so we left them there but knew who to ask if it became necessary. By the time he returned, now happily smoking, and with the 'housewife' and cup, we had stuffed the last few items into the new issue of webbing.

'Report to me on Monday evening at eight o'clock, with everything clean and correct, with webbing over greatcoats and with two pounds in cash and your documents in your pocket.'

Two pounds was more than my week's wages, but I had a Post Office Savings account from which I could withdraw some money if I ran short.

We were both there on Easter Monday evening in good time, waiting for the final details. I had, over the weekend, been trying to think of what might be in store for us, and had almost worked myself up into a nervous state. I wanted to banish the problem from my mind but could not do so, and it was sometimes difficult to get to sleep at night. The warrant officer called us in to the stores.

'Webbing off. Greatcoats off. Jackets off. Empty your pockets. Put it all on the table.' he ordered.

'Stand at ease. Arms outstretched. Whose beret is that on the table?'

'Mine, sir.'

I was not going to get away with anything now.

'I didn't tell you to take it off.'

'No. Sorry, sir.'

I quickly put it back on again as he did a body search and inspected the contents of my pockets, making really sure that I had no more than £2, and no means to get any more. Then I saw him do a similar search on Barry. He was satisfied and we put our kit back on. The warrant officer had been a senior NCO in the RAF and I had been trained to respect those of higher rank. He was being abrupt and very positive tonight, so standing still and taking on the role of an airman during initial training seemed to be what he was expecting of us. I stood with my back to the stores wall. Barry took the hint and did likewise. The warrant officer eyed us from the other side of the stores, and gave us each an envelope.

'In those envelopes are your detailed instructions. You are going to Edinburgh. There is an address to report to when you get there, and a few telephone numbers in case of difficulty. I shall count out your money when you get back and I shall need an explanation of every penny gained and every penny spent. Any questions?'

I thought for a few moments, then Barry spoke.

'But that must be four hundred miles away.'

'I did not ask for facts. I asked for questions.'

'But how do we get there?'

'Ever heard of initiative?'

'Yes, sir. But...'

'Dismiss. I shall be here for another ten minutes or so, then you are on you own until Friday.'

Barry had had a huge shock to his system. I was not far off it either. We were very silent for a few moments. I had never been to Edinburgh before and neither had Barry. I was beginning to wonder whether my parents had been aware of this when they signed the form giving their permission. Neither Barry nor I was sure about it. I had a vision of mountains, sheep, whisky, peculiar accents, bagpipes and everybody wearing a kilt.

It was now nearly 9.30 p.m. and we had to get going. I was thinking about lots of things. We had clothing and food. We agreed that we needed to look at the map. I took it out of my pocket. I was glad that one of my best subjects at college was geography. London was at the bottom of the map and Scotland at the top, with the A1 between them. We could thumb it up the A1 like servicemen did when they went on leave, thus avoiding having to pay train or coach fares. Unless our badges were studied in great detail, we even looked like genuine poor and underpaid RAF recruits. I put the point to Barry. Although still slightly shocked, he agreed. A fare of 4d each on the bus and we were most of the way to the A1. We walked the remaining mile to a well-lit roundabout. I had been past Apex Corner before. It was a well used thumbing spot. We saw two civilians trying their luck some distance up the road. We asked and they told us that they had been thumbing for fifteen minutes or so. Barry suggested that we stood right by the exit of the roundabout, where traffic was naturally slower and would sweep the footpath with its headlights. A couple of drunken, unshaven chaps stopped first, driving a decrepit old heap of a car. I did not like the idea of travelling with them, so I asked if they were going to Brighton. They took off into the night without a word, torturing the engine and producing a cloud of oily smoke from the exhaust pipe. I dread to think what might have happened if I had mentioned a place that was on their route.

The next vehicle to stop was a van going only ten miles. It was no good for us, but it took away the competition. It was another ten minutes before a lorry stopped. He had to turn the engine off before we could make intelligible conversation. It was certainly not a local accent, but he was going to Hull. Our luck had changed. It was certainly in the right direction and was going to be a great help. Conversation was possible in the cab as the engine noise was reduced with the door shut. It was also pleasantly warm. All was very quiet and uninteresting for a couple of hours, except when we tried to make intelligible conversation with the driver. Somewhere around the Peterborough area, Barry spotted what he thought were the two drunks, with the bonnet of their car open at the side of the road. After that I must have dozed off for a while.

I woke up with a jolt. It was dark outside and the engine noise had ceased. Barry was more awake than I was. The driver announced that he was stopping for breakfast. I rummaged under the thick cuffs of my greatcoat and tunic to peer at the watch that I had earned by passing my college exams. It was nearly 4 a.m., not really a civilised time for a visit to a transport café. However, he was offering us food, and we could not refuse. We followed him through the doors, their hinges squeaking to announce our arrival. I was conscious of many heads looking up from their plates of hot food.

'Where have you parked your aeroplane mate?' came a shout from somewhere in the depths of the feeding masses. Our driver told us that we had saved the country from Jerry and he would be delighted to repay the debt with two big breakfasts. Apart from the overdose of grease, it was much better than my mother's cooking.

After breakfast, our driver stood up and, over the hubbub of the café, asked, 'Anybody with two seats for Edinburgh this morning?' Until then it had not dawned on me that it was Tuesday morning, but it quickly became obvious as I collected my thoughts. There were shouted replies of Carlisle, Geordie-land and Sunderland, but no mention of Edinburgh until a better dressed, inoffensive character came to the table and quietly asked our actual destination in Edinburgh. We looked at our instructions.

'The gate at Edinburgh castle,' I said. He did not bat an eyelid. He said that he would be back in fifteen minutes. On the way out to the lorry park, I noted the registration number and address on the side of the first lorry, with the intention of writing a letter of thanks as soon as I could get to some writing materials.

'Just call me Jock,' said our next driver in a beautiful Scottish accent. We walked with him to a quiet corner where a gleaming Rolls-Royce was parked. This was something that all the cadets in the squadron were going to hear about! We wondered just how it got out of the parking area and up to 60 mph without making a noise. It was now five o'clock in the morning and it would be another hour and a half before we saw daylight. There was absolutely no chance of sleep while I was enjoying the thrill of speeding along the road in such luxury. The first glimmer of daylight came when I spotted a signpost to Barnard Castle. I was going to say something to Barry but he was laying across the rear seat, sleeping soundly. I consulted my map and watch again, and I calculated that we would be in Edinburgh by ten o'clock. We stopped at another café for a cup of tea and other serious necessities of life. I thought it must be my turn to do the buying this time. There was an awful lot of khaki around. They looked really browned off but had their own methods of surviving in there. They clasped their hands round their mugs for warmth and drank hot soup slowly, between bouts of swearing. By the state of their dress, they had been fighting a fictitious battle in the local training area. They did not try to start a conversation so we drank up and got back to the luxury of the Rolls.

Eventually we saw Edinburgh castle towering over the city. The shops were open and we were respectable. We elected to get out and thanked the driver for his help in the last stage of our expedition. That splendid piece of mechanical perfection purred away along Princes Street and out of sight. The guardroom at the castle was our destination. It was more of a climb than we expected and it was almost eleven o'clock before our struggling ceased and we found someone in authority. He knew all about us. No, they were not all wearing kilts and playing their bagpipes. In fact, we considered the place to be respectably normal, except for its outstanding beauty. The keeper at the gate used the telephone without us hearing any of the conversation, and we were asked to wait. The wind was gusty and I realised how practical these berets were, compared to the forage cap that I had recently discarded. Barry still looked tired but within twenty minutes a car arrived, driven by a young lady, with a boy in the passenger seat. Her house was three miles away. The cadet in the car had volunteered her for looking after us until Thursday.

I had to explain carefully that we had already eaten one breakfast somewhere on the A1, and had a cup of tea since then. I was not very hungry and I could certainly wait an hour or so if that was their normal meal time. The cadet introduced himself as Angus, followed by Mc—something or other that I could not quite grasp. He wanted us to have a quick look round the city, before we did anything else. His city tour took us to a little shop not far from the castle. Angus was well known in there and the owner took no persuading at all to make us each a present of some tartan cloth. I was certain that my mother would appreciate that.

Mrs Mc—whatever her name was made us very welcome. She made sure that this initiative exercise was more of a holiday. We were both invited to the squadron that evening. The parade of cadets in kilts looked superb. We asked why the English did not do things like that. There was no answer except that the words 'tradition' and 'national pride' kept coming up. At final parade, the CO made an announcement about our journey between London and Edinburgh and said that we had beaten his two cadets by forty minutes. It was not until then that I had any idea that there was a reciprocal arrangement. We had a lovely evening and a good night's sleep in a stationary bed. Angus took us round more of the tourist attractions during the next two days, including his pet haggis and chip shop for lunch.

Barry and I were both a little bit hesitant about going to their squadron on Thursday evening. Angus was very positive about it and the cadets were on parade much earlier than usual for our benefit. Their CO met us at the entrance and took us straight to his office. We were not quite sure whether it was formal or otherwise.

'Sergeant, I have been authorised to make you an offer. It started off by the squadron suggesting that we ought to present you with something for your outstanding effort in getting here. This has the approval of your own CO. I have here one set of flight-sergeant's stripes and one set of sergeant's stripes for yourself and Corporal Jenkins, but on one condition.'

Barry looked at me with a great smile on his face. He had been desperately after a third stripe for a long time. Barry accepted immediately. I was not going to be beaten by Barry but although my answer was 'yes', we both wanted to know what the condition was. The CO looked amused.

'The condition is that when you go back to London tonight, and on your next parade you will be wearing kilts instead of trousers. If you default then you are going to lose this promotion. Do you understand?'

'Yes, sir.' Came the reply from Barry.

'Flight-sergeant?'

'It's a hard bargain. Yes, sir.'

'Then go into the stores. One of my NCOs will organise it.'

The stores were vast and every shelf was packed to capacity. I did not detect any shortages here. Some delightful little girls had accepted the challenge of sewing on stripes, and we watched as they got going. The storekeeper took charge of our gaiters, trousers and civilian socks and put them in our packs. I had a terrifying thought then. Were my knees clean, and what should I wear under my kilt? I knew about the standard jokes south of the border relating to kilts, but now all was soon to be revealed. It was all well taken care of, and we were released to join the parade amidst cheers from the cadets.

During the middle of the evening we left to make our way home. I had an idea. The first stage of our journey home was to be by bus for a short distance to Princes Street. At the bus station and I found the inspector in his office. I poured out a pathetic story about losing my money in Edinburgh, and I turned out my pockets to prove it. The uniforms helped. Either he had to help with transport to London or we would have to suffer the night trying to scrounge a lift all the way. He felt sorry for us and had a word with a coach driver. There did happen to be some vacant seats, and we could sit on them. It would be over an hour before the coach left and we decided to wander round for a while.

Barry and I walked along the road until we found a seat.

'You're a scheming sod, flight-sergeant.'

'Why?' I said.

'You take on the challenge of this initiative exercise, get to Scotland, get all these gifts and then you persuade an inspector to get us back to London for free.'

'Well, so what. It's initiative.'

'So why didn't I think of that?'

'Easy. It's because you're only a sergeant.'

Barry was speechless for a moment.

'What are we going to do about this kilt I'm wearing?'

'Just wear it. What's the problem?'

Barry protested.

'But I can't go home like this. I shall be a laughing stock.'

'I can go home like it. Just tell the English how stupid they look wearing those trousers. You wear shorts without complaining and what you've now got round your bum is only a different colour. Anyway, we are reporting to the squadron first when we get back. Then we are going to my house for something to eat, then back to the squadron for parade in the evening, depending on the time, of course, both wearing these beautiful kilts.'

'But...'

Barry was not winning the argument, but I had to do something about his protests.

'Look here, Sergeant Jenkins, I'm a flight-sergeant now and I give the orders. We are going to wear these lovely kilts with our uniform until you get home after parade tomorrow. And the other point I want to make is that we do not go and buy anything on the way back because we are not supposed to have any money on us. All the grub we need is in our webbing, and if you want to drink we use water, and that's an order as well.'

'Yes, flight.'

We made our way back to the coach.

'Oh, I nearly forgot. No talking about anything that has happened since we set out on Monday. We might give the game away.'

'Yes, flight.'

We found the coach, avoided putting our kit in the boot, and made ourselves comfortable in the back seat. I reckoned that most passengers would prefer to be at the front, and we might have the whole of the back seat to ourselves. I enquired if the coach could drop us off at Apex Corner on the way back. It did not seem to be a problem. Some kind ex-serviceman asked where we were going and, after some quick thinking, I told him that we were due at RAF Hendon in the morning. It sounded genuine. We slept for the rest of the journey, between the areas of bumpy road. We found tasty morsels of food in our kit. We saw our second daybreak that week. Someone spoke to his partner in the seats in front of us and pointed out Hatfield aerodrome. I consulted the map and decided that Apex Corner would soon be upon us. Jenkins and I tidied ourselves and our kit and we moved carefully to the front of the coach as we approached Apex Corner. The coach driver remembered to stop. We thanked him and landed on the damp pavement outside a telephone box. I wanted to ring the warrant officer to let him know that we were in the area. With all that kit on my back there was no room for Barry and his kit as well, so he had to wait outside. I dialled the number, pressed button A, heard the coins drop and wished him a good morning. We would be at the squadron in about an hour and he said that he would meet us there.

Barry complained that he had just discovered a real problem with his kilt. Everybody was looking at him and it was cold and draughty. When we got on the coach in Edinburgh, we were both correctly carrying our greatcoats over our left arms. If Barry was cold and wanted to put on his greatcoat, then I was quite willing to wait while he adjusted all of his webbing and put it on. He dismissed the idea as being too much trouble. We retraced our route to get to the bus, and paid another 4d to get to the squadron. Just in case the warrant officer was looking, we marched that last 200 yards.

He was there to see us arrive. We heard his words of congratulations for our new ranks, and a polite comment on our smartness. We had beaten the time record on our northbound journey by a considerable margin. I was able to produce £1.3.5d of the £2 that I started off with, and Barry, due to his greater eating requirements, produced £1.1.11d. What little emergency food that we had not eaten we were now tucking into as a breakfast. The warrant officer needed a report of our expedition so we sat down and wrote our individual reports while the adventure was still fresh in our minds. Barry added a note to his version that he did not like kilts or haggis or corporal's stripes, but he wanted to have another go at this kind of thing at some time in the future.

My mother was at home when I arrived there with Barry, and she was highly amused with our new dress sense. She reminded me of my firm objections to wearing short trousers again after I had obtained long trousers when I started college. I pointed out that I had the same trouble with Barry before we left Edinburgh. She did not know until then that we had been to Edinburgh, so my father was almost certainly in for a roasting from her when he got home. I almost forgot to give her the tartan cloth. She was delighted and had instant ideas for making a new dress.

My mother had made lunch for the two of us. Judging by the pile of food, she must have thought that we had been on a starvation diet for four days. Pam came home from school towards the end of the afternoon. She wanted to know why we were wearing frocks and when my father arrived home from work, as we were leaving to go to the squadron, he could offer no more than a hefty grunt. It must have been an awfully bad day for him at the office. We were both the centre of attraction at the squadron that evening, initially attracting all kinds of saucy remarks, but later bombarded with more serious questions. Barry was not happy, except that his new rank enabled him to keep control of the situation. Just to deal the last final blow, we locked his trousers in the stores, promising that, if he turned up dressed in the Scottish uniform for four parades, he would be allowed to have his trousers back afterwards.

In a way, I suppose that I felt sorry for Barry. I had wound him up by getting his trousers locked up in the stores for a while. He considered the kilt a little embarrassing to wear, so I tried to think of a way to alleviate matters. I decided that on Sunday morning I would cycle to the squadron and go out of my way to call on him. I located the house. It was slightly more modern than ours. The street shelters had been demolished and there were trees of many varieties in the small traffic islands at the turn of the road. Barry was walking out of the side door when I spotted him. He stopped in his tracks, surveying my Scottish attire and my ancient old bicycle. He went back to get his super lightweight multi-coloured new bike out of the garage.

'I'm glad you came,' he said.

'Why?'

'Well, it's this kilt that you lumbered me with. I had not thought about riding a bike wearing a kilt.'

'To start with, Barry, it was a deal. You either had three stripes and a kilt, or two stripes and trousers.'

'Yeah, I suppose so.'

'I actually came over to meet you because I guessed that you might be embarrassed about it.'

'Good heavens, no. Mum and Dad were so impressed that we all went up to London to do some shopping yesterday and see what it was like after all the war damage. My only problem was on the tube on those seats facing each other. No wonder the girls adjust themselves carefully when they sit down. I got another five bob out of dad, just 'cos he bet me that I hadn't got the guts to do it.'

I kept silent for a moment. This was interesting. On a nice level section of road, he started chatting again.

'You know, I feel different after going to Edinburgh, but I would never have dared to do it on my own.'

'Nor would I.'

'Just think of all those people who helped us, and those officers and cadets in Edinburgh. I can't believe that my parents allowed me to go.'

'Was it worth that third stripe, then?'

'Not 'alf.'

We were almost at the squadron. When we got to the driveway, I heard little giggles aimed at Sergeant McJenkins and Flight-Sergeant McJudd. Apart from inquisitive looks and silly questions, the cadets seemed to accept it all. Barry Jenkins admitted that he was conscious of everyone looking at him but this happened when he first got his uniform too. I suppose that it was the same for me.

On final parade that Sunday morning I was detailed to be the NCO in charge of the parade. When it was time for the CO to hand over the parade for dismissal, he asked for the Scottish flight-sergeant. I very proudly marched out, with kilt swinging, to a point between the front rank of cadets and the CO and saluted.

'Will you dismiss the cadets, flight-sergeant?'

'Och, aye, Sir.' in my best Scottish accent.

26
Children's hour

It was not unusual, but on my arrival at the squadron one Sunday morning in the middle of May there was a message to the effect that as soon as I appeared, the CO wanted to see me. Now that I had risen to the rank of flight-sergeant, this was a common occurrence. I had learnt through experience that there was never any point in guessing, as I often came to the wrong conclusion. As soon as I had closed his office door behind me, I knew that there was nothing wrong because of his brief smile. Being asked to sit down on his visitors' chair was always another good sign, but I was not going to get that treatment this morning. He was not going to ask a favour, today he was dispensing orders. He reminded me that since the war the enthusiasm to recognise Empire Day had been waning and he wanted the cadets to return to the tradition of going to school in uniform on that day. It would be excellent publicity and would possibly encourage more cadets to join.

There was a challenge for me here. I needed to find the names of cadets and link them with the schools they attended, and this information was in the adjutant's office. Before the morning's training was over, I had selected a number of cadets and had spoken to them about the COs orders for Empire Day. I nominated one cadet from each school to monitor the scheme. On the following evenings and on Sunday morning I repeated the exercise and briefed them. There was more enthusiasm among the cadets than I had anticipated. There was also a lot of interest from headmasters. My boss at work had been very understanding about granting me leave for my cadet activities but I could not justify asking for another day off work for something in which I was not personally involved.

It was not until the evening of Empire Day that I began to hear the results of the cadets' efforts. At a debrief, some cadets admitted that they had left home that morning feeling really excited about the day ahead, but had grown apprehensive as they approached the school gates and at first in the classroom. Having confronted the class, there was no chance whatever of doing anything about the situation and they were committed to demonstrating their loyalty to the ATC for the rest of the day. During breaks between classes they had met a constant barrage of questions about the cadets and lots of requests to try a uniform on to see what it looked like on them. The cadets had been briefed to offer a standard reply and that was 'call in at the squadron and see for yourself'. The principle of giving away a free drink on their first attendance had been proved to be popular over the years and still applied. The results could not be judged for a couple of weeks, but the squadron saw a sudden increase of about thirty cadets and all except two of them were still attending a month later.

The second year of my studies at evening classes was now at an end and the exams were over. It was a relief and I felt exhausted for a week afterwards. My father was pleased and he was looking forward to the results so that I could enrol for another year. At least I was confident about them, but I was not looking forward to the work involved for three more years before the final examinations came, bringing with them the hope of a qualification at the end of it all. Nor was I looking forward to seeing less of Betty, as the pressure of work was sure to grow. The summer would bring some relief from the gloom but I had already used up four out of my annual allocation of ten official working days holiday. I decided that, except for weekends, I was not going to forfeit any more time to the ATC this year because I wanted a week's real relaxing holiday.

I went to see Betty late on a Saturday afternoon. She was good at restoring a bit of sanity to me when everything else had failed. I was now legally old enough to go to the pub for a pint and that was where we went to unwind. I poured out the gloom and despondency and she understood the situation. She listened carefully and put forward the idea that perhaps evening classes after work on three nights a week, plus all the homework, was not the answer. I already had a good knowledge of the important basic subjects and had been concentrating on building surveying as a speciality. Was there a similar trade that did not need quite so much effort? Maps fascinated me. They had not been available during the war years for security reasons, and the talents of the cartographers had been needed elsewhere. Here was a possibility. My innocent intention to have just a pint got a little bit out of hand but Betty stopped me well before total incapacity set in. I took Betty as far as her front door, slightly under her supervision, then decided that walking would be more hazardous than usual, so I got the bus to complete my journey home.

I was in a bit of a dream on Sunday morning, probably due to the urgent need to relieve the water pressure in my body in the early hours of the morning, and not getting enough satisfactory sleep afterwards. I arrived at the squadron on time as usual, but it was not until the warrant officer called me into the office and told me my fortune that I realised that it was just not my morning for doing things right. Now I always seemed to wear a worried expression, and was not so jolly as I had been. Betty had said it and the warrant officer had commented on it. There was something wrong and, back at home, after lunch I went up to my bedroom to think about it. My father had found a small desk, so that I could work, tucked away in my bedroom if I wanted to. In case my father came to find me I spread some college papers out on the desk to make things look authentic. I had to think about the long-term future. Perhaps a change of job would be the answer, but there was one dominant, outstanding issue that had not resolved itself. That was National Service. I was back to the old problem of whether or not they still wanted two years of my life. I had thought about it on many occasions and when I raised the matter with Betty's father, I had had a negative reply, but now my priorities were changing. I supposed that HM government would catch up with me in due course.

I took a day off work. The rules said that I was allowed to have two weeks' holiday, but it was usually frowned upon if they were taken in odd days. However, I was on the right side of my boss and he agreed without asking any difficult questions. I told my parents that I wanted to get something for Betty's birthday and to do some shopping for things I needed for the ATC. I had the remains of my wages in my pocket and I had not had the opportunity to wander leisurely in London for some time. At my normal time of travel the underground was crammed with hot human bodies, only a few of them expecting a seat but all jockeying to get inside the carriage before the doors closed, and then coughing over each other like animals going to market. This morning, I was much later and I had the choice of a seat.

I stood outside the Royal Navy recruiting office for some time, daring myself to go in and wondering whether I was doing the right thing. Whichever way things went, the end result was going to be the same. In two years' time I would have finished my National Service and possibly still be alive and much fitter. I hated the thought of the Navy and of perhaps meeting Tony, but at Ronnie's party those Royal Marines were impressive. I directed my feet up several steps and ventured inside. I soon found myself standing in front of a very smart Royal Marine boasting three stripes, gleaming metal buttons, badges and medal ribbons on his blue uniform. Instinctively, cadet training came into play and I came to attention and addressed him by his rank. I sat down opposite him at an official issue desk, in a small room with a carpet and lots of glossy recruiting posters covering the otherwise bare plastered wall. I explained the circumstances and the depressing nature of life at work and college, showed my identification card and proof of registering, and asked to join the Royal Marines. The details were meticulously recorded on the official forms. Then the sales talk and cross-examination came. It was now obvious that I had been a cadet, but why I was choosing the Royal Marines was difficult to explain. Although I was not a lover of the sea, I had been persuaded at Ronnie's party. Certainly it was the uniform that had 'switched me on'. I did not think that the interview went very well, and I was sure that the Royal Marines would push me off to one of the other services. Afterwards, I made my way back to the street, convinced that I was a miserable failure.

I knew where the Army recruiting office was. The soldier at the interview desk was an intelligent National Service type who understood. We talked about what I was good at before he started writing the details down. I made it very clear to start with that the Guards were at the very bottom of the list, assuming that I was ever going to have a choice. There were possibilities here that I had never considered before. The war had generated years of outstanding bridge building work, demolition and land surveying. The range of possibilities was enormous and just what I wanted. There was also a catch. If I wanted one of these goodies it would have to be for longer than the two years that I had in mind, but he could sign me on immediately if necessary. As the interview drew towards its natural end, there were a few bits of advice that he wanted to offer. The first was that I ought to go away and think about it more seriously before signing on and the second was that if I did want to pursue the matter further then, as a cadet, I would be expected to turn up in uniform for the next interview. I was not too happy about all that. I was getting hungry so I sought lunch down a side street, in a café that was not too expensive. I searched for some time for a suitable present for Betty then arrived at the tube well before the evening rush hour started to make travelling uncomfortable.

My mother was quite excited when I let myself in by the front door. The postman had delivered an important letter. It was in a standard buff envelope clearly marked OHMS with the word 'Private' in bold black letters. If it contained anything dramatic my mother would notice my reaction straight away so I took the standard precaution of going upstairs to my bedroom to open it in private. It was a preprinted document to which the references and my name had been added in ink, and it merely stated that the government would not need me for National Service. No further explanation was given. Not so much as a thank you for going to their nice medical or an apology to my employer for being told to give me time off from work. It was like them telling me to buzz off because I was a nuisance. What an anti-climax after months of concern and of trying to manoeuvre the situation to my advantage. If only this letter had arrived earlier it would have saved a valuable day's holiday from work. I laid on my bed, full of relief, wondering how it all came about. What, I thought, would I tell my parents and Betty? Or was necessary to tell them at all? What could I say to my boss after he had allowed me to have all that time off for cadet activities? Perhaps it would be better to say nothing, and let them all draw their own conclusions. All I needed to do was to make sure that the letter was not found at home, but it was certainly important enough to be kept. The best plan might be to put it in my desk at the office, or even in my wallet or season ticket case.

✳ ✳ ✳

My uncle was a railway employee and, before the railways were nationalised in 1948, he had been offered promotion and a move from London to Crewe. He had invited us to visit him and the whole family had arranged to go. For me it was to be my first 'civilian' holiday since the war. My father, mother and Pam had their free tickets on the train. Preferential fares for railway employees and their families were very useful for the holidays, but now that I went out to work I discovered that I was not entitled to them. That gave me the chance to be totally independent in my travel arrangements. I searched around for the alternatives and discovered that a daily coach service was running from London. I liked that idea, and I decided I would try it.

My only suit came out of the cupboard and my only pair of rubber-soled shoes were treated to the polishing that was normally reserved for my ATC boots. I found a clean white shirt and selected that gaudy tie that I had bought a year earlier and which my father hated, then I packed my case and was off to Victoria. My father was not going to have a say in what I took with me. He would just have to put up with the things that came out of my case at Crewe. I knew that he would never burst into a fit of temper in front of our relations, as that would be more undignified than that gaudy tie.

This was my first long-distance coach journey on my own and I wanted to enjoy it. The coach was scheduled to stop at many of the major towns on the way, and I particularly liked the scenery between Oxford and Stratford-upon-Avon. It was time for lunch when we entered the beautiful area around Lichfield and we were directed to an expensive hotel with a restaurant. I remembered my training at the meal table at home and came away without a stain on my clothes or my character. Once back on the coach, an hour and a half on the road brought me to The Square at Crewe.

It was one of those places to which I took an instant dislike. It was all red brick buildings with slated roofs and with tall chimneys on top of factories and houses belching out smoke and adding to the choking industrial atmosphere. I saw my mother standing alone on the footpath looking worried. The coach was late and she must have imagined all kinds of disasters. She was very relieved to see me arrive safely, without any superficial damage, and even more relieved to learn that I was not hungry. Travelling was the best bit of that holiday. Accompanying my auntie and uncle on their shopping expeditions was depressing and a visit to the park to see the council's display of flowers was even worse. Auntie was most particular about everything and took on the role of the driving force in the house. She was much older than my mother, and her ideas on how I should be entertained for the week were not of any interest to me. The bus stopped almost outside her door once an hour, having travelled up the street emitting miscellaneous clanking noises. Then it coughed and rattled before resuming its journey past the railway station, the town square, several factories, a desolate park and an ancient collection of factory workers' gloomy terraced houses, without any flowers, before it came back again. I had no desire to spend my pocket money paying fares to ride on that old heap and secretly thought that the driver must have been crackers to drive this bus for a living. I knew that my father and uncle had plans to go out for a drink or two on several evenings. I needed to remind them both that I was now of age and I knew what drinks I liked. They were not quick to take the hint but I got the invitation. I think that my father wanted to discuss things in private with uncle and I must have foiled his plans. The rest of my stay at Crewe was quite tedious and the only glimmer of light at the end of the tunnel was the thought of a relaxing coach journey home. How I wished for a chance to be at an annual camp among my cadet friends, getting in some flying and even the occasional bollocking for deviations from the rules.

At the beginning of September I had very reluctantly enrolled for another session of evening classes. Nobody enquired about my National Service but I did watch the gradual disappearance of many of my friends to do their two-year stints. The squadron had wanted my attendance at the Battle of Britain Weekend at North Weald, and my parents had received a special invitation to go to see my aunt at Loughton on the same weekend. Initially there was a family dilemma until it was established that the two locations were not too far apart, so I started negotiations with the bandmaster, my relations and my parents to have me for a day each. During the war, and until that time, auntie had been a nurse. For most of the time when she worked at the hospital she had lived alone, since my uncle was in the Army and had spent most of his time in North Africa. As the war progressed he moved northwards and, as far as I knew, at that time he was in Italy. We arrived in Loughton on the Saturday morning. Auntie had a problem with the plumbing and she had tried to mend the lavatory cistern without turning the water off first. I was detailed to assist by trying to stem the flow, but my attempts at repairs soon turned into a disaster and my best suit got drenched. Because the ATC wanted me on the following day I had my uniform with me, so I was able to wear that while my suit was drying out.

My auntie was not normally of a nervous disposition, but we all detected something unusual was due to happen. Eventually she could not keep it from us any longer: she broke the news that my uncle, having been away for almost seven years, was due to arrive at any moment. The neighbours knew about it and were waiting and chatting to each other in their front gardens. When he finally appeared, climbing out of a taxi, there was a great deal of clapping and waving. He came into the house, dumped his kit in the hall and spoke to us all in turn, in the manner of an officer doing his rounds. I was the last in line.

'Hello. Why the uniform?' We shook hands.

'There was a problem with the lavatory and my suit got wet during the course of repairs. Auntie wanted it to work before you got here,' I explained.

'But there must be another reason.'

'Yes. I'm due at North Weald tomorrow. I think I shall be on television. Would you like to come too?'

'I'll have to consult the wife, because we've only spoken to each other twice a year since I got called up.'

The explanations and exchange of family news carried on for the rest of the afternoon, almost delaying the production of tea, and then continued into the late evening.

Auntie, with help from her neighbours, had found some camp beds and we slept the night. Sunday was to be my great day. The band was already at North Weald and I was expected there as soon as I could make it. The bus took us all to Epping, where we got off and patiently waited for another to take us the last couple of miles. I was talking to uncle and taking no particular notice of other things, when I became aware of a rather smart RAF uniform at close quarters. It's wearer was a warrant officer, also going to North Weald. We travelled together. When we arrived, I found our bandmaster, and I made the formal introductions.

Once the morning rehearsal was over, I discovered that the band was playing music for BBC Children's Hour, and many other squadrons were giving displays for the same programme. Television sets were a novelty, and although programmes were being transmitted before the war, the service did not resume until well after hostilities had ceased. We were situated against a background of trees with the late afternoon sun shining on them which were hiding a poorly painted aircraft hangar. I felt important and could not avoid looking directly towards the business end of a television camera. The realisation that anybody with a television set only had to switch it on to be able to see us brought instant terror. Whatever the band did, every viewer in the country would notice. It had a salutary effect on those who did not normally concentrate fully on the matter in hand. We played a varied programme of classical music for about fifteen minutes before the cameras switched to show other activities of the ATC. When the filming was over we turned to the favourite cadet cure for all problems – food. Between the serious business of eating and drinking, we heard lots of words of congratulation from all kinds of people. The warrant officer that I had met earlier that day at Epping got talking to my uncle and they discovered that they had both served in the Army and had in common knowledge of Egypt and North Africa.

240

I was hoping to go back home on the coach with the rest of the cadets, but before I could confirm this, I had to persuade my mother to rescue my suit, after the previous day's episode, and take it home with her. Naturally she agreed. The cadets had not been able to embark on the usual pranks that day, despite the intention being there, but the opportunity arose on the journey home. The coach driver needed to stop on the road alongside Epping Forest to obey the call of nature and this allowed a few of us to do likewise. We accidentally came upon a gang of boys observing a gang of girls who were modelling their new bikinis in the shelter of the trees. It was not too long before the rest of the cadets began to wonder about our prolonged absence and they joined us to spy upon the scene. On the way back to the coach, we came upon their disrobing area and were delighted to find several pairs of extremely frilly clean knickers amongst the undergrowth. Gleefully, we took them away with us as a reminder of the occasion. When we arrived back at the squadron they were added to our collection of rare winnings and memorabilia. With suitable inscriptions, they were placed in a secluded corner of the band store.

I was not thinking of anything in particular as I walked into the office on that Monday morning. I offered pleasant 'good mornings' to everybody while I was trying to recall things that were left over from the previous week . There were more people in the office than usual and it would seem that all of their new television sets had been switched on to see Children's Hour on Sunday afternoon. Pointed remarks about being a star on the television dominated their conversation. I had not appreciated just how many of my colleagues were the proud owners of television sets. I was a minor hero for most of the day, and even received several requests for autographs.

27
Finale

O ctober had arrived. I had been in the ATC for several years, and I had achieved the dizzy height of a flight-sergeant. My first annual camp at a fairly young age had torn me away from my mother's apron strings and my father's dominant control of the family policies for a week. It was not that I objected to what my parents said or did, because at the end of the day I realised that they had considered matters thoroughly before they had taken any decisions. Both of my parents had lived through hard times during the early 1900s. They had seen two disastrous wars, poor conditions at home and shortages of money and food, so discipline had to prevail. They did not wish those awful conditions upon my sister or me and they did their best in the circumstances and during their own personal difficulties. I was always aware that if ever I went home bringing any discredit at all upon the family, I should be in trouble and should never dare to repeat the offence.

Having survived my first camp without coming to any physical harm, I looked back on it as a good laugh which provided a wealth of unique experiences that I could not have gained elsewhere. The camps that followed got better because the RAF, who took us under their wing, did not as the years rolled by have the same urgency thrust upon them to concentrate on warfare. As a cadet though, once I had seen three camps, I had been through most of the training available. I had mixed with cadets who were much older than myself and I respected them for their wealth of experience and even the pranks that they carried out with precise planning and great effect.

Once I had come to appreciate fully the extent of the damage caused by war, I really wanted to do something about it. As fate would have it, that possibility suddenly disappeared when that little note came through the door saying that the armed services did not want me. I wondered what I was supposed to do then. Was my next move to rush to the doctor and find out what was wrong with me? Until then I had never felt the need to go banging on his surgery door. Should I start now? As far as I knew, my brain and the rest of my body were intact and working properly, so I was stumped for an answer. I faced several more years of evening classes with just a gap during Christmas and a couple of months break during the summer. Then there was Betty who had dared to put her hand on my knee in public one day, and was obviously thrilled to associate with a male of her own age who was encased in a khaki uniform. We had been the best of friends ever since we met. Betty had always been very supportive of my involvement with the cadets, and both our sets of parents had been keen on the idea too.

I persuaded myself that the time had come for me to do some serious thinking about the future. I was now committed to more studies and spending a lot of extra time on college work if I wanted to get somewhere in life. The more I thought about it, the more I was convinced that it was time to abandon the ATC. By the time the next lot of exams was over I would have seen off another birthday. I poured out all my troubles to Betty one Saturday evening while supping a pint in the Red Lion, but before I got too deeply involved, Betty revealed that she had her own set of problems. Betty's father was due to be posted from his job in the depths of government in Whitehall before the end of the year, and the best guess was that it was going to mean a move to Edinburgh. We each had to have another pint while I briefed her on the beauties of Edinburgh, then we agreed that it was much too far away for us to communicate except by post.

On the following morning I put my uniform into my mother's shopping bag, ready to take it to the squadron. I looked lovingly at those boots that I had bought when I first joined. They were in the bottom of my wardrobe, with their beloved metal studs, partly eroded by so many miles of cadet service, still gleaming and fit for further wear, but now the only solid reminder of my time in the ATC. I very sadly took my uniform back to the squadron, and broke the news that I had decided to leave. The officers wanted me to stay on, but I could see the pressure of work continuing for at least another couple of years before the situation improved. The Army Cadet uniform that I had acquired from college was also in my wardrobe and had not been used on a regular basis. I really thought that was the end of the matter but on Saturday afternoon of the following weekend I had a visit from a group of NCOs inviting me out to a party that evening at the squadron headquarters. My suit came out again and I made contact with Betty. I had a pleasant surprise when she greeted me at the door. Despite the continuing problems of food rationing, someone had worked hard to lay out a buffet and the music was coming out from a speaker in the corner of the hut. It was very jolly. We chatted and danced the evening away. During the interval, mainly reserved for the hungry ones, I was presented with a writing set. I think that this must have been the first time that I had been caught out, totally unprepared to give a short speech in reply. Neither had I realised before how popular I had been among my cadet friends.

A week later it felt most strange having Sunday breakfast without putting a uniform on, and then followed the unique experience of not having anything positive to do until lunch time. In desperation, I turned to the homework. It was also the first Sunday evening for a long time that I had actually put the previous week's work away before eight o'clock. The news that I had taken my uniform back was filtering through the system. The first visitor on that Sunday evening was Paul from next door. He brought news of his brother, Stephen, who had left college and the CCF and had joined the Army for his contribution under the National Service Act. The CCF, in conjunction with college, had been a great source of delight to him, but he considered that the Army was an inexcusable waste of time and he would have been much happier if he had been able to embark on some specialised education at the same time.

Tony had gone into the Navy and his parents had not heard from him for a long time. One of his old acquaintances even suggested that he might be with his second wife by this time but this was dismissed as just a rumour. Ronnie was known to be safe and well and I had occasional visits from him and his lady friend when he came home from leave. Ronnie had changed since his removal from Poplar to what he thought was a posh area out in the country. His instinct for work in the markets had vanished and he was now a professional soldier with all the smartness and dedication that he could muster.

The problem that remained for me was that of finding enough time to do everything that I wanted to. Perhaps that pair of shorts and a good run over the golf course would be my best bet in any future times of crisis.

In the event, my college friends, many of my acquaintances from my employment and certainly most of the ATC cadets all seemed to keep in contact. I built up a rich network of friends, reinforced by correspondence and cards over the holiday and Christmas periods. I even managed a satisfying progression in seniority through business. I am convinced that my cadet service made a considerable and valuable contribution to my life.

Fisher Miller Publishing provides a service for authors. We arrange editing, typesetting, printing or a complete self-publishing package, at cost but to professional standards, tailored to your requirements and your pocket. We specialise in short print runs and books which mainstream publishers find uneconomic to publish. You, the author, keep control, and you receive the profits. If you are interested in our services, please contact us at 17 The Drive, Oakley, Basingstoke, Hanpshire RG23 7BA (Tel 01256 781050   Fax 01256 782850 email j.a.miller@mail.ndirect.co.uk).